D1688629

ZEITRÄUME | TIME SCALES

zeit-räume

time scales

Zeitgenössische
deutsche Landschafts-
architektur

Contemporary
German Landscape
Architecture

Birkhäuser
Basel

Bund Deutscher Landschaftsarchitekten bdla (Hg. | Ed.)

Wir danken den Förderern des Deutschen Landschaftsarchitektur-Preises für ihre freundliche Unterstützung dieser Publikation | We would like to thank the sponsors of the German Landscape Architecture Prize for their kind support of this publication:

Allianz Umweltstiftung

Bruns-Pflanzen-Export GmbH & Co. KG

Bundesverband Garten-, Landschafts- und Sportplatzbau BGL

ComputerWorks GmbH

Deutscher Mieterbund e.V.

GdW Bundesverband deutscher Wohnungs- und Immobilienunternehmen

RINN Beton- und Naturstein GmbH & Co. KG

Redaktion im Auftrag des bdla | Editor for bdla Vera Hertlein · Thies Schröder, ts|pk thies schröder planungskommunikation, Berlin

Redaktionsbeirat | Editorial Board Ulrike Böhm · Elisabeth Lesche · Andreas Müller · Martin Prominski · Till Rehwaldt · Jutta Sankowski · Nicole Uhrig

Übersetzung ins Englische | Translation from German Julian Reisenberger, Weimar

Redaktion der Übersetzung | Copyediting of translation Michael Wachholz, Berlin

Gestaltung, Layout und Typographie | Graphic design, layout and typography Miriam Bussmann, Berlin

Die Abbildungen der Beiträge „Unser vornehmster Begriff", „Intelligentes Engineering im Anthropozän", „Palmen am Chiemsee" und „Von Entitäten zu Identitäten" zeigen Projekte, die zum Wettbewerb Deutscher Landschaftsarchitektur-Preis 2013 sowie zu den Sonderpreisen „Infrastruktur und Landschaft" und „Wohnumfeld" eingereicht wurden.

The illustrations and photos accompanying the articles "Our most illustrious term", "Intelligent engineering in the anthropocene", "Palm trees on Lake Chiemsee" and "From entity to identity" show projects that were submitted for the German Landscape Architecture Prize, the Special Prize for Infrastructure and Landscape and the Special Prize for Residential Environments in 2013.

A CIP catalogue record for this book is available from the Library of Congress, Washington D.C., USA.

Bibliographic information published by the German National Library The German National Library lists this publication in the Deutsche Nationalbibliografie; detailed bibliographic data are available on the Internet at http://dnb.d-nb.de.

This work is subject to copyright. All rights are reserved, whether the whole or part of the material is concerned, specifically the rights of translation, reprinting, re-use of illustrations, recitation, broadcasting, reproduction on microfilms or in other ways, and storage in databases. For any kind of use, permission of the copyright owner must be obtained.

© 2013 Birkhäuser Verlag GmbH, Basel
P.O. Box 44, 4009 Basel, Switzerland
Part of De Gruyter

Printed on acid-free paper produced from chlorine-free pulp. TCF ∞

Printed in Germany

ISBN 978-3-03821-567-7

9 8 7 6 5 4 3 2 1
www.birkhauser.com

Inhalt

| 6 | **Vorwort** | *von Andrea Gebhard*
| 8 | **Unser vornehmster Begriff** · Ein Streifzug durch das Wortfeld „Nachhaltigkeit" | *von Ulrich Grober*
| 26 | **Intelligentes Engineering im Anthropozän** | *Prof. Dr. Klaus Töpfer im Gespräch mit Thies Schröder*
| 38 | **Nachhaltigkeit ist unsichtbar** | *von Günther Vogt*

| 48 | DEUTSCHER LANDSCHAFTSARCHITEKTUR-PREIS 2013
| 50 | **hutterreimann Landschaftsarchitektur GmbH · Park am Löbauer Wasser, Löbau** | *von Till Rehwaldt*
| 60 | WÜRDIGUNGEN | 60 · relais Landschaftsarchitekten · Der Christliche Garten (Gärten der Welt), Berlin | 62 · WGF Landschaft · Grüngürtel: Impuls 2012, Köln | 64 · club L94 Landschaftsarchitekten GmbH · Elsbethenareal und Schrannenplatz, Memmingen | 66 · lohrer.hochrein landschaftsarchitekten bdla · Park Phoenix West, Dortmund | 68 · Lützow 7 Cornelia Müller, Jan Wehberg, Landschaftsarchitekten · Elisengarten, Aachen | 70 · Stefan Fromm Landschaftsarchitekten · Drei neue Parks für Nagold | 72 · TOPOTEK 1 Gesellschaft von Landschaftsarchitekten mbH · Superkilen, Kopenhagen/Dänemark | 74 · Straub Thurmayr Landschaftsarchitekten und Stadtplaner · Folly Forest, Strathcona School, Winnipeg/Kanada
| 78 | SONDERPREIS INFRASTRUKTUR UND LANDSCHAFT | **RMP Stephan Lenzen Landschaftsarchitekten, ASTOC Architects and Planners, Landschaft planen + bauen, Norbert Post · Hartmut Welters, Architekten und Stadtplaner GmbH · Masterplan emscher:zukunft**
| 82 | WÜRDIGUNGEN
| 88 | SONDERPREIS WOHNUMFELD | **herrburg Landschaftsarchitekten · BIGyard Gartenhof, Berlin**
| 92 | WÜRDIGUNGEN

| 100 | PETER-JOSEPH-LENNÉ-PREIS 2012
| 100 | **Strategie Stadtlandschaft** | *von Michael Müller*
| 102 | **Peter-Joseph-Lenné-Preis 2012** | *von Christoph Rosenkranz*

| 116 | **Palmen am Chiemsee** | *Karlheinz Steinmüller und Björn Theis im Gespräch mit Johannes Böttger, Andrea Gebhard, Arno Sighart Schmid, Cornelia Schmidt und Thies Schröder*

| 134 | **Von Entitäten zu Identitäten** | *von Nicole Uhrig*

| 152 | ANHANG | 154 · Über die Preisträger Deutscher Landschaftsarchitektur-Preis 2013 | 162 · Über den bdla und die Autoren | 168 · Über die Förderer der Publikation | 170 Personen- und Projektregister | 174 · Ortsregister | 175 · Bildnachweis

Contents

| 6 | **Foreword** | *by Andrea Gebhard*
| 8 | **Our most illustrious term** · An exploration of the semantic field of "sustainability" | *by Ulrich Grober*
| 26 | **Intelligent engineering in the Anthropocene** | *Prof. Dr. Klaus Töpfer in conversation with Thies Schröder*
| 38 | **Sustainability is invisible** | *by Günther Vogt*

| 48 | GERMAN LANDSCAPE ARCHITECTURE PRIZE 2013
| 50 | **hutterreimann Landschaftsarchitektur GmbH · Löbau River Park, Löbau** | *by Till Rehwaldt*
| 60 | COMMENDATIONS | 60 · relais Landschaftsarchitekten · The Christian Garden (Gardens of the World), Berlin | 62 · WGF Landschaft · Green Belt: Impuls 2012, Cologne | 64 · club L94 Landschaftsarchitekten GmbH · Elsbethenareal and Schrannenplatz, Memmingen | 66 · lohrer.hochrein landschaftsarchitekten bdla · Park Phoenix West, Dortmund | 68 · Lützow 7 Cornelia Müller, Jan Wehberg, Landschaftsarchitekten · Elisengarten, Aachen | 70 · Stefan Fromm Landschaftsarchitekten · Three new parks for Nagold | 72 · TOPOTEK 1 Gesellschaft von Landschaftsarchitekten mbH · Superkilen, Copenhagen/Denmark | 74 · Straub Thurmayr Landschaftsarchitekten und Stadtplaner · Folly Forest, Strathcona School, Winnipeg/Canada
| 78 | SPECIAL PRIZE FOR INFRASTRUCTURE AND LANDSCAPE | **RMP Stephan Lenzen Landschaftsarchitekten; ASTOC Architects and Planners; Landschaft planen + bauen; Norbert Post und Hartmut Welters Architekten und Stadtplaner GmbH · Emscher Future master plan**
| 82 | COMMENDATIONS
| 88 | SPECIAL PRIZE FOR RESIDENTIAL ENVIRONMENTS | **herrburg Landschaftsarchitekten · BIGyard garden courtyard, Berlin**
| 92 | COMMENDATIONS

| 100 | PETER JOSEPH LENNÉ PRIZE 2012
| 100 | **Urban Landscape Strategy** | *by Michael Müller*
| 102 | **Peter Joseph Lenné Prize 2012** | *by Christoph Rosenkranz*

| 116 | **Palm trees on Lake Chiemsee** | *Karlheinz Steinmüller and Björn Theis in conversation with Johannes Böttger, Andrea Gebhard, Arno Sighart Schmid, Cornelia Schmidt and Thies Schröder*

| 134 | **From entities to identities** | *by Nicole Uhrig*

| 152 | APPENDIX | 154 · About the prize winners of the German Landscape Architecture Prize 2013 | 162 · About the bdla and the authors | 168 · About the sponsors of the publication | 170 · Index of persons and projects | 174 · Index of places | 175 · Illustration credits

Vorwort
Foreword

von · by Andrea Gebhard

Landschaftsarchitektur ist selten allein auf den kurzfristigen Erfolg orientiert. Dass zum Entwurf auch Entwicklung und Pflege – also Zeit – gehören, um einen überzeugenden (Lebens-)Raum zu gestalten, ist quasi eine gärtnerische Binsenweisheit. Der jahrzehntelange Weg von der Gartenkunst zur Landschaftsarchitektur ist selbst ein solcher Weg der Entwicklung gewesen, ein Weg der Pflege von Stärken ebenso wie der ständigen Erneuerung und Innovation.

Das einhundertjährige Bestehen des Bundes Deutscher Landschaftsarchitekten ist vor allem eine Entwicklungsgeschichte des stetigen Wachstums an Wissen und Qualität, an Aufgabenfeldern und Methoden. Daraus erwuchs die grundlegende gesellschaftliche Bedeutung, die der Landschaftsarchitektur zukommt.

Die Bedeutung der Freiräume, der Grünflächen und Landschaftsräume für die Überlebensfähigkeit der Gesellschaft ist heute anerkannt und führt zu immer größeren Erwartungen. Das Leben in den Städten wird weltweit als größte ökologische und soziale Herausforderung verstanden, die Chancen der ländlichen Räume werden vor allem in Europa intensiv diskutiert, und Lebensqualität und Freiraumqualität werden heute quasi gleichgesetzt. Die Profession der Landschaftsarchitektur hat viele Schlüssel zur Zukunft in den Händen.

Vor 30 Jahren erschien das Buch *Grün in der Stadt* von Michael Andritzky und Klaus Spitzer mit dem verheißungsvollen Untertitel *Von oben, von selbst, für alle, von allen*. Für viele Studierende war das damals ein entscheidender Meilenstein im Selbstverständnis der Profession. Denn Grün wurde erstmals als strategische Frage von gesamtgesellschaftlicher Bedeutung diskutiert. Plötzlich wurde aus dem Stadtgrün weit mehr als ein schmückendes Beiwerk. Es trat in den Mittelpunkt des zu erringenden guten Lebens. Aus diesen Anfängen wurde teilweise ein neuer

Landscape architecture is rarely solely about short-term goals. Gardeners know that successful (living) environments are as much the product of development and cultivation – in other words time – as they are of the initial design. For the profession, the decades of transition from Garden Art to Landscape Architecture have likewise been a path of development, of the cultivation of competencies and of continual renewal and innovation.

The one-hundred-year history of the bdla, the Federation of German Landscape Architects is, above all, one of continual growth – of knowledge, in quality, in the scope of work and the methodologies applied. It is through this process that landscape architecture has acquired the fundamental social importance it is accorded today.

The importance of open spaces, of green space and landscapes for the continuing survival of society is now recognised, and with this come ever greater expectations. Making cities liveable is today regarded as the greatest ecological and social challenge facing society around the world, and the chances presented by rural spaces are being debated intensively, especially in Europe. The quality of our outdoor spaces is seen as determining our quality of life. The profession of landscape architecture therefore holds many of the keys to our future in its hands.

Thirty years ago, the book *Grün in der Stadt* (Green in the City) by Michael Andritzky and Klaus Spitzer was published with the promising-sounding subtitle *Von oben, von selbst, für alle, von allen* (From above, by itself, for all, by all). For many students at that time it represented a milestone in the self-conception of the profession because it was the first book to discuss urban green spaces as a strategic issue of relevance to society as a whole. Suddenly, urban green was more than merely decorative.

Lebensstil, vor allem aber eine neue Bürgergesellschaft. Es gibt keine politische Partei oder gesellschaftliche Institution mehr in Europa, die der Umwelt, der Mitwelt, der Lebenswelt keine Schlüsselbedeutung zuerkennt.

In den letzten Jahren hat die politische Öffentlichkeit erkannt, dass die Frage der Strategien der Städte und Stadtregionen (unter diesem Begriff sind verkürzt die Disziplinen der Ökologie, der Stadtsoziologie und der Planung des öffentlichen und privaten Freiraums subsumiert) eine der Fragen ihrer Zukunft ist. Gerade im Wettbewerb um die besten Wissens- und Arbeitskräfte – ein Wettbewerb, der gerade erst beginnt – sind die „weichen" Standortfaktoren einer Region ausschlaggebend. Die innovativen und dynamischen Ansätze zur Gestaltung und Nutzung der Freiräume entwickeln die Landschaftsarchitekten.

In diesem Werk zum Jubiläumsjahr des bdla kommen Autoren zu Wort, die sich den grundlegenden Werten unserer Profession widmen. Nachhaltigkeit ist für die Landschaftsarchitektur weit mehr als ein Modewort – Ulrich Grober untersucht Herkunft und Zukunft dieses Begriffs. Günther Vogt erklärt, wie aus Worten Werte werden im landschaftsarchitektonischen Handeln. Im Interview mit Klaus Töpfer steht – neben seinem Einfluss auf die globale Umweltpolitik – die Frage nach den Möglichkeiten des Entscheidens für Ingenieure und Künstler im Mittelpunkt. Und in einem Zukunftsdialog stellen sich Landschaftsarchitekten den Fragen der Zukunftsforschung an die Profession.

Neben diesen Blicken zurück und weit nach vorne bildet die Dokumentation des Deutschen Landschaftsarchitektur-Preises 2013 den Kern dieses Buches. Eine Auswahl aller Einreichungen des Jahres 2013 begleitet auf der Bildebene auch die Essays von Ulrich Grober und Nicole Uhrig, das Interview mit Klaus Töpfer sowie den Zukunftsdialog. Denn in Vergangenheit und Zukunft sind und bleiben zwei zentrale Themen ausschlaggebend für die Landschaftsarchitektur: die Qualität der Planung und die Feststellung, dass für jede gesellschaftliche Fragestellung der Entwurf als dreidimensionales Ordnungsgebilde unverzichtbar ist. Gute, wegweisende Antworten der Gegenwart auf diese Fragestellungen bieten die Arbeiten, die der Deutsche Landschaftsarchitektur-Preis 2013 würdigt. Das Buch zeigt diese Räume in Wort und Bild.

It became central to what constitutes a good life. These beginnings were to bring forth a new way of life, and more importantly a new sense of citizenship. Nowadays, there are no political parties or social institutions in Europe that do not see the natural and social environment as being of vital importance.

In recent years, politics has recognised that urban and regional strategies (a term that encompasses the disciplines of ecology, urban sociology and the design and planning of public and private green space) are critical for the future. In the competition to attract highly qualified and skilled workers – a competition that is just getting under way – it is the "soft" location factors of a region that make the difference. And it is here that landscape architects are called on to develop innovative and dynamic solutions to the design and use of outdoor spaces.

In this book, published on the occasion of the centenary of the bdla, the authors explore the fundamental values of our profession. Sustainability is for landscape architecture far more than a buzzword: Ulrich Grober examines the origins and future of this term, while Günther Vogt describes how such words are translated into values in our work as landscape architects. In an interview, Klaus Töpfer discusses – in addition to his influence on global environmental policies – the possible directions available to engineers and artists. And in a futures dialogue, landscape architects reply to the questions of foresight researchers on the future of the profession.

In addition to looking back into the past and far into the future, the core section of this book documents the German Landscape Architecture Prize 2013. A selection of project photographs and plans drawn from all the submissions also accompany the essays by Ulrich Grober and Nicole Uhrig, as well as the interview with Klaus Töpfer and the futures dialogue. They show that, whether in the past or in the future, two main themes are fundamental for landscape architecture: good-quality planning and the essential value of design as a three-dimensional ordering medium for addressing social issues. The projects distinguished by the German Landscape Architecture Prize 2013 and featured in the texts and illustrations of this book represent valid, forward-looking responses to these issues.

Unser vornehmster Begriff
Ein Streifzug durch das Wortfeld „Nachhaltigkeit"

Our most illustrious term
An exploration of the semantic field of "sustainability"

von · by Ulrich Grober

Nachhaltigkeit – soviel scheint klar, ist ein total unsinnliches Wort: *Nach* und *halt* und *-ig* und *-keit*. Ächz, würg, gähn! Zu lang, zu schwerfällig! Eine massive Anhäufung von stimmlosen Verschlusslauten, Reibelauten, rauen Hauchlauten! Sie erfordern von den Stimmorganen beinahe akrobatische Fähigkeiten im Blockieren und Verschließen. Besonders gefordert ist der Rachenbereich, das ist der Bereich, in dem auch die Schnarchgeräusche entstehen. Der Wortkörper erlaubt kaum einen dynamischen Luftstrom, kaum Vorwärtsbewegung. Ein verschnarchtes Wort, eins, das bereits im Mund Blockaden hervorruft. Für alle, die Deutsch als fremde Sprache lernen, muss es ein Horror sein. Weg damit! Oder?

Alle reden von Nachhaltigkeit, *sustainability, chi xu fa zhan, desarollo sostenible* ... Im globalen Vokabular des 21. Jahrhunderts hat kein anderer Begriff eine so steile Karriere hinter sich. Unweigerlich geriet er dabei in das Feuerwerk der Reklamesprache und der politischen Propaganda: Im Speckgürtel von Zürich baute man die „nachhaltigste Autobahn aller Zeiten"; Experten fordern die „Nachhaltigkeit von Militäreinsätzen", Gewerkschafter eine „nachhaltige Stärkung der Kaufkraft"; die deutsche Bundesregierung erhob „nachhaltiges Wachstum" zum Programm; die Produktinformation meines Haar-Shampoos verheißt mir „nachhaltige Befreiung der Kopfhaut von Schuppen". Wie wär's mit einem „*sustainable Las Vegas*"? Kein anderes Wort wurde so brutal entkernt, verwässert, weichgespült. Steiler Aufstieg, heftiger Absturz? Ist der Begriff schon verbraucht? Verbrannt?

Ich halte dagegen: „*In an age in which we are denuding the resources of the planet as never before and endangering the very future of humanity, sustainability is the key to human survival.*" Nachhaltigkeit – der Schlüssel zum Überleben der Menschheit in einer Epoche, in der wir den

Everyone talks about sustainability, *Nachhaltigkeit, chi xu fan zhan, desarollo sostenible…* In the global vocabulary of the 21st century, no other word has risen so rapidly to such importance. In the process it has inevitably entered into the language of advertising and political propaganda: the "most sustainable motorway ever" has recently been built on the outskirts of Zurich; experts argue for "a sustainable use of military interventions"; trade unions demand a "sustainable improvement in purchasing power"; the German government has made "sustainable growth" a key part of its programme; and the product details on my shampoo bottle promise "sustainable freedom from dandruff". And what about a "sustainable Las Vegas"? No other word has been so brutally robbed of its substance, diluted or washed out. Rapid ascent, or perhaps sobering downfall? Has the term lost its lustre? Is it burnt out?

I would instead venture that "in an age in which we are denuding the resources of the planet as never before and endangering the very future of humanity, sustainability is the key to human survival." In this succinct description, the Sri Lankan judge and former Vice-President of the International Court of Justice, Christopher G. Weeramantry, summarises the status still accorded to this concept in the thinking of the international community – a status to which the UN Rio+20 conference, despite the otherwise varied reception of its results, renewed its commitment in summer 2012.

So what are we to believe? Sustainable freedom from dandruff? Or sustainability as the key to survival? I suggest we step back for a moment and take a closer look at the term itself.

When asked in the 6th century BC what he considered the first thing to be done if he were to run the govern-

▲ Die historische Kulturlandschaft der Toskana stand im Vordergrund eines Masterplanverfahrens zur Gestaltung des Golf Resort Castelfalfi in Montaione, Italien. Entwurf: Rainer Preißmann, Maximilian Freiherr von Wendt, Essen

The historic cultural landscape of Tuscany serves as a main reference in the master plan Castelfalfi Golf Resort in Montaione, Italy. Design: Rainer Preißmann, Maximilian Freiherr von Wendt, Essen

Planeten und dessen Ressourcen wie nie zuvor plündern und damit sogar die Zukunft der Menschheit gefährden. So prägnant drückte es der frühere Vizepräsident des Internationalen Gerichtshofes, der sri-lankische Jurist Christopher G. Weeramantry, aus. Damit umreißt er den Status, den dieses Konzept im Denken der internationalen Gemeinschaft nach wie vor einnimmt. Die UN-Konferenz Rio+20 – wie auch immer man ihre Ergebnisse ansonsten bewerten mag – hat im Sommer 2012 diesen Rang neu bekräftigt.

Was denn nun? Befreiung der Kopfhaut? Oder Schlüssel zum Überleben? Ich schlage vor, einen Moment lang innezuhalten und einen Schritt zurückzutreten. Wie wär's mit ein wenig Arbeit am Begriff?

ment, the Chinese sage Confucius answered: "definitely, to rectify the names". *Zheng ming*, the concept of rectification of names, literally "the correct use of terms", remains a central aspect of Chinese philosophy today.

The arbitrariness with which the term is used today leads to conceptual confusion. But as long as we have no other word with the same range of meaning, with the same degree of gravity and elasticity, there is only one alternative to renouncing its usage entirely: to head in search of the core meaning of a word that has become increasingly hollowed out. This search takes us on a journey into history. It is in the early days of a new concept that the fundamental elements of its meaning are negotiated. This is where the original substance of the term

Auf einer Fläche von 17 Hektar über 1,7 Kilometer Länge wurden am Neckar bei Ludwigsburg vielfältige neue Lebensräume geschaffen, darunter ein Umgehungsgerinne und neue Auenbiotope mit verschiedenen Fließgeschwindigkeiten. Entwurf: Landschaftsarchitekturbüro Geitz & Partner GbR, Peter Geitz, Stuttgart

17 hectares of land over a distance of 1.7 kilometres along the River Neckar near Ludwigsburg have been converted to create new habitats, including a bypass channel and floodplain biotopes with different flow rates. Design: Landschaftsarchitekturbüro Geitz & Partner GbR, Peter Geitz, Stuttgart

Auf die Frage, was er als Erstes tun würde, wenn ihm der Kaiser die Regierung des Staates anvertraute, antwortete im 6. Jahrhundert vor unserer Zeitrechnung der chinesische Weise Konfuzius: „Unbedingt die Bezeichnungen richtigstellen." *Zheng ming* – die Richtigstellung der Worte, wörtlich übersetzt „auf korrekte Begriffe halten" – steht noch heute im Zentrum chinesischer Philosophie.

Die Beliebigkeit bei der Verwendung des Begriffs macht uns begriffslos. Doch solange wir kein anderes Wort mit demselben Bedeutungsumfang, mit derselben Gravität und Elastizität haben, gibt es nur eine Alternative zum totalen Verzicht auf einen Begriff: der schleichenden Entkernung die Suche nach seinem Kern entgegenzusetzen. Diese Suche führt uns in die Geschichte. In den Anfängen einer Begriffsbildung wird immer Elementares verhandelt. Hier wird die Substanz entwickelt, die später ihr Potenzial entfaltet, aber im Prozess der Operationalisierung und Anwendung zu verschwimmen droht. Suchen wir also nach den historischen Quellen, in denen wir unseren Gebrauch des Wortes spiegeln und überprüfen können – und, wenn's gut geht, seine Würde neu erfahren.

NACHHALTIGKEIT VERSUS KOLLAPS

Mein Favorit im Dickicht der Definitionen ist schon 200 Jahre alt. Er findet sich in Joachim Heinrich Campes *Deutschem Wörterbuch* von 1809: „Nachhalt ist das, woran man sich hält, wenn alles andere nicht mehr hält." Nur ein kurzer Satz. Man sollte ihn sich freilich auf der Zunge zergehen lassen. Denn Campes Definition öffnet einen Zugang zur Tiefendimension des Wortes. Nachhaltigkeit erscheint auf einmal in einem neuen Licht: als Gegenbegriff zu dem, was nicht mehr hält, zu: Kollaps.

Dasselbe Denkbild liegt dem Neustart des Begriffs im 20. Jahrhundert zugrunde. Am Anfang stand der Bericht an den Club of Rome. Seine Autoren suchten 1972 nach developed that would later reveal its greater potential but now, in the process of operationalization and application, is losing its contours. Let us therefore go in search of historical sources with which we can reflect on and reassess our use of the word – and, with a bit of luck, rediscover its core value.

SUSTAINABILITY VERSUS COLLAPSE

My favourite definition among the jungle of alternatives is already 200 years old. It can be found in the *Dictionary of the German Language* published in 1809 by Heinrich Campe in which *Nachhalt* (the root of *nachhaltig*, the German word for sustainable) is defined as "that which one holds on to when nothing else holds any longer". It's a short sentence, but one that we should take the time to savour. Campe's definition offers us a glimpse of a deeper dimension of the word. It shows us sustainability in a new light: as the antonym to that which no longer holds, to "collapse".

It is this same notion that is at the root of the renaissance of the term in the 20th century. It began with the report to the Club of Rome. Its authors were searching for a model for "a world system that is sustainable", that is resistant to "sudden and uncontrollable collapse" and "capable of satisfying the basic material requirements of all of its people." This is what is written in the famous report on the *Limits of Growth*, a report that was hastily – too hastily – declared obsolete. Here too "sustainable" is used as the antonym to "collapse" and corresponds very closely to our contemporary notion of "resilience".
Is that too intangible? Anyone who has renovated a house and lent a hand in repairing its loadbearing walls knows that this is something very real and tangible. It is the lasting durability and loadbearing elements of a construction that lend it a feeling of being habitable. It caters

einem Modell für ein „Weltsystem, das nachhaltig (*sustainable*)" ist. Und das heißt: gegen einen „plötzlichen und unkontrollierbaren Kollaps" gefeit und „fähig, die materiellen Grundansprüche der Menschen zu befriedigen". So steht es in der berühmten und schnell – vorschnell – für obsolet erklärten Studie über die *Grenzen des Wachstums*. Und wieder ist *sustainable* Gegenbegriff zu Kollaps! Und sehr dicht an dem, was wir heute als *resilient* bezeichnen.

Ist das unsinnlich? Wer schon mal ein Haus renoviert hat und an den tragenden Wänden mit Hand angelegt hat, weiß, dass es sich dabei um etwas sehr Sinnliches handelt. Erst die nachhaltenden, dauerhaft haltbaren und tragfähigen Elemente einer Konstruktion vermitteln das Gefühl von Bewohnbarkeit. Sie antworten auf das Grundbedürfnis nach Sicherheit. Nachhaltigkeit als Gegenbegriff zu Kollaps ins Spiel zu bringen, halte ich für brandaktuell. In Zeiten, wo der Planet sich aufheizt und ein höllisches Klima droht, wo Solidarität und Gemeinsinn so schnell schmelzen wie die Gletscher der Polarkappen, wo *global players* über Nacht kollabieren, Gemeinwesen, ja ganze Staaten zu „scheitern" drohen, wird Nachhaltigkeit zum Mega-Thema. Nicht als Sahnehäubchen auf dem Kuchen einer Überflussgesellschaft, sondern als Schwarzbrot einer ökologischen Überlebenskunst.

Diese Idee ist weder eine Kopfgeburt moderner Technokraten noch ein Geistesblitz von Ökofreaks der Generation Woodstock. Sie ist ein geistiges Weltkulturerbe. Es war der „grüne Prinz", der britische Thronfolger Prinz Charles, der vor einigen Jahren die Frage aufwarf, ob nicht „tief in unserem menschlichen Geist eine angeborene Fähigkeit existiert, nachhaltig im Einklang mit der Natur zu leben (*to live sustainably with nature*)".

for a basic human need for security. The notion of sustainability as the antonym of collapse is, I believe, more relevant than ever. In a time in which the planet is warming and the climate is threatening to change drastically, where solidarity and public spirit are melting as quickly as the glaciers of the polar ice caps, and where global players fall apart overnight and communities or even entire states are on the point of "failing", sustainability has never been more topical than it is today. Sustainability is not the icing on the cake of an affluent society but the daily bread of an ecological art of survival.

This idea is neither an abstract theory dreamt up by modern technocrats nor a wild fantasy hatched by Woodstock-generation eco-freaks. It is a form of spiritual world cultural heritage. It was Prince Charles, the "green prince" and heir to the British throne, who a few years ago posed the question as to whether there is, "deep within our human spirit ... an innate ability to live sustainably with nature".

REFLECTIONS

While the idea is universal, the term itself first began to take shape in 17th-century Europe. One of its forerunners was also a pioneer of landscape architecture: the English landscape gardener, landowner, art historian, beekeeper, bestselling author and courtier John Evelyn. At that time too, it was a crisis of resources that precipitated action. In the same way that we today talk about *peak oil* (the point at which the rate of oil production starts to decline, heralding an end to our oil resources), the dwindling of oil resources, the people of the day were concerned about a looming shortage of timber if the rate

SPIEGELUNGEN

Die Idee ist universell, die Begriffsbildung freilich begann im Europa des 17. Jahrhunderts. Einer ihrer Wegbereiter war gleichzeitig ein Pionier der Landschaftsarchitektur: der englische Gartengestalter, Großgrundbesitzer, Kunsthistoriker, Bienenzüchter, Erfolgsautor und Höfling John Evelyn. Auch damals gab eine Ressourcenkrise den Anstoß. So wie wir heute *peak oil*, das Überschreiten der maximalen Erdölfördermenge, wahrnehmen und ein Versiegen der Ölquellen absehbar wird, sah man damals einen bevorstehenden Mangel an Holz voraus – wenn man so weitermachen würde. In England sorgte man sich nicht zuletzt um den Schiffbau des Landes und das „hölzerne Bollwerk Britanniens", die Marine. Im Auftrag der von ihm mitgegründeten Royal Society setzte Evelyn einen Diskurs über Auswege aus der Ressourcenkrise in Gang. 1664 erschien in London sein Buch mit dem Titel *Sylva or a Discourse of Forest Trees and the Propagation of Timber*.

of consumption were to continue unabated. In England, the authorities were particularly concerned about the impact on shipbuilding and the navy, the "wooden bulwarks of the nation". Commissioned by the Royal Society, which he had helped to found, Evelyn initiated a discourse on possible ways out of the predicted crisis of resources. His book *Sylva or a Discourse of Forest Trees and the Propagation of Timber* was published in London in 1664. His overarching vision was of an "Elysium Britannicum", a reconstruction of the Garden of Eden on the British Isles. His response to the problem is "to manage woods discreetly" – that is to manage them carefully in accordance with their respective characteristics. Evelyn sees their future in "providential planting" and is convinced that the human mind can impose a new order on wild nature, indeed that in the interests of coming generations it must. He proceeds to back up his passionate plea, "Let us arise and plant…", with examples of good practice

◀ Umweltbildung in historischer Kulisse betreibt der Verein ProSpecieRara in den Merian Gärten in Basel, Schweiz. Pflanzenraritäten und selten gewordene Nutztierrassen werden hier gepflegt. Entwurf: pg landschaften, Pascal Gysin, Sissach/Schweiz

The ProSpecieRara Association offers environmental education in the historical Merian Gardens in Basel, Switzerland. The association cultivates rare plants and keeps uncommon livestock breeds. Design: pg landschaften, Pascal Gysin, Sissach/Switzerland

▶ Schulklassen kommen regelmäßig zu Projekten in den Park mit seinem angeschlossenen Landwirtschaftsbetrieb

Schoolchildren take part regularly in the projects offered in the park and its associated farm

Evelyns überwölbende Vision: ein „*Elysium Britannicum*", die Rekonstruktion des Paradieses auf der britischen Insel. Seine Forderung: „*to manage woods discreetly*" – die Wälder „unterscheidend", also ihre jeweilige Eigenart beachtend, und behutsam managen. Ihre Zukunft sieht Evelyn im „*providential planting*", dem vorausschauenden Pflanzen. Er ist davon überzeugt, dass der menschliche Geist der wilden Natur eine neue Ordnung geben könne und – nicht zuletzt im Interesse der nachfolgenden Generationen – geben müsse. Seinen leidenschaftlichen Aufruf: „*Let us arise and plant*" – erheben wir uns und pflanzen wir – untermauert er mit zahlreichen Beispielen für gute Praxis aus ganz Europa. Sein eindringlichstes Plädoyer – und das Leitmotiv seines Buches – gilt der Vorsorge für die *posterity*, die Nachwelt. Jede Generation – so zitiert er ein lateinisches Sprichwort – sei *non sibi soli natus* – nicht für sich allein geboren. Sie sei vielmehr „*born for posterity*" – für die Nachwelt geboren. Seine eigenen Zeitgenossen aber, fügt er anklagend hinzu, seien offenbar „*fruges consumere nati*" – geboren, um die Früchte der Erde zu konsumieren. In Abgrenzung von diesem Zeitgeist entwickelt Evelyn die Ethik einer vorausschauenden, vorsorgenden und verantwortlichen Gesellschaft.

Ein junger sächsischer Edelmann, Hans Carl von Carlowitz, hatte um 1666 auf seiner *peregrinatio academica*, seiner mehrjährigen Bildungsreise durch Europa, die englische Bewegung intensiv verfolgt. Später übernahm er leitende Funktionen im erzgebirgischen Silberbergbau, wo der Holzmangel bedrohliche Ausmaße anzunehmen drohte. Am Ende seines Lebens, 1713, veröffentlichte Carlowitz sein Buch *Sylvicultura Oeconomica*. Vor 300 Jahren taucht in diesem Buch unser Begriff zum ersten Mal in seiner modernen Bedeutung auf. Gegen den Raubbau am Wald setzt die *Sylvicultura Oeconomica* die eiserne Regel,

drawn from all over Europe. His most urgent plea – and the leitmotif of his book – concerns making provision for posterity, for the future. Quoting a Latin saying, he argues that each generation is *non sibi soli natus* – not born for itself alone, but rather born for posterity. His own contemporaries, he observes accusingly, seem *fruges consumer nati* – born to consume the fruits of the earth! Taking a critical attitude to the spirit of his contemporaries, Evelyn goes on to formulate an ethics for a provident and responsible society.

In 1666, a young Saxon nobleman, Hans Carl von Carlowitz, had closely followed the movement in England while on his *peregrinatio academica* – his educational grand tour of Europe that lasted several years. Some time later he was appointed a leading position in the silver mines of the Ore Mountains where the dwindling supply of wood had reached dangerous proportions. Towards the end of his life in 1713, he published his book *Sylvicultura oeconomica*. This, some 300 years ago, is where our term was first formally mentioned in the meaning that we use it today. To counter the over-exploitation of the forests, the *Sylvicultura oeconomica* establishes an iron rule: "that wood should be used with care". Carlowitz goes on to pursue the question as to "how such a conservation and cultivation of wood can be arranged so as to make possible a continuous, steady and *sustaining* use, as this is an indispensable necessity, without which the country cannot maintain its Being." Here, in the convoluted language of the Baroque, we encounter this word for the first time. And even at this early juncture the motivation is the same: sustainability as a means of protecting society against impeding collapse.

Carlowitz was not only responsible for coining the word; he also outlines the "three pillars of sustainability"

Das neue Wohngebiert Tübinger Mühlenviertel entstand auf einer ehemaligen Industriebrache, es wird von einem Grünzug entlang des offengelegten und renaturierten Mühlbaches durchzogen. Entwurf: Stefan Fromm Landschaftsarchitekten, Dettenhausen

The new residential quarter in Tübingen's Mühlenviertel was built on a former industrial site. The Mühlbach (mill brook) has been restored and turned into a green corridor that flows through the quarter. Design: Stefan Fromm Landschaftsarchitekten, Dettenhausen

„daß man mit dem Holtz pfleglich umgehe". Und Carlowitz geht der Frage nach, „wie eine sothane" – eine solche – „Conservation und Anbau des Holtzes anzustellen / daß es eine continuirliche beständige und nachhaltende Nutzung gebe / weil es eine unentbehrliche Sache ist / ohne welche das Land in seinem Esse nicht bleiben mag". In diesem Satz, verkleidet in einer barocken Sprache, taucht das Wort zum ersten Mal auf. Ohne den *nachhaltenden* Umgang mit den Wäldern kann das Land in seinem *Esse* – in seiner Existenz – nicht bleiben. Schon hier: Nachhaltigkeit als Selbstschutz der Gesellschaft vor dem existenzbedrohenden Kollaps.

Nicht nur das Wort, auch das „Dreieck der Nachhaltigkeit" aus Ökologie, Ökonomie und sozialer Gerechtigkeit erscheint bei Carlowitz in klaren Konturen. Die Natur ist „milde". Es ist eine „gütige Natur". *Mater natura* – Mutter Natur. Carlowitz spricht vom „Wunder der Vegetation", von der „lebendig machenden Krafft der Sonnen", von dem „wundernswürdigen ernährenden Lebens=Geist", den das Erdreich enthalte. Die Pflanze ist „*corpus animatum* … ein belebter Cörper … welcher aus der Erden auffwächset / von selbiger seine Nahrung an sich zeucht, sich vergrössert und vermehret". Heute sprechen wir von … Biomasse! Ausgangspunkt des ökonomischen Denkens ist die Feststellung, dass sich der Mensch nicht mehr im Garten Eden befinde. Er müsse der Vegetation der Erde „zur Hülffe kommen" und „mit ihr agiren". Er dürfe nicht „wider die Natur handeln", sondern müsse ihr folgen und mit ihren Gaben „ökonomisch" (= haushälterisch) umgehen. Im Einklang damit formuliert Carlowitz seine sozialethischen Grundsätze: Nahrung und Unterhalt stehen jedem zu, auch den „armen Unterthanen" und der „lieben Posterität", also den nachfolgenden Generationen. Seine Begriffsbildung etablierte sich in der Fachsprache des Forstwesens, zuerst im deutschsprachigen Raum, dann im

in clear terms: ecology, economy and social fairness. He describes nature as being "mild", *Mater natura* – Mother Nature – as being bountiful and generous. Carlowitz talks of the "wonderful world of plants", of the "life-giving power of the Sun", of the "wondrous and nourishing life force" in the soil. The plant is "*corpus animatum*, a living body which grows out of the earth, feeds itself, grows and multiplies". Today, we would call that… biomass! The starting point for his economic thinking is the realisation that Man no longer resides in the Garden of Eden. He must "come to the aid of" the vegetation of the earth and "work together with her". He may not "act against nature" but must follow it and must be "economical" (= provident) in his use of its gifts. Carlowitz's social and ethical principals follow in the same vein: nourishment and sustenance are for everyone, including the "poor subjects" and "beloved posterity", that is, the future generations. His terminology was later adopted in the language of forestry, first in the German speaking countries, then, in the 19th century around the world. Today we still speak of "sustained yield forestry".

How did ecology then fit into this? A generation after Carlowitz, the Swedish naturalist Carl Nilsson Linnaeus arrived on the European scene. He too was looking for the key to the "*flor*", the flourishing of the land. His delight in the variety of species, his passion for the processes of fertilisation, reproduction, growth, for the whole "*multiplicatio individuorum*" (Linnaeus, 1735), arose out of a vital interest in the "sustainable use" (Carlowitz, 1713) of living resources. Linnaeus' guiding motto was *oeconomia naturae*, meaning the unity of nature, the multiplicity of species, the cycles of growth and decline, symbioses, food chains and energy streams. The world of minerals, of plants and of animals for him formed an interconnected whole. It is a self-regulating and self-sustaining organ-

19. Jahrhundert auch international. Ins Englische übersetzte man sie mit „*sustained yield forestry*".

Wie kam die Ökologie ins Spiel? Eine Generation nach Carlowitz betrat der schwedische Naturforscher Carl Nilsson Linné die europäische Bühne. Auch er suchte den Schlüssel für den „Flor", das Aufblühen des Landes. Sein helles Entzücken an der Vielfalt der Arten, seine Leidenschaft für die Prozesse von Befruchtung, Vermehrung, Wachstum, für die ganze „*multiplicatio individuorum*" (Linné, 1735) entsprangen einem vitalen Interesse an der „nachhaltenden Nutzung" (Carlowitz, 1713) lebendiger Ressourcen. Linnés Leitbegriff war: *oeconomia naturae*. Gemeint war die Einheit der Natur, die Mannigfaltigkeit der Arten, die Kreisläufe von Werden und Vergehen, Symbiosen, Nahrungsketten, Energieströme. Mineralreich, Pflanzenreich, Tierreich bilden für ihn ein vernetztes Ganzes. Es ist ein sich selbst regulierender und erhaltender ism. It ensures that life goes on. For Linnaeus, the answer to the all-important question of the relationship between economy and ecology was clear: it is necessary to synchronise our economy with the unchanging cycles of the *oeconomia naturae*.

Nearly one hundred years after his death, in 1866, his concept was to become the blueprint for the coining of a new term: *ecology*, the science of nature's household. This coinage was the creation of Ernst Haeckel, professor of biology in Jena. Ecology became part of the inner circle of meaning of sustainability: what holds and sustains us are the forces of nature and the cosmos, the light of the sun and the life force of the biosphere fed by the energy of the sun.

In the late 20th century, the forestry term "sustained yield" reached the UN and became the blueprint for the universal model of "sustainable development". Where

Organismus. Dieser sorgt dafür, dass das Leben weitergeht. Die Lösung der allgegenwärtigen Frage nach dem Verhältnis von Ökonomie und Ökologie war für Linné klar: Es muss gelingen, die Abläufe unserer Ökonomie mit den unwandelbaren Kreisläufen der *oeconomia naturae* zu synchronisieren.

Knapp ein Jahrhundert nach seinem Tod, 1866, wurde sein Konzept zur Blaupause für einen neuen Leitbegriff: *Oecologie*, die Lehre von der Haushaltung der Natur. Die Wortschöpfung verdanken wir Ernst Haeckel, Professor der Biologie in Jena. So rückte Ökologie in den inneren Sinnbezirk von Nachhaltigkeit: Was uns hält und trägt, sind die Kräfte von Natur und Kosmos, das Licht der

300 years ago, Carlowitz was concerned with "a continuous supply of wood for burning and other uses for the people" as well as "for posterity", the UN Brundtland Commission in 1987 defined this aim as development "that meets the needs of the present without compromising the ability of future generations to meet their own needs."

How can a concept born out of pre-modern, cameralist thinking for a closed and small-scale central European territory, have such vast potential in the globalised world of the 20th century? A first answer: the photos sent back from outer space in 1970 by the first manned flight to the moon, gave mankind a view of themselves from outside for the first time in history. In this epochal moment of

◀ Die Gestaltung des Zollhallenplatzes in Freiburg/Breisgau wurde komplett aus Abbruchmaterialien des anliegenden ehemaligen Güterbahnhofs realisiert. Entwurf: Atelier Dreiseitl, Überlingen

The redesigned Zollhallenplatz in Freiburg am Breisgau has been made from demolished material recovered from the neighbouring former goods railway station. Design: Atelier Dreiseitl, Überlingen

▲ Urbane Landwirtschaft: Bewohner und ein Weinbauer pflegen gemeinsam die Gemeinschaftsflächen der Wohnanlage Pichlgasse in Wien/Österreich. Entwurf: rajek barosch landschaftsarchitektur, Wien/Österreich

Urban agriculture: residents and a vintner tend to a joint vineyard in the Pichlgasse housing complex in Vienna/Austria. Design: rajek barosch landschaftsarchitektur, Vienna/Austria

Sonne und das von der Sonnenenergie gespeiste Kraftwerk der Biosphäre.

Im späten 20. Jahrhundert erreichte der forstliche Fachausdruck „Nachhaltigkeit" / *„sustained yield"* die UN und wurde zur Blaupause des universellen Leitbilds *„sustainable development"*. Ging es Carlowitz vor 300 Jahren um „eine immerwährende Holtz=Nutzung zum Besten des gemeinen Wesens (= Gemeinwesens)" und „den Nachkommen zum Besten", definierte die Brundtland-Kommission der UNO 1987 als Ziel eine Entwicklung, „welche die Bedürfnisse der gegenwärtigen Generation befriedigt, ohne die Fähigkeit zukünftiger Generationen zu gefährden, ihre eigenen Bedürfnisse zu befriedigen".

contemplation and wonder we saw our first view of the beauty, uniqueness and fragility of the blue planet. It was these three key terms that defined how these iconic images were interpreted at the time. And it was in this moment that the germ of consciousness began to grow in the *global village* that the planet is a set of closed systems: *spaceship earth*. The limits of growth were suddenly apparent and with it the realisation of a need for self-restraint as the only option for preserving the beauty and uniqueness of our living environment and to continue to enjoy it in the future. Here lies the rational, emotional and spiritual matrix of the modern concept of sustainability. Nevertheless, we are still a long way

Das Projekt :terra nova im Rhein-Erft-Kreis westlich von Köln transformiert eine ehemalige Tagebaulandschaft in eine „Energiekulturlandschaft". Teil des Projekts ist das „Biosphärenband" auf einer ehemaligen Erdfördertrasse. Die sukzessive Neubepflanzung wird bewusst sichtbar inszeniert. Entwurf: bbz landschaftsarchitekten, Berlin

The :terra nova project in the Rhine-Erft district west of Cologne transforms a former opencast mining landscape into an energy-oriented cultural landscape. Part of the project is the "Biosphere Band" on a former earth conveyance route. The successive replanting measures have been made visible with distinctive fencing. Design: bbz landschaftsarchitekten, Berlin

Wie konnte ein Begriff aus dem vormodernen, kameralistischen Denken eines geschlossenen, eng begrenzten mitteleuropäischen Territoriums in der globalisierten Welt des 20. Jahrhunderts eine derartige Wirkung entfalten? Eine erste Antwort: Auf den Fotos aus dem Weltall, die um 1970 von den bemannten Mondflügen zur Erde gesendet wurden, sah sich die Menschheit zum ersten Mal in ihrer Geschichte ganz und gar von außen. Ein epochales Ereignis: ein Moment des Innehaltens und des Staunens über die Schönheit, die Einzigartigkeit und die Zerbrechlichkeit des blauen Planeten – dies waren die drei Schlüsselbegriffe bei der zeitgenössischen Deutung der ikonischen Bilder. In diesem Moment keimte im *global village* ein Bewusstsein dafür, dass der Planet insgesamt ein geschlossenes, begrenztes System bildet: *spaceship earth*. Die Grenzen des Wachstums kamen in Sicht und damit der Zwang zur Selbstbeschränkung – als der einzigen Option, um die Schönheit und Einzigartigkeit unseres Lebensraums zu bewahren und weiter genießen zu können. Hier liegt die rationale, emotionale und spirituelle Matrix des modernen Nachhaltigkeitsdenkens. Doch die Tragweite dieses Perspektivenwechsels haben wir noch längst nicht verstanden.

DIE GROSSE TRANSFORMATION

Eine neue Plattform der Reflexion über eine globale Transformation ist gerade im Entstehen. Das Passwort heißt: *peak oil*. Dieses Fördermaximum des Erdöls haben wir vermutlich vor kurzem überschritten. In wenigen Jahrzehnten werden die Ölquellen versiegen. Damit einher geht der Klimawandel als Folge des fossilen Zeitalters. Innerhalb weniger Generationen haben wir die „unterirdischen Wälder", also die fossilen Lagerstätten, geplündert und mit ihrer Verbrennung gleichzeitig unsere Lebensgrundlage, das Klimasystem, zerrüttet. Die Konsequenz: Unsere bisherige Art zu wirtschaften ist nicht länger fortsetzbar.

from understanding the consequences of this change of perspective.

THE GREAT TRANSFORMATION

A new platform for reflecting on global transformation has emerged more recently. The password here is *peak oil*. By all accounts, the peak rate of global oil production now lies behind us, and in a matter of decades the oil reserves will be depleted. And while we burnt fossil fuels, we also brought about climate change. Within the space of just a few generations we have plundered our "subterranean forests", our fossil fuel deposits, and through its combustion simultaneously wrecked our living environment, the climate system. The consequence is clear: we cannot continue to operate on the basis of our current economic model.

The unavoidable need to effect an epochal change of direction also offers a great opportunity. The transition to a genuinely sustainable pattern of production and consumption is possible. Replenishable raw materials, renewable energy sources and appropriate technologies are now becoming the focus of the economy. Knowledge of the "regeneration" of living resources and respect for long-term natural processes are – once again – becoming a vital intellectual resource. A prerequisite is, of course, a radical break with the ideas that have dominated for the last 20 or 30 years, namely those that can be summarised by the slogan *Let's make money*. The growth of the economy as expressed in the permanent expansion of the production of goods, has become a fetish. The monetary aspects of money and earning money have become the sole purpose of the economy. This has even made inroads into the sphere of human rights and the very heart of our concept of freedom. The dream of *one world* was perverted into a concept of boundless rights and the freedom to

Unser vornehmster Begriff | Our most illustrious term | 19

▶ Auf bis zu 100 Meter kann sich der Fluss Kallang, der bisher in einem geradlinigen Betonkanal verlief, heute bei Hochwasser ausbreiten. Der Fluss ist eingebettet in den innerstädtischen Bishan Ang-Mo Kio Park in Singapur. Entwurf: Atelier Dreiseitl, Überlingen

The River Kallang, which was previously confined within a straight concrete canal, may now spread to a width of 100 metres when there is high water. The river is embedded in the Bishan Ang-Mo Kio Park in the heart of Singapore. Design: Atelier Dreiseitl, Überlingen

Der Zwang zu einer epochalen Wende birgt zugleich eine große Chance. Der Übergang zu genuin nachhaltigen Mustern des Produzierens und Konsumierens ist möglich. Nun rücken nachwachsende Rohstoffe, erneuerbare Energien und angepasste Technologien weltweit in den Mittelpunkt der Ökonomie. Das Wissen über das „Nachwachsen" lebender Ressourcen und der Respekt vor den langfristigen Prozessen in der Natur werden – wiederum – zur entscheidenden geistigen Ressource. Voraussetzung ist freilich ein radikaler Bruch mit Vorstellungen, die uns in den letzten 20 oder 30 Jahren beherrscht haben. Sie lassen sich mit dem Slogan *Let's make money* zusammenfassen. Das Wachstum der Wirtschaft, verstanden als permanente Ausdehnung der Warenproduktion, wurde zum Fetisch. Der monetäre Aspekt, das Geld und das Geldverdienen wurden zum alleinigen Zweck der Ökonomie verabsolutiert. Er gelangte sogar in die Sphäre der Menschenrechte und in die Mitte unseres Freiheitsbegriffs. Der Traum von der *einen* Welt wurde zum grenzenlosen Recht und zur Freiheit des Geldverdienens überall auf der Welt pervertiert. Diese Strategie der Globalisierung war ganz und gar vom billigen Öl abhängig.

Nachhaltigkeit dagegen nimmt wieder das naturale Wachstum und dessen Zeitzyklen in den Fokus. In diesem Licht erscheint Ökonomie – wie bei Linné – als Subsystem der Biosphäre. Nachhaltigkeit ist im Wesentlichen eine Strategie der Reduktion des Naturverbrauchs und der maßlosen Gewinnerwartungen. Sie ist der Selbstschutz der Gesellschaft vor der zerstörerischen Dynamik der Märkte. Sie stellt die Frage: Was brauchen wir wirklich? Und in der Folge das, was wir wirklich brauchen, ressourcenschonend zu erzeugen und gerecht zu teilen, ist die Überlebensstrategie, die wir zu befolgen haben – koste es, was es wolle. Nachhaltigkeit ist im Kern ein ethisches Prinzip. Es handelt nicht primär von unseren Freiheiten

earn money all over the world. This strategy of globalisation was utterly dependent on cheap oil.
Sustainability on the other hand focuses on natural growth and its innate time cycles. Seen in this light, economy is – as it was for Linnaeus – a subsystem of the biosphere. Sustainability is essentially a strategy for reducing the consumption of nature and excessive anticipated profits. It is a means by which society can protect itself against the destructive dynamism of the markets. It poses the question: What do we really need? And then goes about producing and fairly distributing what we really need in a resource-friendly way. This is the strategy of survival that we need to follow – whatever the cost. Sustainability is at its core an ethical principle. It is not primarily about our freedom and rights but about responsibility and obligations. With the aim of ensuring that future generations have the option – and the right – to lead a life worth living.

WHAT NEXT?
Can we find new resources for a contemporary practice of landscape architecture in the old semantic meanings of our term? Here's one such glass bead game: let us take the idea of "sustainable use" that Carlowitz spoke of 300 years ago. He used the participial form of the verb *to sustain*, signalising that it was an active process, an action directed towards achieving this state that through its undertaking would actually bring about a sustained and sustaining condition. Its verbal articulation sent shockwaves through the age. He placed the focus squarely on doing and on thinking in systems: you have the right to use, but not the right to "use up" and to contaminate; you are a custodian for future generations. Perhaps this can serve as the impetus we need to loosen our own thinking, to put aside inflexible ideas about sustainability?

Unser vornehmster Begriff | Our most illustrious term | 21

und Rechten, sondern von Verantwortung und Pflichten. Mit dem Ziel, zukünftigen Generationen die Optionen für ein lebenswertes Leben – und das Recht darauf – offenzuhalten.

UND JETZT?
Finden wir in den alten semantischen Aufladungen unseres Begriffs neue Ressourcen für eine zeitgemäße Praxis der Landschaftsarchitektur? Nur ein kleines Glasperlenspiel: Nehmen wir die „nachhaltende Nutzung", von der vor 300 Jahren Carlowitz sprach. Er verwendet noch die Partizipialform des Verbes *nachhalten*. Signalisiert wird damit ein aktiver Vorgang, nämlich eine Handlung, die darauf abzielt und durch ihren konkreten Verlauf tatsächlich bewirkt, dass etwas auf Dauer hält und trägt. Der verbale Ausdruck bringt sein Umfeld zum Vibrieren. Er rückt das Tun und das systemische Denken in den Fokus: Du hast das Recht zu nutzen, aber nicht das Recht zu „verbrauchen" und zu kontaminieren, du bist Treuhänder für kom-

"Let us arise and plant!" was the plea of the English landscape gardener John Evelyn in the 17th century. Careful observers will notice a slight subversive undertone: "arise" (to stand up, or to rise up) is semantically related to "insurrection" (to take a stand), to uprising and revolt. "Planting" too is both a very practical activity, and also a synonym for every kind of productive, creative and life-affirming practice. Could this be the hidden agenda for the "coming uprising" in the context of a looming threat of collapse?

And why not use the new perspective gained through the flights to the moon to improve our own appearance? The sense of wonder that we have for the planet as a whole can be our measure, one that we can then apply to every corner of the biosphere. That means to appreciate the uniqueness, (potential) beauty and fragility of every place, however disfigured it may be, to explore and then repair and gently let it develop its own pattern of life and characteristics. Scarcity, the shortage of resources, can be

◁ Parallel zur Flussumgestaltung wurde der 1960 angelegte Park behutsam saniert

The park from the 1960s was sensitively redesigned as part of the river remodelling

mende Generationen. Ein Anstoß, um eigenes Denken zu verflüssigen, Denkschablonen über Nachhaltigkeit abzulegen?

„*Let us arise and plant!*", war die Parole des englischen Garten-Designers John Evelyn aus dem 17. Jahrhundert. Wer genau hinhört, spürt einen subversiven Unterton. *Arise* (sich erheben, aufstehen) ist semantisch dicht an *insurrection* (Erhebung, Aufstand, Revolte). „Pflanzen" als ganz praktische Tätigkeit, aber dann auch als Chiffre für jede produktive, kreative, lebensbejahende Praxis – ist das die verborgene Agenda für den „kommenden Aufstand" angesichts des drohenden Kollaps?

Und warum nicht die Perspektive der Mondflüge nutzen, um die eigene Optik neu zu justieren? Also an der Pracht des Ganzen Maß nehmen und sich so an jeden kleinen Flecken Biosphäre heranzoomen. Das würde bedeuten, jeden Ort, und sei er noch so kaputt, in seiner Einzigartigkeit, seiner (potenziellen) Schönheit und Zerbrechlichkeit wahrzunehmen, zu erkunden und dann zu sanieren und behutsam sein Eigenleben und seine Eigenart zu entwickeln. Die Armut, also die Knappheit an Ressourcen, zum Konzept zu machen, könnte dann ganz neue Spielräume für die Entfaltung von Imagination und Kreativität öffnen. „Auch Schönheit ist ein Lebens-Mittel" (Toblacher Thesen). Dieser Satz meint das Naturschöne, das Schöne in den zwischenmenschlichen Beziehungen, die Schönheit und Vielfalt in den Kulturen der Welt.

An dem hohen Anspruch einer "schöneren Welt" noch in der tiefsten Krise festzuhalten und ihn in kleinen kreativen Akten zu verwirklichen, scheint mir heute die große Herausforderung. In der Konfrontation mit den Phänomenen des Kollaps entwickelt sich *homo sapiens* zum *homo sustinens*, zum "Hüter des Wachstums", letztlich zum „Hüter des Seins" (Heidegger). Wäre es vermessen zu prophezeien, dass mit ihrer grünen Expertise, ihrem

made into a concept that has the potential to reveal new possibilities for applying one's imagination and creativity. "Beauty, too, is a kind of nourishment" (Toblach Theses) – this refers to natural beauty, to the beauty of interpersonal relationships, the beauty and diversity of the cultures of the world.

To hold on to this ideal of "a more beautiful world" when in the midst of a deep crisis, and to work towards it with many small acts of creativity, seems to me to be the greatest challenge today. In our confrontation with the phenomenon of collapse, *homo sapiens* has become *homo sustinens*, to the "custodian of growth" and ultimately to the "custodian of being" (Heidegger). Would it be too presumptuous to prophesy that landscape architects, planners and gardeners have the expertise, professional knowledge and ethos to assume a key role in a *green economy* worthy of its name? Another world is possible. The Indian writer Arundhati Roy goes one step further: "Another world is not only possible, she is on her way. On a quiet day I can hear her breathing."

▲ Eine ehemalige Mülldeponie in Hamburg-Wilhelmsburg wird zum „Energieberg" mit Photovoltaik-, Windkraft- und Deponiegasnutzung. Eine Plattform bietet ungewohnte Aussichten auf Stadt, Hafen und umgebende Landschaft. Entwurf: Häfner/Jiménez Büro für Landschaftsarchitektur, Berlin

A former refuse tip in Hamburg-Wilhelmsburg has been converted into an "Energy Hill" employing photovoltaic technology, wind power and landfill gas conversion. A platform offers unusual views over the city, harbour and surrounding landscape. Design: Häfner/Jiménez Büro für Landschaftsarchitektur, Berlin

▶ Die aufgeständerte, beleuchtete Brücke wird zum neuen „Horizont" und zur Landmarke

The illuminated raised bridge serves as a landmark and marks the new "horizon"

beruflichen Wissen und Ethos Landschaftsarchitekten, Planer und Gärtner in einer *green economy*, die diesen Namen wirklich verdiente, eine Schlüsselrolle einnehmen? Eine andere Welt ist möglich? Die indische Schriftstellerin Arundhati Roy geht noch einen Schritt weiter: „Eine andere Welt ist nicht nur möglich. Sie ist im Entstehen. An einem stillen Tag höre ich sie atmen."

Zum Weiterlesen
Ulrich Grober, *Die Entdeckung der Nachhaltigkeit – Kulturgeschichte eines Begriffs*, Antje Kunstmann Verlag, München, 2010.

Further reading
Ulrich Grober, *Sustainability: A cultural history*, Totnes, Devon, Green Books; White River Jct., VT, Chelsea Green, 2012.

Intelligentes Engineering im Anthropozän
Intelligent engineering in the Anthropocene

▲ Prof. Dr. Klaus Töpfer

Prof. Dr. Töpfer, in dem von Ihnen geleiteten Institute for Advanced Sustainability Studies (IASS) engagieren Sie sich seit 2009 für multidisziplinäre und internationale Nachhaltigkeitsforschung. Ist ein national arbeitender Verband wie der bdla in Zeiten der globalen Umweltherausforderungen zeitgemäß?

Ich bin davon überzeugt, dass der bdla zeitgemäß ist. Denn ein nationaler Verband beschäftigt sich ja nicht nur mit national relevanten Themen, ganz im Gegenteil. Aus den Kenntnissen, die man selbst im eigenen Umfeld gewonnen hat, lassen sich Entwicklungsperspektiven ableiten, die uns global betreffen. Nur derjenige, der solide Arbeit dort macht, wo er zu Hause ist, wird ernst genommen von denen, die an anderen Stellen Probleme zu bewältigen haben. Dass wir die Qualität unserer Landschaftsarchitektur exportieren sollen und müssen, ist unstrittig.

Ihr Institut widmet sich unter anderem einem „Globalen Gesellschaftsvertrag für Nachhaltigkeit". Wenn man sich die Schwerpunkte Ihres Institutes ansieht – Böden und Ozeane, Energiewende und Klimawandel, Mensch und Atmosphäre im Anthropozän –, fällt auf, dass der Mensch vor allem als Ingenieur eine Chance zu haben scheint. Ist ein intelligentes Engineering im Maßstab Erdsystem Ihre Antwort auf die Umweltkrise?

Wir geben ja bereits seit langer Zeit diese Antwort: Wir gestalten die Natur durch menschliche Eingriffe um. Wir regulieren Flüsse. Wir sehen massive Änderungen der Atmosphäre durch Emissionen von Treibhausgasen. Wir sehen den Einfluss des Menschen überall. Immer mehr Menschen kommen zu dem Ergebnis, dass das, was wir gegenwärtig als Herausforderungen sehen, die Bewältigung negativer Konsequenzen vorangegangenen Engineerings ist, nicht beachteter Konsequenzen menschlichen Handelns.

Prof. Dr. Klaus Töpfer im Gespräch mit · in conversation with Thies Schröder

Professor Dr. Töpfer, since 2009, you have been furthering multidisciplinary and international sustainability research as part of your work as Director of the Institute for Advanced Sustainability Studies (IASS). In an age of environmental challenges on a global scale, is a national association like the bdla in keeping with the times?

I am convinced that the bdla is in keeping with the times. After all, a national association doesn't just address issues that are nationally relevant. On the contrary, the knowledge one gains in one's own context can be used to derive perspectives for developments that affect us globally. And those who do sound work in their home environment will earn recognition from those who have problems to tackle elsewhere in the world. As such, it is quite clear that we should, indeed must, export the quality of our landscape architecture.

Your institute is, among other things, concerned with establishing a "Global Contract for Sustainability". When one looks at the focal areas of your institute – soil management and oceans governance, energy transition and climate change, people and atmosphere in the Anthropocene – it would seem that mankind's greatest chance lies in his role as an engineer. Is intelligent engineering at the scale of the earth system your answer to the environmental crisis?

For a while now we have been giving the following answer: we shape nature through our interventions as humans. We regulate rivers. And we are seeing massive changes in the atmosphere as a result of greenhouse gas emissions. Wherever we look, we can see the impact of our actions. Ever more people are coming to the conclu-

Es geht also nicht darum, ob wir als Ingenieure tätig werden wollen, sondern dass wir schon seit langer Zeit tätig sind. Das Thema des Anthropozän ist von dem Nobelpreisträger Paul Crutzen zur Diskussion gestellt worden durch seinen bemerkenswert kurzen, aber bedeutsamen Artikel „Geology of mankind" im Magazin *Nature* 2002, wo er sagt, der Mensch ist so einflussreich, dass wir eigentlich nicht mehr vom Holozän, einem Erdzeitalter, sprechen können, sondern vom Anthropozän, einem Menschenzeitalter. Darüber wird auch wissenschaftlich sehr engagiert diskutiert.

Wie weit ist eine offene Gesellschaft des Anthropozän in der Lage, Alternativen zu entwickeln?
Diese Frage geht weit über naturwissenschaftliche Fragestellungen hinaus. Der Erfinder der Nachhaltigkeit, Hans Carl von Carlowitz, hat das schon genauso gesehen. Man sagt ja immer, man dürfe nur so viel aus dem Wald an Holz ernten, wie in begrenzter Zeit wieder nachwachsen kann. Häufig wird Nachhaltigkeit daher interpretiert als eine Betonung der Grenzen des Wachstums. Bei Hans Carl von Carlowitz steht im Werk *Sylvicultura Oeconomica* aber auch schon, man solle sich international umsehen und sich fragen, ob es Bäume gibt, die schneller wachsen. Das ist schon ein ingenieurmäßiges Denken. Wenn Sie so wollen, ist Hans Carl von Carlowitz mit seiner Idee der Nachhaltigkeit der Ideengeber für deutsche Fichtenmonokulturen, die ja nichts anderes sind als ein ingenieurmäßiges Entwickeln von Wäldern.

Sie setzen damit einen deutlichen Akzent, nämlich dass die Grenzen des Wachstums nicht die Grenzen des Engineerings sind und dass ein ausschließlich bewahrendes Verhältnis zu Umwelt und Natur möglicherweise nicht das Angemessene ist?

sion that the challenges that we are facing today are largely attempts to come to terms with the negative consequences of earlier engineering, with a lack of regard for the consequences of human actions. The question is not whether we need to take action as engineers, because we have been doing that already for a long time. The idea of the Anthropocene was raised by the Nobel prize winner Paul Crutzen in his remarkably short but important article "Geology of Mankind" in *Nature* magazine in 2002 in which he asserts that mankind now has such a strong impact on the world that we can no longer really speak of the Holocene, a geological epoch, but should speak of the Anthropocene, a human-dominated era. This is an issue that has been discussed at length in scientific circles.

To what degree is an open society of the Anthropocene capable of developing alternatives?
This is a question that goes far beyond purely scientific concerns. Hans Carl von Carlowitz, who is credited with inventing the idea of sustainability, realised that in his day too. The saying goes that one may only remove as much wood from the forest as can regrow within a certain space of time. Sustainability is therefore often interpreted as emphasising the limits of growth. In Hans Carl von Carlowitz's book *Sylvicultura oeconomica*, however, it is also written that one should look beyond one's borders to see if there are trees that can grow more quickly. That is in itself already a step in the direction of engineering. To a certain degree, one could say that Hans Carl von Carlowitz's idea of sustainability was the precursor to the German spruce monocultures, which are in essence nothing other than the engineered development of woodland.

▸ Im Landschaftspark „Das Grüne Quadrat" bei Bitterfeld erfolgt die Transformation einer Bergbaufolgelandschaft in einen Park mit künstlerischen Mitteln. Die Skulptur „Am-Tisch-Sitzen-Sehen" findet man an drei besonderen Orten im Park. Projektleitung: Heike Brückner, Jacques Leenhardt, Gianni Burattoni, Dessau

In the Green Square landscape park near Bitterfeld, a mining landscape has been transformed into a park with the help of artistic interventions. The table sculpture and lookout point can be found in three key locations in the park. Project lead: Heike Brückner, Jacques Leenhardt, Gianni Burattoni, Dessau

Dies kann ich nicht ein für allemal entscheiden. Ein dynamischer Prozess wird nicht dadurch bewältigt, dass wir das Nachdenken über Möglichkeiten des Handelns tabuisieren. Andererseits muss ich auch erkennen, ob ein Handeln über die Verantwortung des Menschen hinausgeht. Die deutschen Bischöfe haben ein Hirtenwort herausgegeben: Der Mensch darf nicht alles, was er kann, und je mehr er kann, umso größer wird seine Verantwortung. Genau das beschreibt den Abwägungsprozess. Gerade um die Schöpfung als solche zu bewahren, genügt es nicht, einen Zaun um sie herum zu ziehen. Denn dass wir weiterdenken und unser Handeln verantworten können, ist ja auch Teil der Schöpfung.

Woher stammt Ihre Motivation, die konkreten Handlungsperspektiven des Menschen zu betonen? Eigentlich sind Sie studierter Diplom-Volkswirt, also eher Analytiker als Planer und Handelnder.
Ich habe die längste Zeit meines beruflichen Lebens damit verbracht, die Realität nicht nur zu analysieren, sondern sie an einem Wertekanon auszurichten, sie mit zu verändern, mit zu gestalten. Wenn Sie acht Jahre lang in Afrika tätig gewesen sind, dann kommen Sie nicht daran vorbei zu fragen: Was ist zu tun, damit Menschen eine gesicherte Zukunft haben? Es geht um existenzielle Not im Hinblick auf Ernährung, den Zugang zu Wasser, zur Ausbildung und um die Gesundheit der Menschen. Wir werden weitere technologische Möglichkeiten brauchen. Die Welt mit neun Milliarden Menschen wird eine friedliche Perspektive nur dann haben, wenn wir über das, was wir jetzt wissen, hinausdenken. Genau darum sehe ich mich in hohem Maße mit in der Pflicht, darüber nachzudenken, wie wir als ein führendes Industrieland in der Welt unsere Energieversorgung auf erneuerbare Energien umstellen können. Natürlich tragen wir statistisch so wenig zur weltweiten CO_2-Emission bei, dass alles Handeln hier nicht einmal ein

What you are saying would seem to suggest that the limits of growth are not the limits of engineering and that an exclusively conservationist approach to the environment and nature may not necessarily be appropriate?
That's not something I can decide once and for all. It's clear that we won't be able to get to grips with dynamic processes by forbidding ourselves from considering different possible avenues of action. On the other hand, I must also be able to recognise when certain activities compromise our sense of responsibility to others. The German bishops issued a pastoral letter in which they state that mankind has not the right to do everything he can, and the more he can, the greater the responsibility he has. That in essence describes the deliberations we face. In order to preserve the whole of creation, it is not sufficient to place a fence around it. Part of creation is that we are able to think ahead and act responsibly.

Where does your motivation to focus on the concrete aspects of human action come from? You studied as an economist, so you are more an analyst than a planner and doer.
I have spent the greater part of my professional life not only analysing the realities of the world but also aligning them with a system of values, contributing to changing the world and shaping it. When you spend eight years working in Africa, you cannot ignore the question of what we need to do to ensure that every person has a secure future. These are existential issues that have to do with having enough to eat, access to water, to education and to a healthy life. We will need to leverage further technological possibilities. A world of nine billion inhabitants will only have a safe prospect when we think beyond what we already know. It is here that I see my responsibility to consider how we, as a leading industrial nation, can effect a transition to a system of energy provision based on renewable energy sources.

Tropfen auf den heißen Stein ist. Aber wir können die neuen Energietechnologien entwickeln, die diese negativen Konsequenzen nicht haben. Wir können diese Technologien in eine ökonomische Dimension bringen, die sie konkurrenzfähig macht gegenüber den hoch subventionierten traditionellen Energien. Das ist der entscheidende Entwicklungsbeitrag, den wir zu leisten haben. Ich möchte zur nächsten Klimakonferenz gehen und sagen können: „Jetzt sind wir soweit, ihr könnt die erneuerbaren Energien nutzen. Es ist kein Hindernis mehr für eure wirtschaftliche Entwicklung. Ihr braucht nicht mehr aus Kostengründen auf fossile oder atomare Energiequellen zurückgreifen, sondern ihr habt Alternativen verfügbar, die dezentral sind und euch unabhängiger machen." Insofern bringen mich die Erfahrungen aus meinem Lebensablauf genau an diesen Punkt, mir mit 75 Jahren immer noch Gedanken zu machen zu den Alternativen des Handelns.

In Ihrer Pflichtvorlesung „Planungstheorie" an der Universität Hannover haben Sie in den 1970er Jahren – so berichten es ehemalige Studierende – das muddling through *propagiert, ein theoretisches Anti-Gebäude zu den damals vorherrschenden Planungsideologien. Hat*

In statistical terms, our contribution to CO_2 emissions is so small that any actions we take here are little more than a drop in the ocean. But we can develop new energy technologies that do not have negative consequences. And we can work to make these technologies sufficiently economically viable that they can compete with the traditional, highly subsidised energy sources. That is the primary contribution that we can make to development. At the next climate conference, I would like to be able to say: "We are now ready. You can now make use of renewable energy. It no longer hinders your economic development and you no longer need to rely on fossil fuels or nuclear energy for cost reasons, but have alternatives at your disposal that are decentralised and guarantee you greater independence." As such, the experiences I have gained over the course of my career have brought me to precisely this point: at the age of 75 years, I am still thinking about alternative paths of action.

In your "Planning Theory" lecture series at the University of Hanover in the 1970s, former students have said you propagated the concept of "muddling through", which was an antithesis to the then prevailing planning ideologies.

sich diese Haltung, auch als wissenschaftliche, bis heute erhalten, also das Abarbeiten von Problemen in der Reihenfolge ihres Auftretens?

Ich habe mich orientiert an dem, was man bei Karl Popper gelernt hat, *dem* Wissenschaftstheoretiker der Zeit, als ich Student war. Sein Buch *Die Offene Gesellschaft und ihre Feinde* von 1945 war im Ostblock verboten. Denn Popper war derjenige, der gegen holistische Großentwürfe angetreten ist, die alle das Problem haben, in demokratischen Willensbildungsprozessen nicht mehr änderbar zu sein. Karl Popper sagte, man brauche ein „*piecemeal engineering*", also ein sequenzielles Denken. Ich frage mich immer, wie wir in einer offenen Gesellschaft, und dies auf globaler Ebene, diesen Prozess organisieren können. Inzwischen bin ich sicher, dass selbstgesteckte Ziele wesentlich für das sequenzielle Denken sind.

Zu Beginn meiner Tätigkeit als Umweltminister hat man mich einen „Ankündigungsminister" genannt. Darüber habe ich mich damals sehr geärgert. Im Nachhinein denke ich, war das eigentlich so schlecht? Du musst auch sagen, wo du hin willst. Dich dann aber nicht zurücklehnen, sondern die Schritte gehen.

Bei Ernst Bloch ist dies der Unterschied zwischen abstrakter und konkreter Utopie: An der abstrakten Utopie, dem großen Entwurf, der alle begeistert und beseelt, hatte ich immer die Kritik, dass wir uns nicht aus einem Zukunftsversprechen ein Alibi für das heutige (Nicht-)Handeln schaffen sollten. Daher sehe ich die holistischen Entwürfe eher in religiösen Dimensionen, in Wertestrukturen. Der von mir in besonderer Weise geachtete Philosoph Balthasar Gracián hat in seiner Schrift *Handorakel und Kunst der Weltklugheit* (1647) gesagt, die Festigkeit gehöre in den Willen, nicht in den Verstand. Das finde ich richtig: Im Verstand haben wir immer die Flexibilität und erhalten uns die Chance des Reagierens.

Has this view – that of dealing with problems in the order in which they present themselves – persisted to the present day, also as a scientific attitude?

As a student, I subscribed to what we learned from Karl Popper, the leading philosopher of science of the time. His book *The Open Society and its Enemies*, written in 1945, was banned in the Eastern Bloc nations, because Popper was critical of sweeping holistic ideologies, as they all suffer from the problem that they cannot change in response to democratic decision-making processes. Karl Popper advocated the idea of "piecemeal engineering", a kind of sequential way of thinking. I often wonder how we, in our open society, and at a global level, could organise this process. I have since come to the conclusion that self-imposed mid-term goals are essential for sequential thinking.

When I first became Federal Minister for the Environment, the press called me the "Minister of Announcements". At the time that angered me, but in retrospect I wonder whether that was really so bad? You have to state where you want to go. Then, rather than leaning back and waiting, you have to follow it through.

For Ernst Bloch, this is the difference between abstract and concrete utopias. I have always been critical of abstract utopias, of grand designs that enthuse and inspire people, when the promise that they hold for the future is used to justify our actions, or rather our lack of them, in the present. Consequently I see holistic visions more in terms of religious dimensions, that is, as a set of values. The philosopher Baltasar Gracián, whom I admire greatly, wrote in his work *The Oracle, a Manual of the Art of Discretion* (1647) that steadfastness should be for the will, not for the mind. That I can subscribe to: in our minds we are always flexible and that means that we have the capacity to respond.

▶ Am Ort vorgefundene Strukturen und Materialien werden für die Umgestaltung aufgenommen. Die Installation „Götter im Exil" besteht aus alten Gleisschwellen

Structures and materials recovered from the site have been used for the redesign. The art installation "Gods in Exile" is made of old railway sleepers

Ein Aspekt Ihrer Arbeit ist vielen in Erinnerung: die Lust am Debattieren und Erklären. Was reizt Sie am rationalen Diskurs?

Ich bin lange in einer politischen Aufgabe in einer Demokratie tätig gewesen. Für das, was ich für sinnvoll halte, was ich ändern will, muss ich Mehrheiten bekommen, ich muss überzeugen. Ich bin viel mehr ein Redner als ein Schreiber und freue mich darüber, wenn da ein paar hundert Leute sitzen und man den Menschen die Dinge so darstellen kann, dass sie sagen: Ich bin möglicherweise nicht dieser Meinung, aber die Argumentation ist bedenkenswert. Ich bin davon überzeugt, dass es ein Kulturverlust ist, dass Rhetorik keinen wissenschaftlichen Lehrstuhl in Deutschland mehr hat. Rhetorik ist nicht die Kunst, jemanden zu überreden, sondern ihn in Argumente mit einzubinden. Das führt mich zu dem Begriff der „Transdisziplinarität". Ziel unseres Institutes ist es, nicht nur die wissenschaftlichen Disziplinen zusammenzubringen, sondern auch die immer besser informierten Bürgerinnen und Bürger in unserer Gesellschaft. „Verändern durch Wissen und Wissen durch Veränderung", so war einer der ersten

One aspect of your work that leaves an impression on many people is that you obviously enjoy debating and giving explanations. What attracts you to rational discourse?

I spent many years working in a political capacity in a democracy. To effect change, to make things that you believe are important actually happen, you need to obtain the support of a majority, and for that you need to convince people. I am more of a speaker than I am a writer, and I enjoy getting up in front of a couple of hundred people and relating something to them in such a way that afterwards they say: "Well, I may not be of the same opinion, but his arguments are certainly worth considering." In my view, the decline of the field of rhetoric in Germany's universities represents a loss to our culture. Rhetoric is not the art of persuading people but of including them in your argumentation or train of thought. That leads me to a further aspect: that of "transdisciplinarity". The aim of our institute is not only to bring together scientific disciplines but also the voices of the ever-better informed citizens in our society. "Transformation through knowledge and knowledge through transformation," was

Workshops des IASS benannt. Wie wird durch die Veränderung in einer offenen Gesellschaft Wissen generiert? Vielleicht war das der Grund, warum man mich gefragt hat, Gründungsdirektor dieses Institutes zu sein, also jemanden, der ein Hybrid ist, halb Wissenschaftler und halb Politiker.

Bekannt sind Sie vor allem als Politiker: Minister für Umwelt und Gesundheit in Rheinland-Pfalz, dann der erste Bundesumweltminister und von 1994 bis 1998 als Bundesminister für Bauwesen, Raumordnung und Städtebau entscheidend tätig für den Regierungsumzug von Bonn nach Berlin. Es folgte die weltweit führende Rolle als Exekutivdirektor des Umweltprogramms der Vereinten Nationen (UNEP). Ist Ihnen die mit diesen Aufgaben verbundene Verantwortung manchmal zu viel?
Diese Entwicklung war ja ein Wachstumsprozess. Ich bin Staatssekretär in Rheinland-Pfalz geworden, als man Umwelt noch sehr viel konkreter aus anderen traditionellen Handlungsfeldern heraus verstand. Umweltpolitik speiste sich aus Gesundheitsfragen. Ich war dann Minister in Rheinland-Pfalz für Umwelt und Gesundheit, übrigens einer der wirklich sinnvollen ministeriellen Zuschnitte, weil eben viele Umweltprobleme negative Konsequenzen für die menschliche Gesundheit haben. Das Umweltministerium, das ich dann in Bonn mit aufbauen durfte, speiste sich aus dem Innenministerium mit dem technischen Umweltschutz, dem Landwirtschaftsministerium mit dem Bereich Naturschutz und dem Gesundheitsministerium. Bisher sektorale Themen wurden in die Klammer der Umweltpolitik eingebunden, was zwingend notwendig war.

Als Leiter der „Ethikkommission für eine sichere Energieversorgung" haben Sie 2011 unter dem Eindruck des Unglücks von Fukushima in kürzester Zeit die Energiewende

one of the opening workshops at the IASS. How does transformation in an open society produce knowledge? Perhaps that was the reason why I was asked to become founding director of the institute: because I am a hybrid myself – half scientist, half politician.

You are most well known as a politician: you were Minister for Health and the Environment in Rhineland-Palatinate, then the first Federal Minister for the Environment; and from 1994 to 1998, as Federal Minister for Regional Planning, Civil Engineering and Urban Development, you were instrumental in effecting the transfer of the government from Bonn to Berlin. Then followed leading global positions as Executive Director of the United Nations Environment Programme (UNEP). Has the responsibility you have shouldered ever been too much?
This development was a growing process. I became State Secretary in Rhineland-Palatinate at a time in which the environment was seen very much in the context of other traditional fields of action. It was health issues that shaped environmental policies. I then become Minister for Health and the Environment in Rhineland-Palatinate, which in my view is one of the more sensible pairings of ministries because many environmental problems have negative consequences for our health. The Ministry for the Environment that I later took part in setting up in Bonn was an amalgamation of the Technical Environmental Protection Department of the Ministry of the Interior, the Nature Conservation Department of the Ministry of Agriculture, and the Ministry of Health. Issues that were previously handled by different sectors were brought together under the roof of environmental policies, which was very necessary.

in Deutschland eingeleitet. Ein „Erfolg" oder eine sachliche Entscheidung?

Nein, das war ein wirklich offener Prozess. Wir waren 17 Persönlichkeiten in dieser Ethikkommission, alles Persönlichkeiten aus ihrem eigenen Recht heraus, die nicht ausgewählt worden waren, weil sie für vorgefasste Meinungen standen. Das gilt für den Kardinal von München genauso wie für den Vorstandsvorsitzenden der BASF oder den Vorsitzenden einer großen deutschen Gewerkschaft und auch für die Wissenschaftler, die teilnahmen. Es entstand ein Prozess der Erarbeitung von gemeinsamen Positionen, der sich intensiv auch mit der Frage beschäftigt hat: Was ist das Ethische an dieser Fragestellung? Es war wirklich eine Ethikkommission. Die harsche Kritik, die Kommission sei nur ein Deckmäntelchen für politische Vorstellungen gewesen, trifft nicht. Der für mich zentrale Satz war, dass „die gesellschaftlichen Werte den ökonomischen und technischen Möglichkeiten vorangehen" – das ist ein unglaublicher Satz, der kaum irgendwo zitiert wurde. Aber aus eben solchen Leitsätzen entstehen Konsequenzen im Konkreten. Das Ergebnis ist dann einstimmig akzeptiert worden und diese Einstimmigkeit hat wesentlich dazu beigetragen, dass im Parlament eine nahezu einstimmige Entscheidung für diese Energiewende zustande gekommen ist.

Wie haben Sie zwischen dem Ereignis in Fukushima und den grundlegenden Überlegungen abgewogen? Sie selbst haben 2007 noch gefordert: „Die Debatte um die Kernenergie wird, und soll, engagiert weitergehen ..."[1] Ist sie nun in Deutschland beendet?

Es gab in Deutschland auch vor Fukushima schon die parteienübergreifende Aussage: „Die Kernenergie ist eine Brückentechnik." Die intensiv diskutierte Frage war: Wie lang ist diese Brücke? Da gab es einen Riss in der Gesellschaft, der zurückgeht auf die Diskussion, die wir nach

In 2011, the Fukushima disaster struck while you were chairman of the "Ethics Commission for a Safe Energy Supply", and you were very quick to initiate the process of energy transition in Germany. Was this a "success" or a carefully reasoned decision?

No, that really was an open process. There were 17 of us in the Ethics Commission, all public figures, each of whom came from their own respective ethical background and were not selected because they represented any preconceived opinion. That applies for the Cardinal of Munich as it does for the chairman of the board of BASF or the chairman of a large German trade union as well as for the various scientists who took part. A process began in which we elaborated joint positions and also discussed at length what the ethical parameters of this issue were. It really was a commission about ethics. The harsh criticism levelled at us, that we were merely a cover for justifying political objectives, does not apply. For me the central phrase was that "society's value judgements ... precede technical and economic aspects" – that is an incredible sentence that was hardly picked up on by the press. Ultimately, it is key sentences like these that have very concrete consequences. The result was accepted unanimously within the committee and this unanimity was a major reason why parliament decided by a large majority to implement the energy transition strategy.

How did you weigh up between the events in Fukushima and the more fundamental considerations? In 2007, you yourself said: "The debate over nuclear power will and must be actively continued..."[1] Is it now over in Germany?

Before Fukushima, there was already a cross-party consensus in Germany that "nuclear power is a bridge technology". The much-debated question was: how long is this bridge? There was already a division in society that

Tschernobyl 1986 hatten. Von daher gesehen haben wir nicht bei Null angefangen, sondern uns gefragt: „Wie schnell kann der Ausstieg aus der Atomtechnologie gelingen und welche Konsequenzen sind damit verbunden?"

Die Debatte um die Kernenergie, die ja schon lange vor Tschernobyl begann, ist deswegen so spannungsreich, weil mit Kernenergie zu Beginn ja nicht eine Brückentechnologie, sondern die Lösung der weltsozialen Frage definiert worden war. Sie selbst werfen im Institut diese Frage erneut auf: „Verändert die Energiewende unsere Demokratie?"

Ich verweise immer auf das Interview, das ich als gerade berufener Bundesumweltminister der Tageszeitung *Die Welt* gegeben habe: „Wir müssen eine Zukunft ohne Kernenergie erfinden." Wir sahen damals mehrheitlich keine Alternative. Deswegen mussten wir sie erfinden. Dass unter meiner Verantwortung das erste „Stromeinspeisegesetz" durchgesetzt wurde, war der Beginn dieses Erfindungsprozesses. Nun waren veränderte Investitionen in Forschung und Entwicklung möglich, die uns weltweit führend auf dem Gebiet der regenerativen Energien gemacht haben.

Mit diesen neuen Technologien haben wir nun eine andere Mitwirkungsmöglichkeit vieler Menschen. Heute gibt es schon über 600 Energiegenossenschaften in Deutschland.

goes back to the discussions that followed Chernobyl in 1986. As such, we didn't have to go back to square one, and instead could ask: "How quickly can we withdraw from nuclear energy and what consequences will that have?"

The debate over nuclear power, which began long before Chernobyl, is such a rich source of tension not least because to begin with nuclear power was not a bridge technology but posited as the solution to the world's social problems. In your institute, you yourself bring up this question once again: "Will the energy transition change our democracy?"

I always point people to the interview I gave shortly after becoming Federal Minister of the Environment to the daily newspaper *Die Welt*: "We must invent a future without nuclear energy". At the time, the majority of us saw no alternative. For that reason we had to invent it. The introduction of the German Electricity Feed Act, which I was responsible for implementing, was the beginning of this process of invention. It made different kinds of investments in research and development possible, which have since helped us to become a world leader in the field of regenerative energy sources.

With these new technologies, we now have another way in which many people can contribute. Today, there

Der Außenraum der Münchener Wohnanlage Gern 64 verbindet wie die Architektur alte und neue Elemente zu einer Einheit auf der Grundlage der ursprünglichen Geometrie der Hofanlage. Entwurf: el:ch landschaftsarchitekten, München

The outdoor areas, like the architecture, of the Gern 64 residential estate in Munich combine new and old elements and follow the geometric layout of the original courtyard. Design: el:ch landschaftsarchitekten, Munich

Die Möglichkeiten der dezentralen Energieerzeugung sind andere als die der großen Einheiten, die sehr kapitalintensiv sind und die deswegen nur von großen, leistungsfähigen Unternehmen getragen werden konnten. Daher ist diese Öffnung hin zu erneuerbaren Energien auch eine Öffnung in die Gesellschaft hinein und eine neue Möglichkeit der Teilhabe, der Mitwirkung an Entwicklungs- und Entscheidungsprozessen. Dies halte ich für einen wichtigen Effekt unserer Energiewende. Denn genau dieser Effekt der dezentralen Verantwortung führt dazu, dass diese Energietechnik globalisierungsfähig ist.

Wie gelangt man zu der Wissensgrundlage, um solche Entscheidungen treffen zu können bzw. politische Mehrheiten dafür zu bekommen? Ist diese Fähigkeit, komplexe Zusammenhänge zu erfassen und zu sortieren, in den Landschaftsplanungs- und Raumordnungsdisziplinen hinreichend ausgeprägt? Oder denkt man aufgrund der Erfolge, die man seit den 1970er Jahren errungen hat, zu sehr in Sektoren und Zuständigkeitsbereichen?

Wenn wir stärker sequenziell denken, wenn wir komplexe Tatbestände auch in ihren Teilbereichen sehen, dann können wir einzelne Entscheidungen treffen und zugleich sinnvoll einbinden, ohne nicht verantwortbare Koordinierungsverluste hinzunehmen. Einzelne Entscheidungen sollten also einem Masterplan folgen, der aber nicht allzu detailliert sein muss, sondern an dem ich jährlich anhand von Indikatoren sehen kann, wie weit wir gekommen sind, wo nachjustiert werden muss, wo Fehlentwicklungen unterbunden werden müssen. Wenn ich beispielsweise sehe, dass wir derzeit keine relevanten Preise für CO_2-Emissionen erzielen, dann muss ich fragen, welche Konsequenzen das hat. Die aktuelle Konsequenz ist der Anstieg an CO_2, weil die alten abgeschriebenen Kohlekraftwerke bei niedrigen Kohlepreisen ökonomisch konkurrenzlos besser

are over 600 energy cooperatives in Germany. The possibilities for generating energy locally are different to those of the large plants that require a vast amount of capital and can therefore only be developed by large and powerful corporations. The move towards renewable energy is also a move towards more openness in society and a new way for people to take part, to contribute to development and decision-making processes. That is, I think, an important effect of our energy transition policy. For it is precisely this effect of decentralising responsibility that can make this kind of energy technology globally viable.

How do you acquire the knowledge basis to make such decisions or to obtain majority political support for them? Is the capacity to identify and to sort such complex interrelationships sufficiently well developed in the spatial planning disciplines? Or are we still stuck in sectorial thinking and areas of responsibility that have consolidated since the successes achieved in the 1970s?

If we start to think more sequentially, if we are able to also see complex circumstances in terms of their constituent parts, then we will be able to make individual decisions and to integrate them sensibly without suffering unacceptable coordination losses. Individual decisions should, therefore, follow a master plan. This need not be overly detailed but can be assessed using indicators each year to see how far we have come, what needs to be adjusted, and where we need to put a stop to undesirable developments. When, for example, I can see that we are not currently achieving relevant prices for CO_2 emissions then I need to ask what the consequences will be. The current consequence is a rise in CO_2 production because the old amortised coal power stations are economically more advantageous when coal prices are low than a modern gas power station with a high degree

sind als ein modernes Gaskraftwerk mit hohem Wirkungsgrad und geringen CO_2-Emissionen. Hier muss dann nachgesteuert werden. Ein Masterplan ist also nicht eine Festlegung ein für alle Mal, sondern Ausdruck der Verantwortung, demokratisch beschlossene Ziele immer wieder zu justieren und voranzubringen. Wenn du mit dem Kopf durch die Wand gehst, ist das weniger intelligent, als wenn du fragst, wo die Tür ist, durch die du gehen kannst, oder nach dem Weg um die Wand herum suchst. Das ist auch eine pragmatische Position, die ich vor allem in den Jahren bei den Vereinten Nationen gelernt habe.

Es wird viel über alternative Ansätze gesprochen: Smart Cities, Smart Buildings, Smart Living. Haben Sie eine Vision für eine „smarte" Landschaft?
Wir sollten eine Landschaft als Vision haben, die wieder den Menschen in der Natur sieht, die den bisherigen Entwicklungen, dass der Mensch die Natur geformt hat, ein Stück begegnet. Wir sind auf absehbare Zeit in Deutschland und in anderen hochentwickelten Ländern eine Gesellschaft mit weniger Menschen, die aber älter werden, auch eine buntere Gesellschaft. Ich möchte gerne eine Landschaft sehen, die wieder etwas ruhiger atmet. Wenn Sie das „smart" nennen, wäre das treffend im Sinne einer neuen Gelassenheit, nicht immer alles sofort fertig stellen zu müssen. Ich habe als Bauminister mal schüchtern den Versuch eingebracht, über eine zeitlich begrenzte Architektur zu diskutieren, so dass auch kommende Generationen ihre Vorstellungen vom Bauen entwickeln können. Meine Vision ist also eine gestaltbare Landschaft, die nicht definitiv ist, sondern auf Änderungen hin ausgelegt.

of efficiency and low CO_2 emissions. This is the kind of thing that needs to be adjusted. A master plan therefore does not set out a plan once and for all but is instead an expression of the responsibility to adjust and push forward democratically reached goals. Rather than trying to force one's way through a brick wall, it is more intelligent to ask where the door is, or to find a way around the wall. That is a pragmatic approach that I learnt particularly during my years at the United Nations.

There has been much talk of alternative approaches: Smart Cities, Smart Buildings and Smart Living. Do you have a vision for a Smart Landscape?
We should have a vision of a landscape that sees people once again as being within nature, that counters the prevailing developments in which people shaped nature. In Germany and in other highly developed countries, we will in the foreseeable future be living in a society with fewer people, who will be older and also more multi-cultural. I would like to see a landscape that once again breathes a little more slowly. If you want to call that "smart", then it is appropriate in the sense that we are more relaxed about not always having to finish things right away. As Minister for Construction, I hesitantly proposed the idea of talking about architecture made for a limited time frame so that later generations can also realise their ideas of building. My vision is, therefore, of a designable landscape that is not definitive but conceived to be able to adapt to changes.

Wir sitzen hier im Institut IASS in Potsdam. Potsdam ist groß geworden mit der Botschaft: „Das ganze Eyland muss ein Paradies werden". Für Sie ist nicht das Absolute des Paradieses das Ziel, sondern die Alternative in der Entwicklung?

Offen zu bleiben auch für neue Erwartungen der Menschen an ihre Region, nicht zu glauben, wir wüssten alles jetzt abschließend: Dies ist wieder das sequenzielle Denken. Ich möchte nicht Landschaften, nicht Städte, nicht Gebäude, die – einmal gebaut – nur durch Abriss verändert werden können. Wenn wir nicht nur in der Kategorie Raum, sondern auch in der Kategorie Zeit denken und uns dadurch selbst immer ein Stück infrage stellen, werden wir Landschaften entwerfen, in denen man gerne ist, weil sie dem Denken des Menschen über Perspektiven, die er in der Landschaft wiederfinden will, gerecht werden.

Wenn Sie mit Studierenden aus Hannover oder Afrika heute wieder auf Exkursion am Lagerfeuer sitzen würden und diese würden Sie fragen: Wie soll ich offen bleiben für das Denken in Alternativen? Wie lautet Ihre Antwort?

Indem man offen und motiviert mit den Menschen spricht und die Fähigkeit nicht verliert, die eigenen Überzeugungen auch in Frage stellen zu können.

We are sitting here in the IASS Institute in Potsdam. Potsdam grew up with the motto: "The whole island must become a paradise". For you, it is not about achieving the absolute vision of paradise but the alternative pathways of development?

To remain open to new expectations that people may have of their region and not to think we have to finish everything off right now: that is once again the principle of sequential thinking. I don't want to have landscapes, cities or buildings that – once built – can only be changed by demolishing them. If we think not only in the category of space but also in the category of time, and all the while call our motives into question, we will be able to design landscapes that one enjoys being in because they reflect how people think in terms of perspectives that they wish to see in the landscape.

If you were to sit around the campfire today with your students from Hanover or from Africa as part of some study trip, and they were to ask you: "How should I remain open for thinking in terms of alternatives?" what would be your answer?

By speaking openly and motivatedly with people, and by maintaining the capacity to question one's own convictions.

---

1 Klaus Töpfer, Friederike Bauer, *Arche in Aufruhr. Was wir tun müssen, um die Erde zu retten*, S. Fischer Verlag, Frankfurt am Main, 2007, S. 177.

1 Klaus Töpfer, Friederike Bauer, *Arche in Aufruhr. Was wir tun müssen, um die Erde zu rettten*, S. Fischer Verlag, 2007, p. 177.

Die in diesem Beitrag gezeigten Projekte stammen, wenn nicht anders angegeben, von Vogt Landschaftsarchitekten, Zürich/London/Berlin

Unless otherwise specified, all projects shown are by Vogt Landschaftsarchitekten, Zurich/London/Berlin

Nachhaltigkeit ist unsichtbar
Sustainability is invisible

von · by Günther Vogt

Die Buchskugel ist ein gesellschaftliches Phänomen. Botanisch wie ästhetisch gesehen liegt die größte Besonderheit der unscheinbaren Pflanze in ihrer Toleranz gegen Beschnitt. Die Form allein aber kann die Beliebtheit der grünen Kugel nicht begründen. Was sie so begehrenswert macht, ist vielmehr die Welt, die in der Kugel steckt und die wir uns gerne stückweise in unseren Garten holen. Die Pflanze erzählt von Königen, von gepuderten Perücken und barocken Gärten, in denen Hofdamen flanieren, von Prunk und Lustbarkeiten. Die Buchskugel ist ein Symbol wie die Justitia der Juristen oder das Reagenzglas des Chemikers. Die Welt in unseren Köpfen besteht mehr denn je aus Bildern. Welches Bild haben wir beim Globalbegriff „Nachhaltigkeit" oder der „nachhaltigen Entwicklung" vor Augen?

Design, das wissen wir seit der entsprechenden These Lucius Burckhardts, ist unsichtbar. Nicht, weil man das Designobjekt nicht sehen würde, sondern vielmehr, weil es Teil eines größeren, unsichtbaren Systems ist, das seinerseits Gegenstand der Gestaltung ist. So ist beispielsweise die Trambahn als gestaltetes Objekt nur ein kleiner Teil des Systems „öffentlicher Verkehr" mit seinen Regeln und Abläufen.

Ähnlich verhält es sich mit der Nachhaltigkeit: Sie ist omnipräsent, doch unsichtbar. Es gibt für sie so viele Bilder, dass jegliche Auswahl so zusammenhanglos wie willkürlich erscheint. Doch egal, ob es sich um ökonomische, soziale oder ökologische Aspekte handelt, der Begriff steht für umfassende Prozesse. Nachhaltige Gestaltung hat wenig mit Naturnähe im Sinne einer Naturgartenästhetik zu tun. Wesentlicher ist der lokale Bezug, was meist mit der Verwendung lokal verfügbarer Materialien einhergeht. Die Idee der Nachhaltigkeit mag global sein, die Umsetzung in der Landschaftsarchitektur ist ortsspezifisch.

Spherical box bushes are a social phenomenon. The greatest asset of this otherwise unspectacular plant, both from a botanical as well as an aesthetic viewpoint, is its tolerance of being pruned. But the form alone cannot explain the popularity that this green ball enjoys. What makes it so desirable is the world that this globe embodies and which we like to bring into our gardens bit by bit. The plant evokes a world of nobility, of powdered wigs and baroque gardens with promenading ladies-in-waiting, and of pomp and festivities. Like Justitia is for lawyers or the test tube is for chemists, the spherical box bush is a symbol. The world in our minds consists more than ever of images. So what do we see in our mind's eye for the global terms "sustainability" or "sustainable development"?

Design is invisible – that much we know since Lucius Burckhardt's seminal essay of the same name. Not because we can't see the designed object in question but rather because it is part of a larger, invisible system that is in turn the subject of design. For example, a tram as a designed object is just a small part of the larger system of "public transport" with its various rules and procedures.

The same is true of sustainability: it is omnipresent but invisible. It has been represented by so many images that whichever we choose seems incoherent and arbitrary. But regardless of whether we are concerned with economic, social or ecological aspects, the term stands for processes that are all-encompassing. Sustainable design has little to do with naturalness in the sense of the aesthetics of a natural garden. What matters is the local connection, which usually involves the use of locally available materials. The idea of sustainability may be global but its manifestation in landscape architecture is site-specific. Depending on the project and its social con-

▲ Sehen ist Wissen: Die Buchskugel fasziniert durch „die Welt, die in der Kugel steckt" – auch im Außenraum der Swiss Re, Rüschlikon

Seeing is knowing: a sphere of box topiary evokes a world of associations, here in the grounds of Swiss Re in Rüschlikon

Sie kann abhängig vom Projekt, den sozialen Bedingungen und naturräumlichen Gegebenheiten ganz unterschiedlich aussehen. Entsprechend bedeutet nachhaltige Landschaftsarchitektur vor allem: tiefgreifende Auseinandersetzung mit dem Ort, denn eine Planung, die in Delhi Ressourcen schont, kann bei einem Projekt in London, Berlin oder Zürich einen negativen ökologischen Fußabdruck hinterlassen. Nachhaltigkeit sehen setzt Wissen voraus.

Der Innenhof des Hotels Greulich in Zürich beispielsweise wurde mit einem Naturschutzpreis ausgezeichnet. Denn die verwendeten Pflanzen, 160 junge Birken, wurden „recycelt": Sie stammen aus dem temporären „Garten der Gewalt" von der Expo.02 in Murten. Mit ihnen entstand auf dem Dach einer Tiefgarage in Zürich ein lichter Birkenhain. Nicht nur die Wiederverwertung der Bäume, auch der Gedanke der Dachbegrünung ist aus Sicht des Mikroklimas wie des Stadtklimas zu begrüßen. Doch ist der Dachaufbau mit den Birken, die bewässert und gedüngt werden müssen, nachhaltiger als die geometrische Rasenlandschaft um das Laban Dance Centre in London? Während der Birkenhain in unser gängiges Naturbild passt und der Beton der Tiefgarage unter ihm verborgen bleibt, ist Nachhaltigkeit rund um die Londoner Tanzschule kaum erkennbar. Doch die geometrische Rasenhügel-Landschaft ist

ditions and natural surroundings, this can take quite different forms. As such, sustainable landscape architecture entails above all a profound examination of the site: for example, a project that conserves resources in Delhi can leave a negative ecological footprint in London, Berlin or Zurich. Sustainability therefore necessitates prior knowledge.

The interior courtyard of the Hotel Greulich in Zurich, for example, was awarded a nature protection prize. Why? Because the 160 young birch trees used for the project were "recycled": the trees came from the temporary "Garden of Violence" created for the Swiss Expo.02 in Murten and were used in Zurich to create a loose arrangement of trees on top of an underground car park. Reutilising the trees was just one aspect; the idea of greening a roof also benefits the local microclimate as well as the urban climate of the city. But is the planting of a roof with birch trees that need to be watered and fed with fertilizers more sustainable than, for example, the geometric lawnscape around the Laban Dance Centre in London? While the grove of birch trees corresponds to our typical notion of what nature is and conceals the concrete of the underground car park, the sustainability of the landscape around the dance centre in London is barely visible. The prismatic landscape of tilted lawns is

nicht nur ökonomisch, sondern auch in Bau und Unterhalt ressourcenschonend und trägt zum Artenschutz bei. Für die Erdmodellierung wurde der Aushub vom Bau verwendet. So musste die kontaminierte Erde des ehemaligen Industrieareals nicht entsorgt und eingelagert werden, sondern konnte vor Ort wiederverwertet werden. Auch der Verzicht auf Baumpflanzungen ist ökologisch begründet. Ein seltener Vogel, der Hausrotschwanz, ist im Gebiet heimisch. Bäume würden Raubvögeln Sitzwarten bieten und die Art damit gefährden.

Potenziale und Strategien im Umgang mit Stadtlandschaft müssen sich aus der stetig fortschreitenden Urbanisierung entwickeln. Landschaft ist eine Ressource geworden, eine Ressource des Urbanen, vergleichbar mit Trinkwasser oder Erdöl. Die Ökologie denkt in Systemen, verknüpft hoch effiziente organische und anorganische Prozesse eines Raums zur Beschreibung eines Lebensraums. Die Erkenntnis, dass in einem Landschaftsraum sehr komplexe Interdependenzen wirken und die Zivilisation mittlerweile überall und andauernd einwirkt, führt zum Begriff der Nachhaltigkeit. Gestaltung städtischer Freiräume bedeutet immer, etwas zu verändern – Wasserhaushalt, Bodenressourcen, soziale und politische Prozesse –, und ist letztlich gezeichnet von unserer Sicht der Landschaft.

not only economical to produce; it also requires fewer resources to build and to maintain and provides a habitat for endangered species. The modelling of the ground was realised using soil excavated from the construction site. The contaminated soil of the former industrial site did not have to be disposed of but could be used on site. The decision to refrain from planting trees also has ecological reasons: a rare bird, the black redstart, is native to the area and trees would have provided birds of prey with a place from which to hunt the endangered species.

Strategies for dealing with the urban landscape and the potential it offers must be developed in response to the steady progression of urbanisation. Landscape has become a resource, an urban resource comparable with water or crude oil. Ecology can be conceived of as a set of systems that link highly efficient organic and inorganic processes within a space to describe a living environment. The realisation that a landscape is subject to very complex interdependencies, and that civilisation now impacts constantly and at all levels, has given rise to the notion of sustainability. Designing urban open spaces always entails changing something – the water balance, soil resources, social and political processes – and is ultimately shaped by our view of what landscape is.

◀ Diese Birken im temporären „Garten der Gewalt" auf der Expo.02 in Murten…

The birch trees in the temporary "Garden of Violence" at the Expo.02 in Murten …

▼ …bilden inzwischen einen lichten Hain über der Tiefgarage des Hotels Greulich in Zürich. Das Projekt gewann einen Naturschutzpreis

… now stand in a loose cluster on the roof of an underground car park for the Hotel Greulich in Zurich. The project was awarded a nature protection award

▲ Ressourcenschonung durch Aushub-Recycling und Artenschutz für den Hausrotschwanz durch den Verzicht auf Bäume verbergen sich hinter dieser geometrischen Rasenlandschaft am Laban Dance Centre, London

This geometric lawnscape around the Laban Dance Centre in London conserves resources by re-using excavated soil and provides a habitat for the endangered black redstart by not providing trees for its predators

▶ „Un-common Venice", Beitrag zur 13. Architektur-Biennale Venedig 2012: Die Erkenntnisse von Passantenbefragungen werden in die Sprache des Kiosks übersetzt. Dieser wird zur gemeinsamen Plattform für eine Vielfalt von Ansichten und Stellungnahmen. Projektentwicklung: Case Studio VOGT, Zürich

"Un-common Venice", 13th Architecture Biennale in Venice in 2012: the opinions of passers-by are translated into the language of the kiosk. This is used as a common platform for a variety of viewpoints and opinions. Project development: Case Studio VOGT, Zurich

Prägend für die heutige Form der Landschaftswahrnehmung in Europa ist ein Ereignis aus dem Jahr 1226: die absichtslose Besteigung des Mont Ventoux durch Francesco Petrarca – eine Anstrengung ohne zwingenden wirtschaftlichen Grund, rein aus dem Wunsch heraus, die Aussicht zu genießen. Das Revolutionäre dieser Bergbesteigung bringt Bazon Brock auf die Formel: „Wenn nicht die objektiven Bedingungen des Überlebens in der Natur, sondern die des subjektiven Erlebens der Natur unsere Haltung ihr gegenüber beherrschen, formen wir sie zur Landschaft um." Bildhaft dargestellt für die Stadt hat das beispielsweise der Filmemacher Guy-Ernest Debord 1957 in seinem *Guide psychogéographique de Paris*, einer Zeichnung von Paris, die mit dem gängigen Stadtplan der Metropole wenig gemein hat. In Debords *Mental Map* liegt das Centre Pompidou direkt neben dem Eiffelturm. Von hier aus mag bei dem einen Betrachter ein Spazierweg zu seinem Lieblingsbistro führen, beim anderen die Métro zum Friseur und für den nächsten wird die Buslinie zum nahen Stadtpark die wichtigste Verkehrsachse sein. Genau hier macht sich die Notwendigkeit einer nachhaltigen Planung bemerkbar, denn gerade die sozialen Prozesse sind nach wie

How we perceive landscape today in Europe can be traced back to an event in the year 1226 when Francesco Petrarca famously decided to climb Mont Ventoux, an undertaking not motivated by a premeditated reason or for material advantage but solely by a desire to admire the view. Bazon Brock expresses the revolutionary aspect of Petrarca's ascent as follows: "When our view of nature is dominated not by the objective conditions of our survival in the natural environment but by our subjective experience of it, we have transformed it into landscape." The filmmaker Guy-Ernest Debord found a similar expression of this for the city in his *Guide psychogéographique de Paris*, a drawing made in 1957 of Paris that has little in common with a normal map of the metropolitan city. In Debord's mental map, the Centre Pompidou lies directly adjacent to the Eifel Tower. Viewers can proceed from here as they please: perhaps on foot to their favourite bistro, or by Métro to their hairdresser, or alternatively by bus to a nearby park – each has their own important axis of movement. Here we can see the need for sustainable planning because it is precisely these social processes that remain invisible: the ability to walk from place to

Nachhaltigkeit ist unsichtbar | Sustainability is invisible | 43

▶ Eine Baumschule als Zwischennutzung in Dagenham Docks, London: Die auf einer Brachfläche gezogenen Bäume werden nach und nach für die Freiräume der Umgebung verwendet

A tree nursery as interim use in Dagenham Docks, London: the trees planted on a wasteland site will gradually be used for other sites in the vicinity

vor unsichtbar und eine fußläufige Verbindung – zum Kindergarten, zur Arbeit und zum nächsten Park – ist sozial nachhaltig.

Unser Beitrag im Rahmen der 13. Internationalen Architektur-Biennale in Venedig 2012, die sich dem „Common Ground" widmete, hat das Thema wörtlich genommen. Den öffentlichen Raum als Allmende verstehend, wurde er im Hinblick auf das Verhältnis zwischen Ressource und Nutzung untersucht. Venedig eignet sich aufgrund der klaren Trennung von öffentlichem und privatem Raum und wegen des Spannungsverhältnisses zwischen lokaler und globaler Nutzung in paradigmatischer Weise für diese Betrachtung. Durch Passantenbefragungen an verschiedenen öffentlichen Räumen in der Stadt wurde versucht, eine differenzierte Wahrnehmung der „Ressource Venedig" und ihr Regelwerk in Bezug auf den gelebten Alltag zu ermitteln. Dabei ging es darum, wie diese Orte benutzt, angeeignet und mental konzipiert werden, wie man sich darin bewegt und orientiert und was ihre spezifischen Merkmale und Qualitäten sind. Das Verständnis von Venedig, genauer von dessen öffentlichem Raum, als „commons" (Allmende) und die Fokussierung auf die subjektive Nutzerperspektive – vom lokalen Bewohner bis zum globalisierten Tagestouristen – soll, gleichsam aus dem Alltäglichen und Gewohnten heraus, einen ungewöhnlichen Blick auf Venedig und einen Ausschnitt aus seinen sozialen Prozessen eröffnen.

Nachhaltige Planung in der Landschaftsarchitektur hat viele Gesichter und ist nicht nur eine Frage des Maßstabs, sondern auch der Möglichkeiten zur Einflussnahme. Am wirksamsten lässt sich das Thema in den interdisziplinären Gremien auf städtebaulicher Ebene angehen. Auf Projektebene geht es dann neben Aspekten des Bauens und des Unterhaltes auch um die gestalterische Umsetzung und Visualisierung der Idee Nachhaltigkeit.

place – to the children's nursery, to work and to the next park – is socially sustainable.

In our contribution to the 13th International Architecture Biennale in Venice in 2012, which was entitled "Common Ground", we decided to address this topic literally. Starting from the premise that public space is common ground, we examined the relationship between its availability as a resource and its utilisation. Venice is a paradigmatic case in this respect because public and private space is so clearly separated and because of the tension between local and global use. By interviewing passers-by in various public spaces in Venice, we attempted to acquire a differentiated perspective of the local "resource" and its regulatory framework in relation to the daily lives of its users. The intention was to examine how these places are used, taken in and mentally conceived, how people move around them and find their way, as well as to identify their specific characteristics and qualities. This understanding of Venice, more precisely of its public space, as common land ("commons"), as well as the focus on the subjective perspective of its users – whether local residents or global day-trippers – aimed to reveal an unusual view of Venice born out of its everyday use and familiar patterns, and to offer insight into the social processes that constitute the city.

Sustainable planning in landscape architecture can take many different forms and the key factor is not only one of scale but of being able to exert an influence. The most effective means is to address the topic in various interdisciplinary urban planning committees. At the scale of the project, one can incorporate these concerns not only in the construction and maintenance concepts, but also articulate them through the design and visualisation of the idea of sustainability.

Pflanzenstrategie · Nursery Planting Strategy

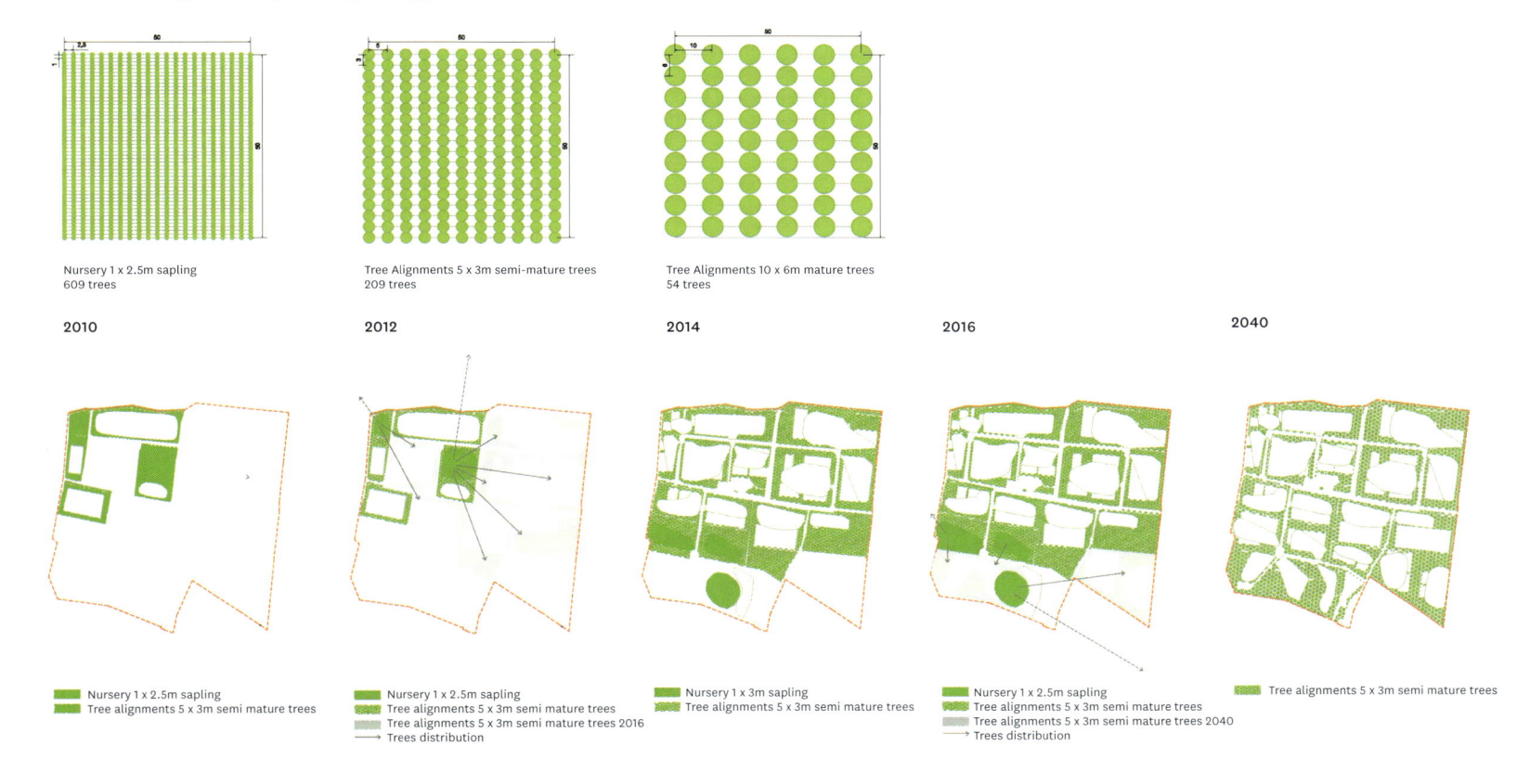

Nursery 1 x 2.5m sapling
609 trees

Tree Alignments 5 x 3m semi-mature trees
209 trees

Tree Alignments 10 x 6m mature trees
54 trees

2010　　2012　　2014　　2016　　2040

- Nursery 1 x 2.5m sapling
- Tree alignments 5 x 3m semi mature trees

- Nursery 1 x 2.5m sapling
- Tree alignments 5 x 3m semi mature trees
- Tree alignments 5 x 3m semi mature trees 2016
- Trees distribution

- Nursery 1 x 3m sapling
- Tree alignments 5 x 3m semi mature trees

- Nursery 1 x 2.5m sapling
- Tree alignments 5 x 3m semi mature trees
- Tree alignments 5 x 3m semi mature trees 2040
- Trees distribution

- Tree alignments 5 x 3m semi mature trees

Die Baumschule als Zwischennutzung – ein Konzept, das für das Projekt Dagenham Docks in London entwickelt wurde – operiert auf städtebaulicher wie projektbezogener Ebene auf der Grundlage von Überlegungen zur Nachhaltigkeit: Temporäre Brachen sollen dort – im Sinne einer Baumschule vor Ort – mit Jungbäumen bepflanzt werden, die später für die Freiräume in der Umgebung verwendet werden können – eine Lösung, die, bedenkt man Transport und Kosten von Großbäumen, ökologisch wie ökonomisch sinnvoll ist.

Doch was, wenn es den Grund, auf dem man plant, noch gar nicht gibt? Wenn einzig klar ist, dass er sich während der nächsten zwei Generationen stetig wandeln wird, wie auf dem geplanten Kiesabbaugelände Rectory Farm in der Nähe des Londoner Flughafens Heathrow? Dabei geht es zunächst weniger um die Frage, wo welcher Baum stehen soll, sondern vielmehr um ein Programm für den Ort. Die Ausbeutung des Bodens, Vegetation, Regenwassermanagement stehen zur Debatte, aber auch soziale und ökonomische Fragen stellen sich – und all das sind Prozesse, die es zu steuern gilt. Interdisziplinarität ist hier wieder das Schlüsselwort. Dennoch stellt der Entwurf von heute ein Idealbild dar. Politische, wirtschaftliche und soziale Interessen an der Gebietsentwicklung werden sich

The interim use of a site as a tree nursery – a concept that was developed for the Dagenham Docks in London – addresses sustainability concerns at both an urban and project-specific level. By planting temporary wasteland sites with young trees – creating as it were an on-site tree nursery – plants can be grown for later use elsewhere in open spaces in the vicinity. Given the cost and effort involved in transporting large trees, this solution makes sense both ecologically as well as economically.

But what can one do when the ground for planning does not yet exist? When all that we know is that it will be subject to constant change over the next two generations, as is the case with the planned Rectory Farm gravel pit site near London Heathrow Airport? Initially, it is not possible to design where which tree should stand; instead the design involves developing a programme for the location. The exploitation of the ground resources, the vegetation, the rainwater management as well as social and economic factors are just some of the aspects to be considered – and all of these are also processes that need to be steered. Once again, an interdisciplinary approach is key. Even then, the design we produce today represents an ideal case: it is conceivable that political, economic and social interests in the development of the

▲ Rectory Farm, London: Das zukünftige Programm für dieses geplante Kiesabbaugebiet lässt sich noch nicht festlegen

Rectory Farm, London: the future programme for this former gravel pit area cannot yet be determined

▶ Der Entwurf einer Parklandschaft erfolgt in Phasen und steuert Schlüsselprozesse wie Regenwassermanagement und sozialökonomische Entwicklung interdisziplinär

The phase-by-phase design for this park landscape takes an interdisciplinary approach to determining key processes such as rainwater management and socio-economic development

voraussichtlich noch einige Male bis Projektende ändern. Ein Programm, das flexibel genug ist, darauf zu reagieren, kann sicherstellen, dass die Parkgestaltung dennoch nachhaltig, sozial verträglich und gestalterisch hochwertig entwickelt werden kann.

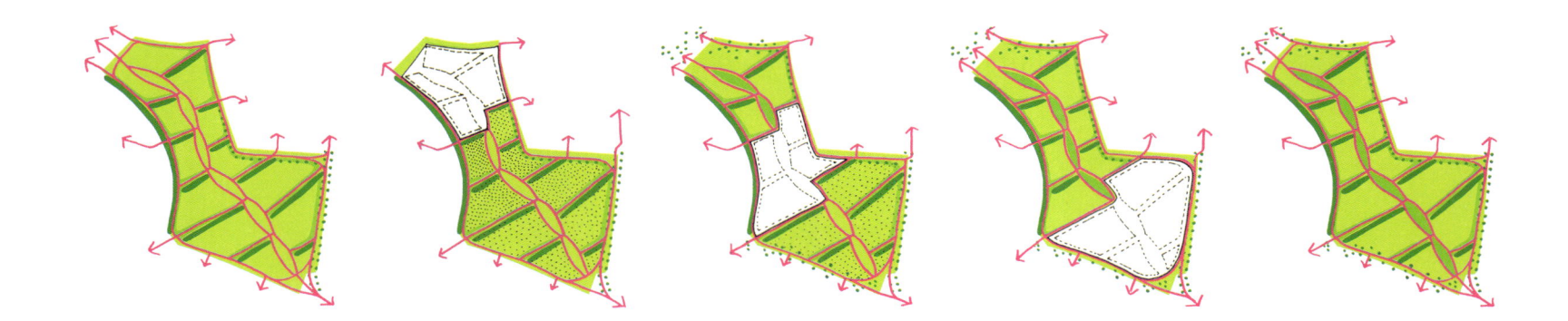

Lucius Burckhardt leitet aus der These vom unsichtbaren Design das Ideal des integrierten Entwerfers ab. Ob der integrierte Landschaftsarchitekt Utopie oder Zukunftsvision ist, bleibt abzuwarten – aber die Landschaftsarchitektur sollte ihren Platz an der Schnittstelle von Forschung und Praxis für intensivere interdisziplinäre Zusammenarbeit nutzen. Die Freiraumgestaltung bietet die Möglichkeit, Nachhaltigkeit nicht nur baulich umzusetzen, sondern sie auch in einzelnen Aspekten sichtbar zu machen und ihr Bild in der Öffentlichkeit zu schärfen.

Die Vielfalt der Aspekte und die Komplexität ihrer Vernetzung zeigt: Nachhaltigkeit ist vom einzelnen Menschen nicht erfassbar. Wie komplexe Computerbetriebssysteme nur noch vom Kollektiv der Entwickler, nicht aber von einzelnen Programmierern begriffen werden können, entgleitet auch die Idee der Nachhaltigkeit – ein Thema für Wissenschaft und Wirtschaft, Politiker und Ideologen – unserer Kontrolle. Übergreifende Studiengänge wie die Umweltwissenschaften sollen Verbindungen schaffen – und stehen vor einer schwierigen Aufgabe, denn die Nachhaltigkeit ist keine exakte Disziplin. Die Ökologie als Lehre analysiert die Wechselbeziehungen zwischen Organismen und ihrer belebten wie unbelebten Umwelt, ohne zu werten. Nachhaltigkeit dagegen basiert zwar unter anderem auf den Erkenntnissen der Ökologie, ist aber, wie schon vom Wort impliziert, ein Prozess und stets mit einer klaren Wertung verbunden. Sie ist alles andere als uneigennützig. Nachhaltigkeit ist eine Werthaltung mit klarem Ziel: der Werterhaltung.

region will change a few times before the project is concluded. A programme that is flexible enough to respond to change can ensure that the park design can still be sustainable, socially acceptable and of a high quality.

From his thesis of invisible design, Lucius Burckhardt went on to derive the ideal of a designer of integrated design strategies. Whether this can also be applied to the landscape architecture profession remains to be seen, but in the meantime landscape architecture should exploit its position at the intersection of research and practice for more intensive interdisciplinary collaboration. The design of open spaces offers a means not only of building sustainably but also of visualising individual aspects of sustainability and lending it a clearer profile in the public eye.

The vast range of aspects and the complexity of their interconnections shows that sustainability cannot be grasped by any one individual. In the same way that complex computer operating systems require a collective of developers, the idea of sustainability – a topic for scientists and economists, politicians and ideologists – exceeds our individual control. Interdisciplinary study programs such as environmental sciences aim to establish connections and at the same time are faced with a difficult task because sustainability is not a precise discipline. The field of ecology analyses the interactions between organisms and their living and lifeless environment without passing judgement. Sustainability, on the other hand, although it is based among other things on the findings of ecology, is, as the word implies, a process and thus always involves passing clear judgement. It is anything but altruistic. Sustainability means partaking of a set of common values, with the clear aim of sustaining value.

DEUTSCHER LANDSCHAFTSARCHITEKTUR-PREIS

| 50 **Park am Löbauer Wasser, Löbau**
hutterreimann Landschaftsarchitektur GmbH mit thoma architekten
„Es ist das große Verdienst der Landschaftsarchitekten, die besonderen Potenziale des Ortes erkannt und daraus ein schlüssiges, in seiner bildhaften Sprache auch allgemeinverständliches Konzept entwickelt zu haben. Unter dem Motto ‚Alles auf Zucker' ist ein Neustart gelungen, der die Geschichte der fast verschwundenen Zuckerfabrik in poetischen Bildern erzählt."

WÜRDIGUNGEN

| 60 **Der Christliche Garten (Gärten der Welt), Berlin**
relais Landschaftsarchitekten
„Sprechender noch ist der semiotische Kunstgriff, aus Buchstaben, aus Worten, aus christlichen Texten einen ganzen Kreuzgang zu formen. Der Wandelgang ... schafft einen Raum des Geistes, der Sprache, der Kommunikation, der die Besucher in Beschlag nimmt."

| 62 **Grüngürtel: Impuls 2012, Köln**
WGF Landschaft
„Mit dem neuen Planwerk ist der Äußere Grüngürtel wieder als Erholungs- und Freizeitpark für die Bewohner der angrenzenden Wohnquartiere und auch für die Gesamtstadt in das Bewusstsein gerückt."

| 64 **Elsbethenareal und Schrannenplatz, Memmingen**
club L94 Landschaftsarchitekten GmbH
„Das zurückhaltende, fein abgestimmte landschaftsarchitektonische Konzept und die hohe Material- und Ausführungsqualität machen diese öffentlichen Räume zu jeder Jahres- und Tageszeit interessant."

| 66 **Park Phoenix West, Dortmund**
lohrer.hochrein landschaftsarchitekten bdla
„Man darf gespannt sein, wie sich das Zusammenwirken von Freiraum und Bebauung, von ökologischen Faktoren und Ästhetik, von lokalen Akteuren in Planung, Bau, Nutzung und Pflege in den nächsten Jahrzehnten entwickelt."

| 68 **Elisengarten, Aachen**
Lützow 7 Cornelia Müller, Jan Wehberg, Landschaftsarchitekten
„Ein jahrelang eher beiläufig genutzter Stadtplatz wandelt sich zu einem modernen, elegant und urban anmutenden Raum."

| 70 **Drei neue Parks für Nagold**
Stefan Fromm Landschaftsarchitekten
„Das Element Wasser dient als verbindendes Thema. ... Die drei neuen Parkanlagen schaffen mit ihrem Charakter als Quartiersparks völlig neue Aufenthaltsqualitäten, für Bürger wie für Besucher der Stadt."

| 72 **Superkilen, Kopenhagen/Dänemark**
Topotek 1 Gesellschaft von Landschaftsarchitekten mbH
„Das Projekt entfernt sich ganz bewusst von der herkömmlichen Haltung, in der sich ein Stadtraum möglichst ruhig, homogen diszipliniert und dadurch ‚zeitlos' in den Kontext einzuordnen hat."

| 74 **Folly Forest, Strathcona School, Winnipeg/Kanada**
Straub Thurmayr Landschaftsarchitekten und Stadtplaner
„Ungewöhnliche Herstellungsmethoden und der konsequente Einsatz gebrauchter Materialien ließen einen überraschend unkonventionell anmutenden Raum entstehen."

GERMAN LANDSCAPE ARCHITECTURE PRIZE

150 **Löbau River Park, Löbau**
hutterreimann Landschaftsarchitektur GmbH with thoma architekten
"The landscape architects must be credited for recognising the special qualities of the site and for developing a concept for its use that is both convincing and accessible in terms of its visual language. The project uses sugar as a springboard for a new beginning that tells the story of the now barely visible sugar factory in a series of poetic images."

COMMENDATIONS

160 **The Christian Garden (Gardens of the World), Berlin**
relais Landschaftsarchitekten
"More telling is the semiotic device of forming the entire cloister walkway out of letters, of words that together constitute Christian scripture. The cloister walkway ... creates a place of spiritual contemplation, of language and of communication that is enthralling for the visitor."

162 **Green Belt: Impuls 2012, Cologne**
WGF Landschaft
"The new planning framework has raised general awareness of the potential of the Outer Green Belt as a space for leisure and recreation among the residents of the neighbouring quarters and the city as a whole."

164 **Elsbethenareal and Schrannenplatz, Memmingen**
club L94 landschaftsarchitekten GmbH
"The restrained and carefully balanced landscape architecture concept and its high quality of execution ensure that these are interesting public spaces at every time of day or year."

166 **Park Phoenix West, Dortmund**
lohrer.hochrein landschaftsarchitekten bdla
"It will be interesting to see how the combination of outdoor areas and buildings, of ecological factors and aesthetics, and of the different local interests in the planning, building, use and upkeep of the area, will develop over the coming decades."

168 **Elisengarten, Aachen**
Lützow 7 Cornelia Müller, Jan Wehberg, Landschaftsarchitekten
"A city square that for years has led a sideline existence has been transformed into a modern, elegant and suitably urban space."

170 **Three new parks for Nagold**
Stefan Fromm Landschaftsarchitekten
"Water serves as the uniting element. ... The three new parks serve as local centres of their respective quarters and create an entirely new quality of life for the citizens as well as for visitors to the town."

172 **Superkilen, Copenhagen/Denmark**
Topotek 1 Gesellschaft von Landschaftsarchitekten mbH
"The project consciously takes a different approach to conventional urban designs, which are typically expected to be quiet, orderly, homogeneous and to fit 'timelessly' into the local context."

174 **Folly Forest, Strathcona School, Winnipeg/Canada**
Straub Thurmayr Landschaftsarchitekten und Stadtplaner
"Unusual production methods and the consistent use of recovered materials have resulted in a surprising and unconventional space."

DEUTSCHER LANDSCHAFTSARCHITEKTUR-PREIS | GERMAN LANDSCAPE ARCHITECTURE PRIZE | 2013

Park am Löbauer Wasser
Löbau River Park

von · by Till Rehwaldt

Auf dem Gelände der ehemaligen Oberlausitzer Zuckerfabrik in Löbau ist eine neue Landschaft entstanden. Wie viele andere Regionen im östlichen Deutschland sah sich auch diese Gegend in den letzten Jahrzehnten einem gravierenden Strukturwandel ausgesetzt. Doch hier, im Tal des Löbauer Wassers, haben wir es nicht mit einer dieser sich in trauriger Weise ähnelnden Industriebrachen zu tun, deren Bilder manchmal ganze Stadtviertel beherrschen. Vielmehr treffen wir auf ein komplexes Areal, das auf eine sehr intensive Weise mit dem landschaftlichen Ort verknüpft ist und seine fast schon anmutig zu nennende Einbindung in die Umgebung als ein wertvolles Startkapital in eine zukünftige Entwicklung einbringt.

Von der Fabrik aus wurden die Abwässer der Zuckerproduktion früher über mehrere Reinigungsbecken in das etwa 20 Meter tiefer liegende Flüsschen geleitet, was der Gesamtanlage eine topografische Dramatik verleiht. Diese räumliche Konstellation und der Umstand, dass die Fabrik für mehrere Generationen ein bedeutender industrieller Standort und somit auch ein Ort kultureller Identifikation war, ließen nach der Einstellung der Produktion 2002 erste Ideen einer Nachnutzung reifen. Mit der Wahl als Ausrichtungsort einer Landesgartenschau wurde die Chance genutzt, die sehr weitgehenden Abrisspläne zu modifizieren und zumindest einen Teil der Anlagen für künftige Generationen zu erhalten.

Es ist das große Verdienst der Landschaftsarchitekten hutterreimann, die besonderen Potenziale des Ortes erkannt und daraus ein schlüssiges, in seiner bildhaften Sprache auch allgemeinverständliches Konzept entwickelt zu haben. Unter dem Motto „Alles auf Zucker" ist ein Neustart gelungen, der die Geschichte der fast verschwundenen Zuckerfabrik in poetischen Bildern erzählt. Als Umformung einer industriellen Brache fügt sich das Projekt

Out of the remains of a former sugar factory in Löbau, a new landscape has arisen. Like many other regions in eastern Germany, the region of Upper Lusatia has been subject to major structural transformations over the past two decades. The situation here in the valley of the River Löbau is not, however, the same as that of the all too familiar areas of industrial decline that sometimes blight entire quarters of towns. Instead, we see a complex terrain that is intimately connected with the landscape of the site and is embedded almost gracefully into the surroundings, providing a valuable starting point from which to develop the site.

The wastewater from the sugar production in the factory was previously passed through a series of troughs and cleansing basins before it was discharged into the river on the valley floor 20 metres below, lending the complex a sense of topographical drama. This spatial constellation and the fact that the factory was a major industrial facility and employer for several generations, and is therefore anchored in local cultural identity, meant that ideas were soon sought for its re-use after production stopped in 2002. The selection of Löbau as the site for the State Garden Show presented an opportunity to rethink existing plans for the factory's extensive demolition and, as such, to save at least a part of the complex for future generations.

The landscape architects hutterreimann must be credited for recognising the special qualities of the site and for developing a concept for its use that is both convincing and accessible in terms of its visual language. The project uses sugar as a springboard for a new beginning that tells the story of the now barely visible sugar factory in a series of poetic images. As a conversion of an

▼ Leuchtend rostroter Stahl markiert eine neue gestalterische Schicht – als Mauerkrone, Steg, Geländer, Wasserband, Rankhilfe oder Beetbegrenzung – und wird selbst zur ikonografischen Landmarke

The bright, rust-red steel denotes a new layer of design – used for wall-copings, walkways, balustrades, water channels, plant supports or planting bed edging – and becomes an iconographic landmark in its own right

ORT	LOCATION	Landesgartenschau Löbau · Löbau State Garden Show
ENTWURF	DESIGN	hutterreimann Landschaftsarchitektur GmbH, Berlin mit · with thoma architekten, Berlin/Zeulenroda
BAUHERR	CLIENT	Landesgartenschau Löbau 2012 GmbH
PLANUNG/BAU	PLANNING/COMPLETION	2010 – 2012

Fischzucht und Schwäne in bizarrer Kulisse: Wassergarten in einem der ehemaligen Rübenwaschwasserreinigungsbecken

Fish farming and swans in a bizarre setting: the water garden in one of the former sugar beet wash water purification basin

damit ebenbürtig in eine Reihe respektabler Vorgänger ein und setzt darüber hinaus ganz eigene Maßstäbe.

Räumliche Konzeption und gestalterische Leitbilder werden aus den prägnanten Merkmalen des Ortes entwickelt, aus der eigentümlichen Spannung zwischen dem Tal des Löbauer Wassers und dem höhergelegenen Plateau der alten Fabrik. So begegnen sich die spröden Funktionsflächen der fast vollständig beräumten Produktionsanlagen und der grün wuchernde Landschaftsraum des Tales in einer gegensätzlichen, aber auch belebenden Beziehung. Diese Verschränkung vermittelt sich hauptsächlich durch sehr sorgsam geführte Wegelinien, die auch schwierige Orte ansteuern, Höhen kunstvoll überwinden und überraschende Ausblicke eröffnen.

Besonders wohltuend wirkt dabei der entspannte Umgang mit Normen, Gewohnheiten und politischer Korrektheit in unserer barrierefreien Welt. Die großen Höhendifferenzen führen hier nicht zu einer alternativlos durchgeplanten „Verrampung" der Landschaft, vielmehr werden sie als eine theatralische Vorführung topografischer Sensationen inszeniert. Das Auf und Ab der Routen bietet vielfältigste Raum- und Geschwindigkeitserlebnisse, lässt Eltern schwitzend Wagen schieben und hält auch die Älteren in sportlicher Form. Mit großen Bewegungen durchmessen die Berg- und Talpromenaden das Areal, führen durch abwechslungsreich installierte Szenerien, sind die roten Fäden des Konzeptes. So wird der Weg zum Ziel.

Im Umgang mit den vorgefundenen, dem Abriss entkommenen Strukturen zeigen hutterreimann sowohl eine große Sensibilität als auch den Willen, den geschichtlichen Kontext aus einer individuellen Perspektive zu betrachten. Reste der ehemaligen Industrieanlagen werden nicht nur als aus der Zeit gefallene, nostalgisch anmutende Fragmente vorgezeigt, sondern in ihrer skurrilen Situationskomik lustvoll ausgekostet. So erleben wir in

industrial wasteland site, the project can hold its own alongside many other respectable precursor projects and at the same time marks a fresh departure in the genre. The spatial concept and key formal motifs build on the most distinctive characteristics of the site, and on the specific tension between the valley of the River Löbau and the higher plateau on which the former factory stood. The hard, industrial surfaces of the almost completely cleared production facilities enter into a refreshing contrast with the lush greenery of the valley landscape. This interleaving is made palpable by the very careful routing of the pathways that don't shy away from difficult terrain, artfully descending the considerable height while revealing surprising views into the valley.

A particularly pleasant aspect is the relaxed approach to the interpretation of norms, conventions and the politically correct obligation to provide barrier-free access. Instead of overcoming the significant height difference by turning the terrain into innumerable ramps, the routing of the pathways delights in theatrically presenting a series of topographic sensations. The ups and downs of the routes create spaces of varying sizes and velocities that will keep older generations fit and might even cause pram-pushing parents to break into a sweat. The promenades weave their way across the hillside into the valley through a variety of installation-like scenarios, and serve as a common thread passing through the site. Here the path is made the goal.

In their use of the relics of the factory that survived the demolition, hutterreimann have demonstrated both great sensitivity as well as the will to allow the historical context to be seen from an individual perspective. Rather than just presenting the remains of the former industrial facilities as nostalgic fragments of objects from the past,

tiefen Betongräben arrangierte Gärten, die mit edler Eleganz ihren Verhau zu sprengen scheinen, oder verwinkelte Treppen, die den Abstieg ins Tal in eine burgähnliche Szenerie verlegen.

Das Grundmotiv des Kontrasts dominiert in konsequenter Weise auch die thematische Durcharbeitung des Entwurfs bis hin zum Detail des einzelnen Objektes. Vor allem die Freiräume unten am Fluss entfalten eine ganz eigene Qualität, wobei das Element des Wassers in seiner artifiziellen Verwendung eine wichtige Rolle spielt. Im so lieblichen wie geschundenen Tal werden die Potenziale deutlich, die die postindustrielle Landschaft bietet, wenn sie nicht nur einer Renaturierung, sondern darüber hinaus einer kulturellen Inwertsetzung unterzogen wird.

Die großformatigen Becken, genauer Rübenwaschwasserreinigungsbecken, wurden als Bauwerke erhalten, frisch befüllt und künden auch in Zukunft – wie schon die hohen Bögen des steinernen Bahnviadukts – vom geschichtlichen Selbstverständnis einer ganzen Region. Dies gelingt vor allem deshalb, weil auch die Becken nicht allein als respektvoll konservierte Reste bewahrt, sondern in einem kühnen Akt der Neuinterpretation zu Funktionselementen

the designers delight in savouring the bizarre and even humorous situations that they provide. Visitors pass through deep concrete troughs converted into sunken gardens that add a touch of cultivated elegance to their rough-hewn surroundings, and winding steps add a touch of castle-staircase atmosphere to the descent into the valley.

The underlying motif of creating contrast is elaborated consistently at all levels of the design right down to the detailing of individual objects. The outdoor areas down by the river acquire a particularly special quality of their own, in which the element of water is employed in artificial form. This setting – a valley that has been devastated and is simultaneously bucolic – reveals the potential that a post-industrial landscape has to offer when the industrial legacy is not given over entirely to nature but also invested with cultural meaning.

The large-format troughs, the sugar beet wash water purification basins as they are called, have been retained in their structures, refilled with water and now speak to us as a testimony – like the high arches of the stone viaduct – to the historical identity of an entire region.

▲ 20 Meter Höhenunterschied liegen zwischen dem Plateau der ehemaligen Zuckerfabrik und dem Talraum des Löbauer Wassers

There is a 20 metre height difference between the plateau of the former sugar factory and the valley of the River Löbau

▶ Die Raumfolge führt die Besucher durch die skurrilen Relikte der ehemaligen Rübenwaschwasserreinigungsbecken hinunter ins Tal

The succession of spaces leads the visitor through the bizarre relic of the former sugar beet wash water purification basins down into the valley

einer auf neue Weise nutzbaren Landschaft erklärt werden. Äußeres Zeichen dieser kulturellen Umformung sind rostleuchtende Stahlabdeckungen, die in markanter Weise die alten Beckenmauern neu verklammern und in ihrer Stringenz zu einer ikonografischen Landmarke werden. Doch nicht nur die Form, auch der Inhalt steht für das Neue. Die Bassins verwandeln sich durch gezielte Eingriffe und Zutaten in eine vielfältige, phantasievoll drapierte Wasserwelt. Eine stählerne Steganlage durchbricht die Umfassungsmauern und führt den Weg in das Innere der Beckenanlage, der Kontakt zum Wasser wird unmittelbar. Sogar Enten, Fischzucht und einen kleinen Strand gibt es in dieser bizarren Kulisse.

Von hier aus führt die Wegelinie weiter am Löbauer Wasser entlang und lässt die unterschiedlichsten Landschaftsräume erleben, bevor endlich auch der echte Fluss in einer Furt durchquert wird. Auf dem Spaziergang be-

What makes this particularly compelling is the fact that, instead of merely respectfully conserving the basins as industrial remains, the landscape architects have also boldly reinterpreted them as functional elements, declaring them to be usable parts of the landscape. This cultural reconfiguration is signified outwardly through the use of bright, rust-coloured steel copings that crown the tops of the concrete walls of the basins, and through their striking appearance mark them out as an iconographic landmark. But it's not just the form that is new; the content is too. With a few carefully chosen interventions and new ingredients, the basins have been transformed into a diverse and imaginative water world. A steel walkway breaks through the perimeter wall and leads across the pool, providing direct access to the water, and visitors may encounter ducks, a fish farm and a small beach within these bizarre surroundings.

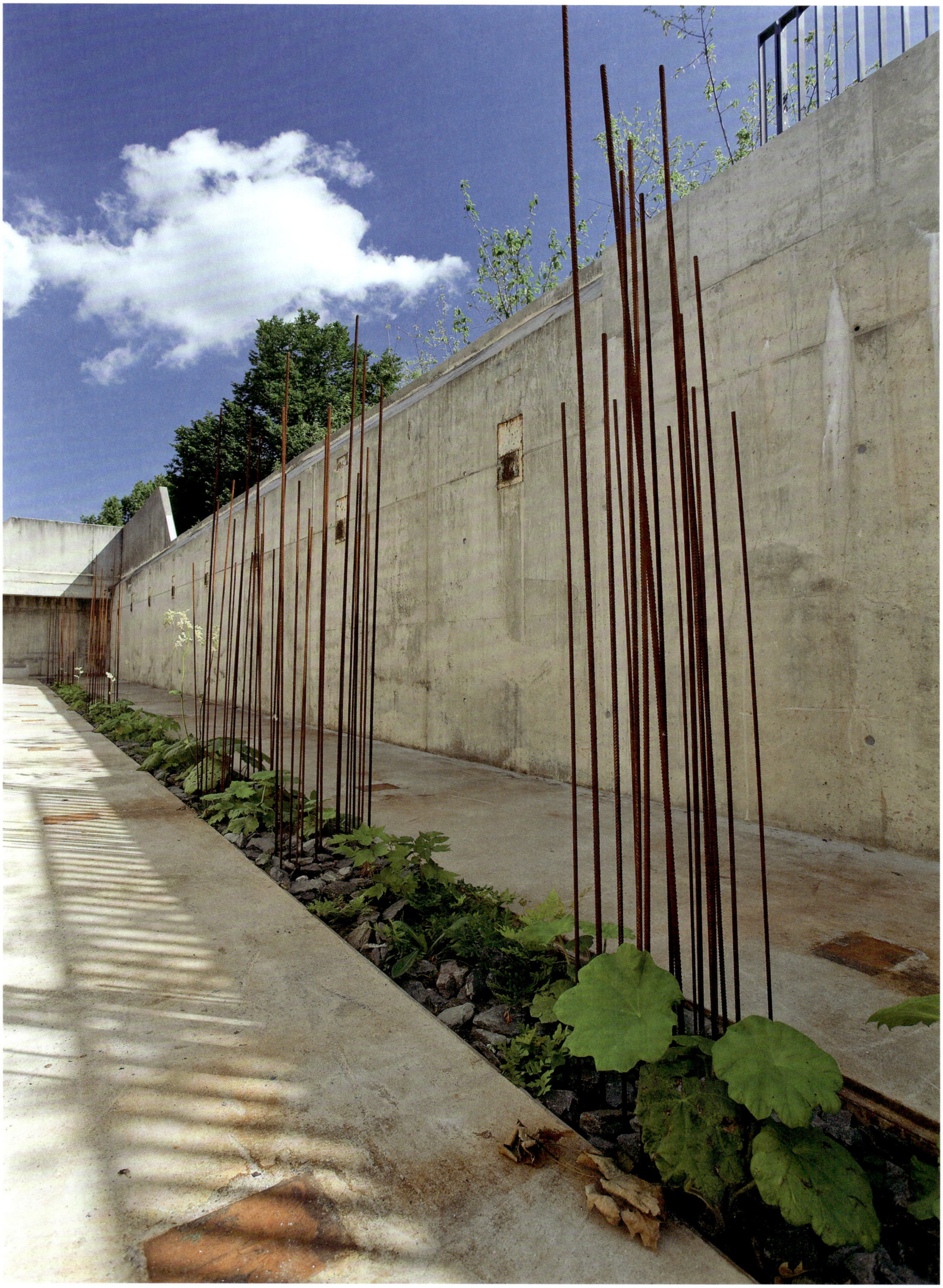

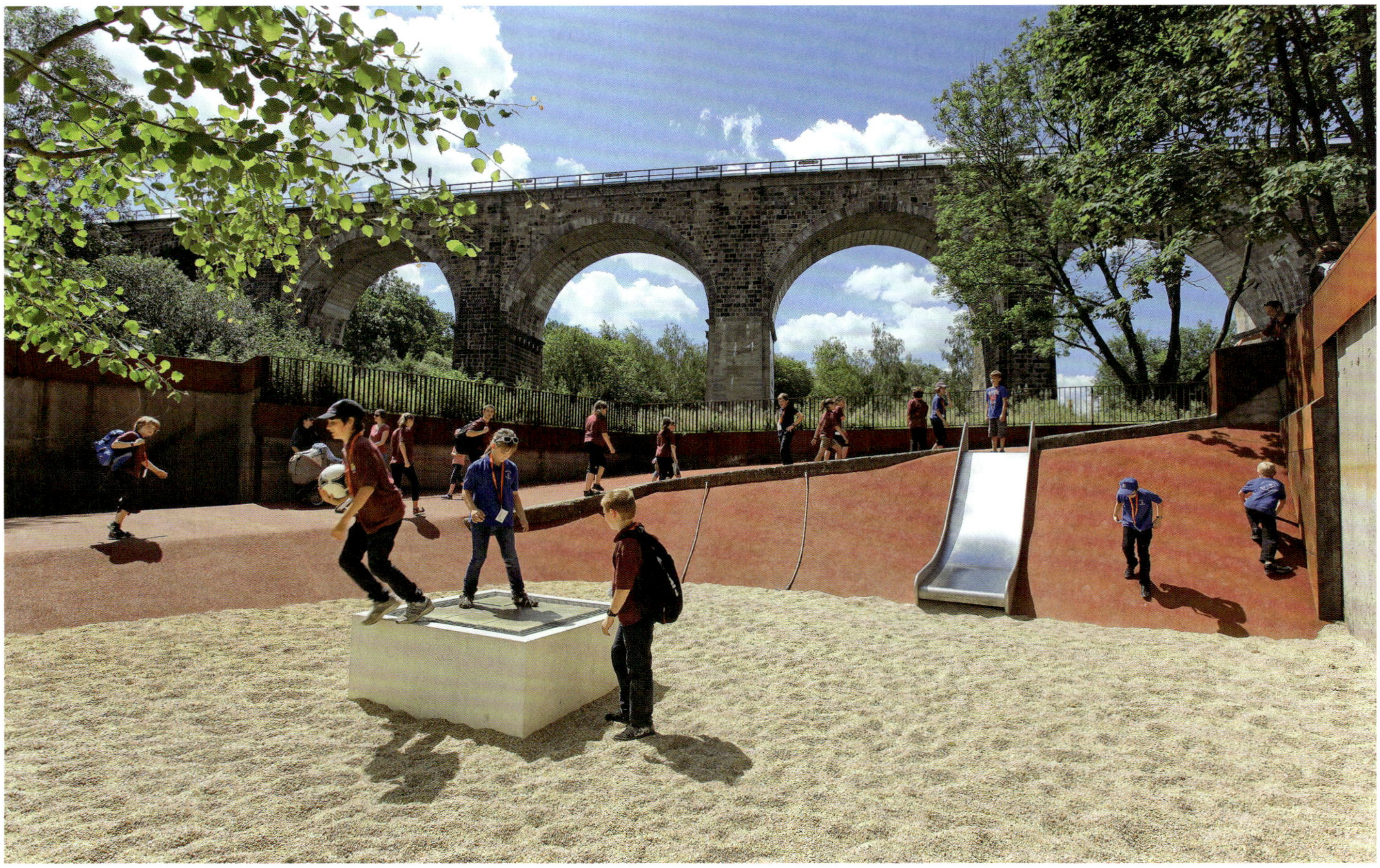

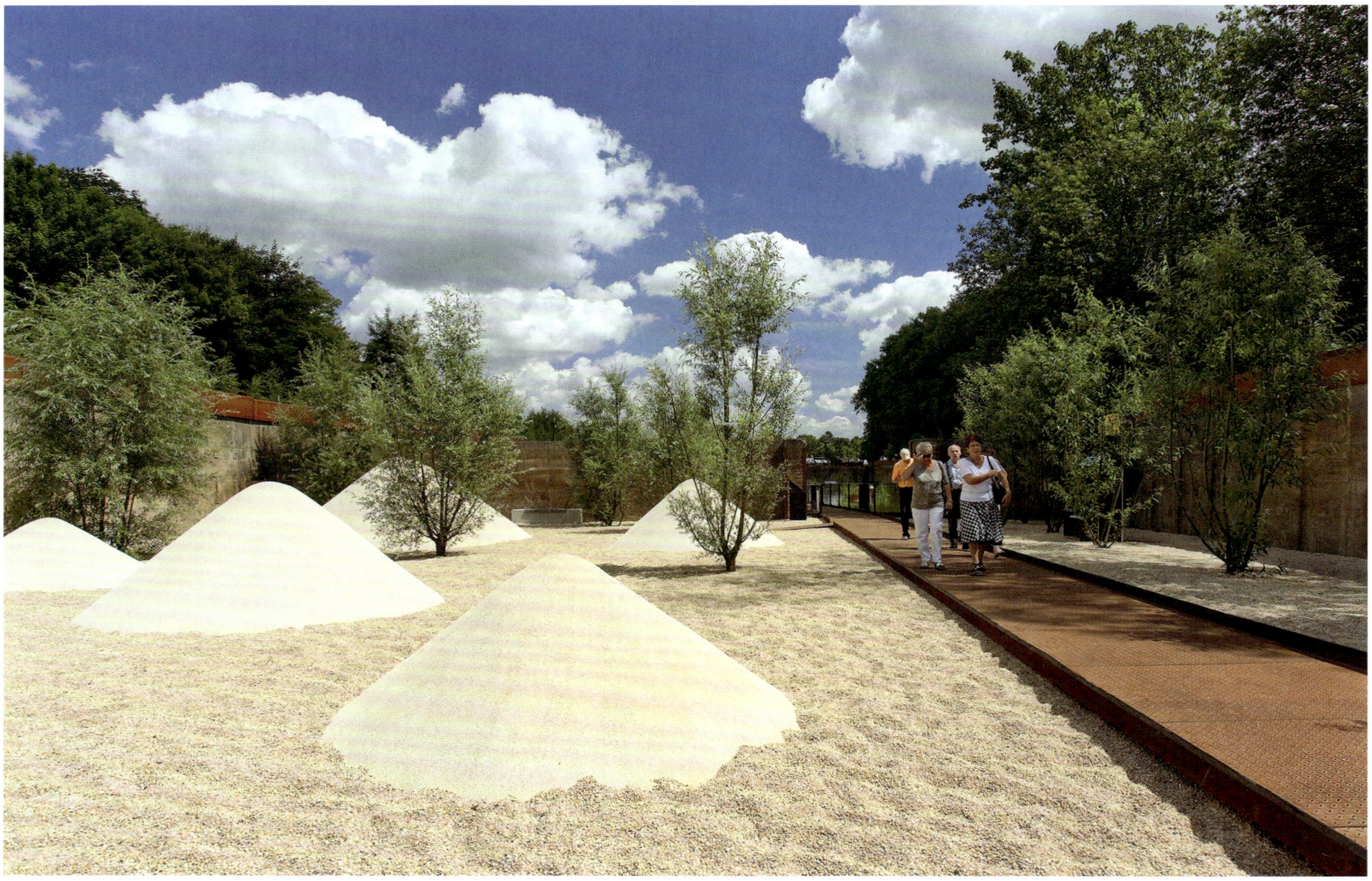

◀ In zwei Senkgärten mit „Würfelzuckern"...

Two sunken gardens with "sugar cubes"...

◀ ... und „Zuckerhüten" entstanden ungewöhnliche Spielbereiche in den ehemaligen Fabrikbecken

... and "sugar cones" serve as unusual playgrounds inserted into troughs from the former sugar factory

▶ Die vorgefundenen Strukturen und der neue Kontext sind sensibel und poetisch verknüpft

The existing structures and the new context have been sensitively and poetically woven together

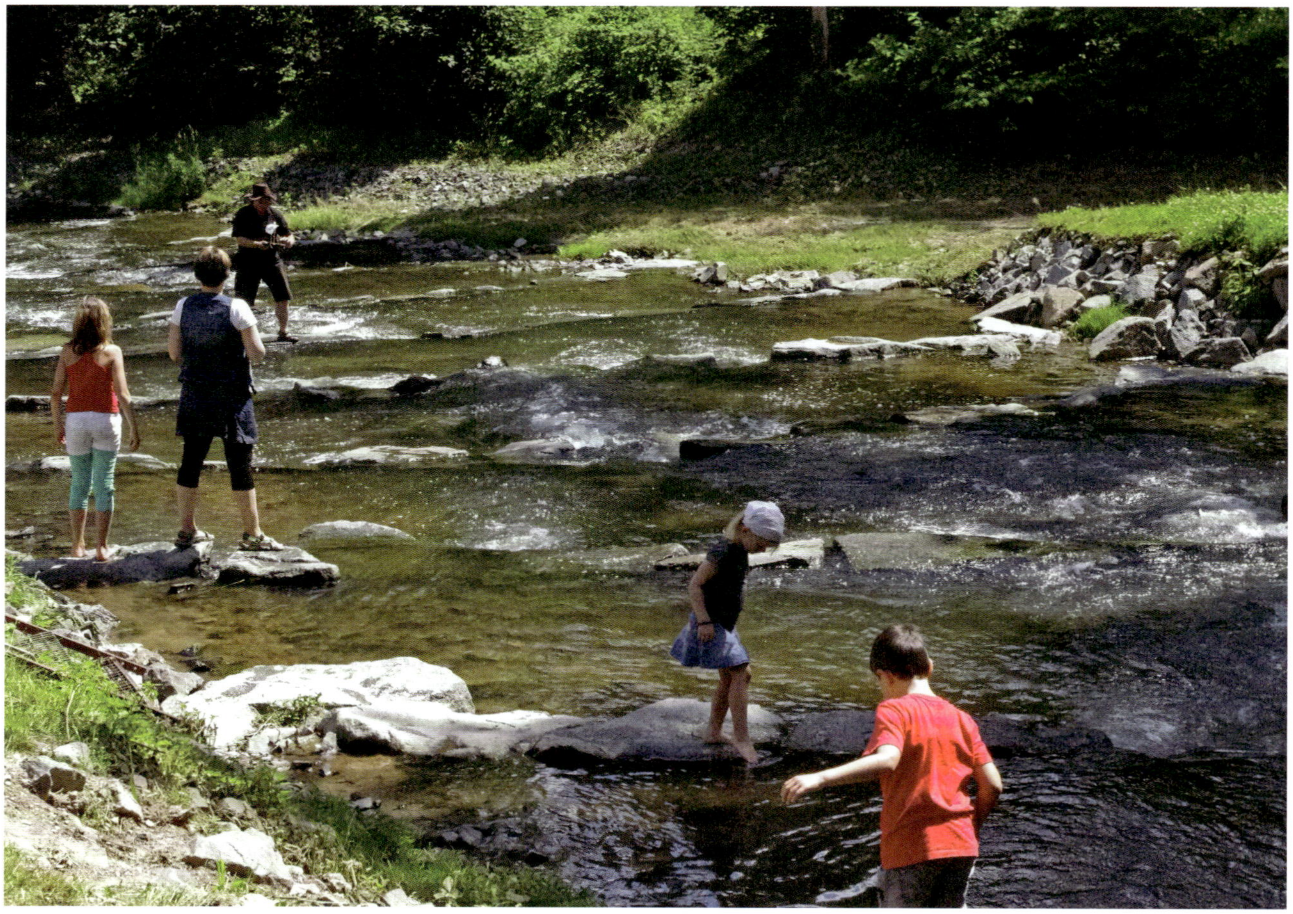

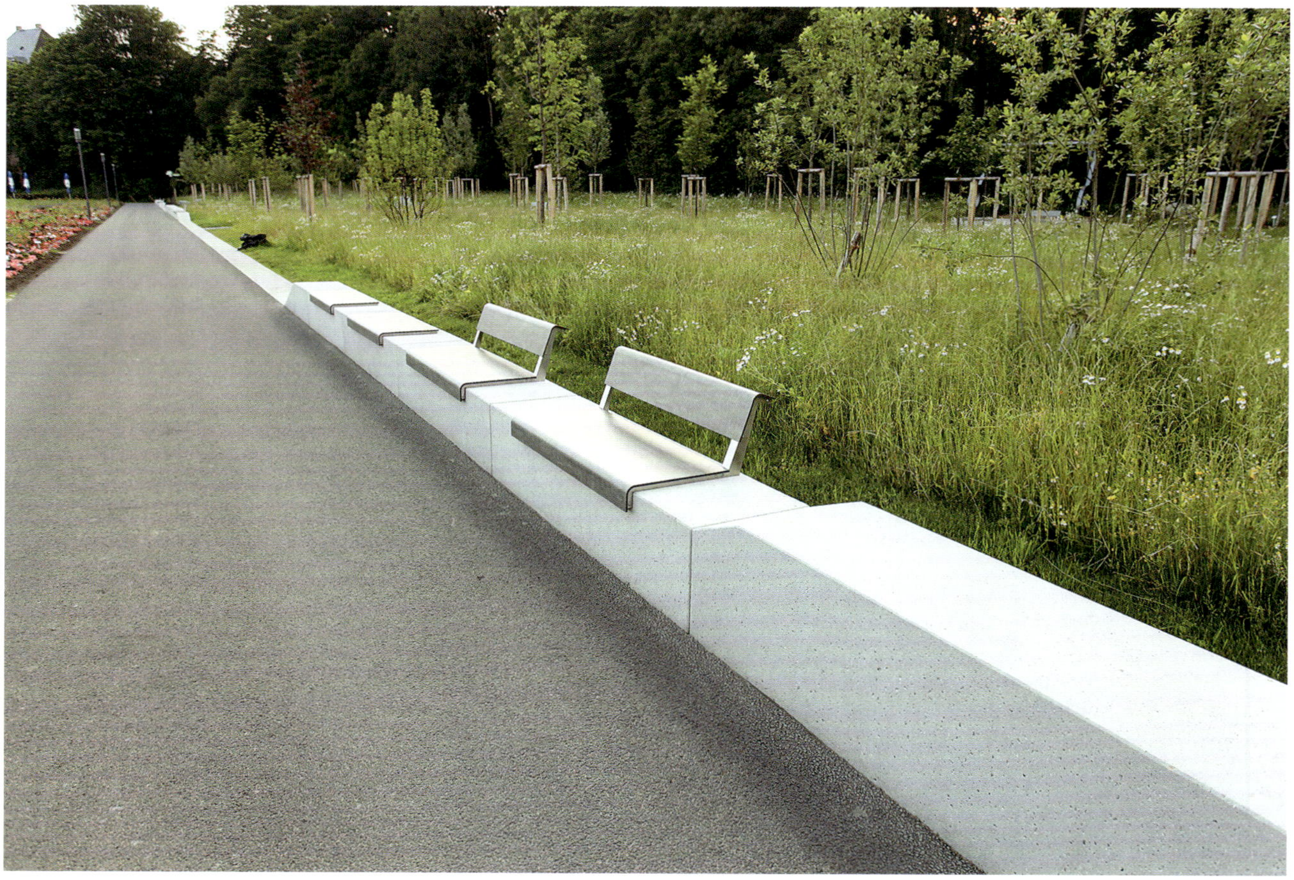

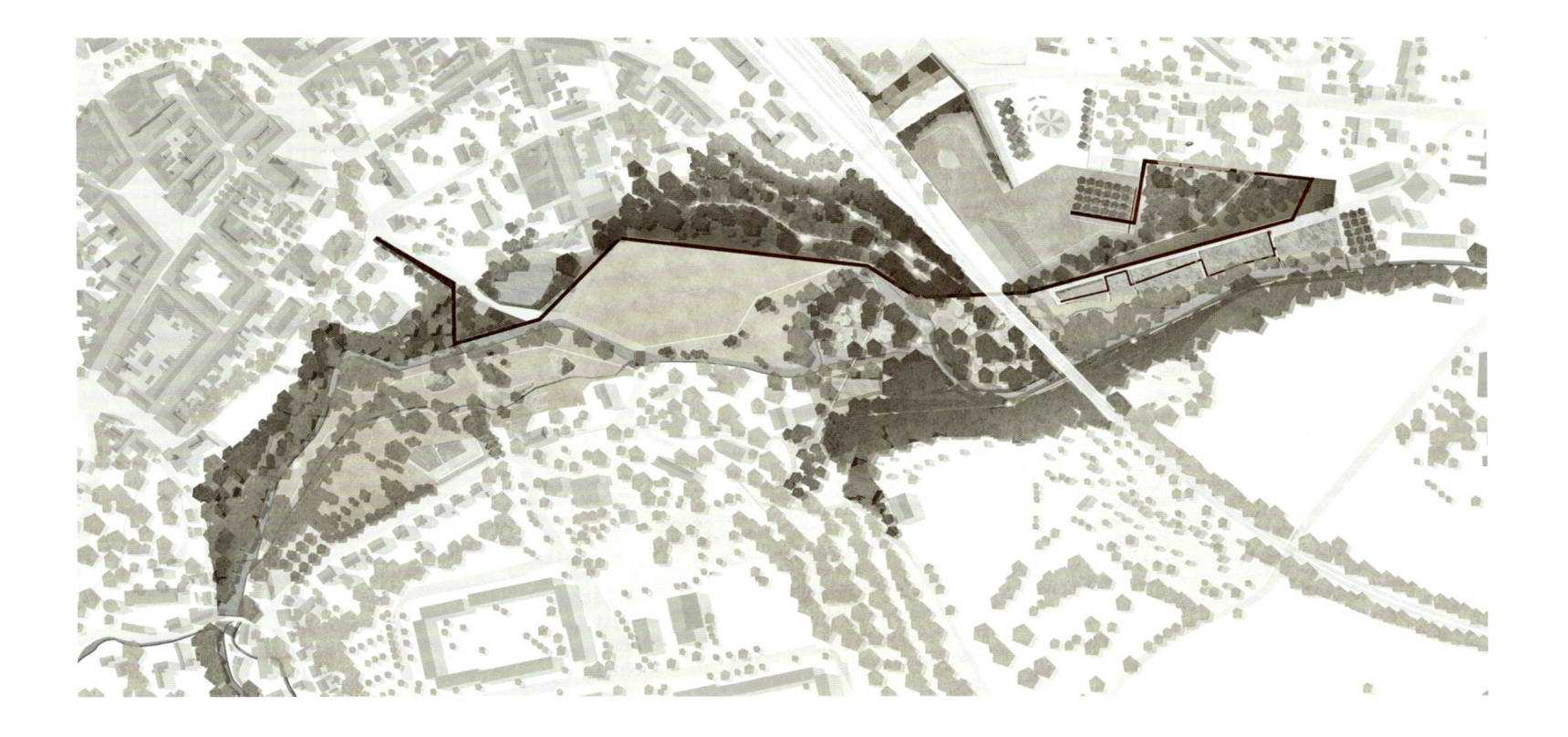

◂ Das namengebende Löbauer Wasser selbst ist Teil des abwechslungsreichen Raumerlebnisses

The River Löbau is itself part of the series of diverse spatial experiences

◂ Die Berg- und Talpromenade bildet das Rückgrat des topografisch bewegten Gartenschaugeländes

The hill and dale promenade forms the spine of the rolling topography of the Garden Show site

▴ Mit der Anbindung der ehemaligen Zuckerfabrik an die Stadt gewann man mit der Landesgartenschau Löbau 2012 den Talraum des Löbauer Wassers zurück

By connecting the site of the former sugar factory to the town, the Löbau State Garden Show 2012 has reclaimed the valley space for the town

gegnen wir immer wieder seltsamen Gärten und Dingen, oft als (nicht nur für Kinder) spielerisch nutzbare Orte entworfen. Wie beim Gang durch die kleine Welt der „Zuckerhüte" oder weißen „Würfelzucker" spüren wir überall in diesem Wunderland die alten und neuen Landschaftsgeister, die sich hier in der Oberlausitz versöhnen.

Mutig gesteuerter Strukturwandel und konzeptionelle Innovation haben der Stadt Löbau einen wertvollen Landschaftsraum zurückgegeben. In einem meisterhaften Werk aus räumlicher Komposition und detailreicher Feinarbeit haben es hutterreimann vermocht, der schmerzenden Romantik verlorener Industriekulturen eine moderne Idee entgegenzustellen. Die präzise gesetzten und in einer eigenen ästhetischen Sprache formulierten Interventionen lassen es zu einem sinnlichen Ereignis werden, den Wegelinien am Löbauer Wasser zu folgen.

From here the pathway leads on past a series of quite different landscapes alongside the River Löbau before, finally, visitors can cross the actual river via a ford. The route leads past all manner of strange objects and gardens that have been transformed into playful, inhabitable spaces that are fun for children and adults alike. As we pass through the enlarged miniature wonderland of "sugar cones" or white "sugarcubes", we can sense the spirits of the old and the new landscape that come together here and are reconciled in this corner of Upper Lusatia.

With the help of a courageous approach to structural transformation and an innovative concept, a valuable stretch of landscape has been reclaimed for the town of Löbau. In this masterful work of spatial composition and meticulous attention to detail, hutterreimann have succeeded in offering a modern idea to counter the painful romanticism of a lost industrial culture. The assured placement of the interventions and their particular aesthetic vocabulary turn the winding journey down the valley of the River Löbau into a festival for the senses.

WÜRDIGUNGEN | COMMENDATIONS | 2013

Der Christliche Garten (Gärten der Welt), Berlin
The Christian Garden (Gardens of the World), Berlin

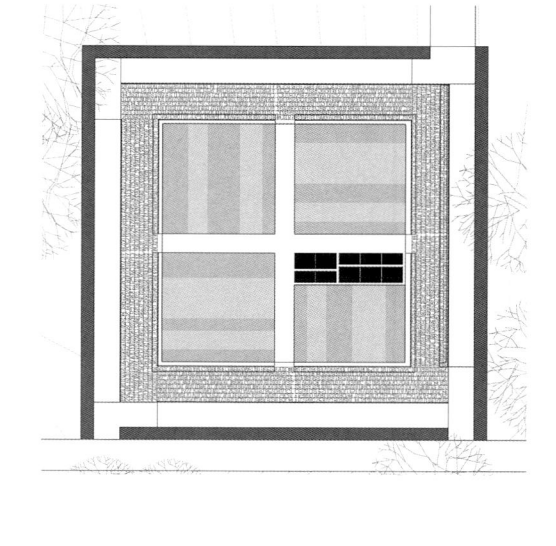

Motive des Hortus conclusus und des Kreuzgangs werden im Christlichen Garten im Erholungspark Berlin-Marzahn aufgenommen

Motifs of the *Hortus conclusus* and the cloister walkway have been incorporated into the Christian Garden at Berlin-Marzahn Recreation Park

„Der Christliche Garten" ist einer der „Gärten der Welt" im Erholungspark Marzahn, Berlin. Die zugrundeliegenden Idee, einem „christlichen Garten" die Form eines klösterlichen Kreuzgangs zu geben, liegt nahe, ist der Kreuzgarten doch die einzige gestalttypologisch festgelegte christlich konnotierte Form des Gartens. Auf diese Weise wird eine allbekannte Reminiszenz abgerufen. Die hier verwendeten Heilpflanzen sowie symbolträchtigen Rosen und Lilien sind aus traditionellen Klostergärten übernommen. Auch der Brunnen als ein in Kreuzgärten geläufiges Element wird zitiert, auf eine eher beiläufige Art allerdings, nicht als Zentrum im Schnittpunkt der gekreuzten Wege, sondern nebenbei, als „Wasserstein" in einem der Quadranten.

Sprechender noch ist der semiotische Kunstgriff, aus Buchstaben, aus Worten, aus christlichen Texten einen ganzen Kreuzgang zu formen. Der Wandelgang aus in Erz gefasster christlicher Philosophie schafft einen Raum des Geistes, der Sprache, der Kommunikation, der die Besucher in Beschlag nimmt. Er erinnert an klösterliche Architektur und interpretiert zugleich auf ungewöhnliche Weise ein genuin gartengestalterisches Element, nämlich die Pergola.

Bei der inhaltlichen Interpretation der vermittelten Botschaft bedarf es keiner allzu komplexen Transferleistung, was auch angemessen ist, handelt es sich doch um einen stark frequentierten Publikumsgarten. Hinzu kommt die ausgesprochen ästhetische Erscheinungsform der Anlage, das spannungsreiche Zusammenspiel der Naturerscheinungen und der Artefakte, an dem sich die Besucher erfreuen können.

"The Christian Garden" is one of the "Gardens of the World" at Marzahn Recreational Park in Berlin. The fundamental idea of designing a "Christian Garden" in the form of a monastic cloister is an obvious choice as the cloister garden is the only kind of ecclesiastical garden to have a prescribed typological form. Consequently, it evokes memories that are familiar to us all. The medicinal plants and the symbolically significant use of roses and lilies are likewise carried over from traditional monastic gardens. The fountain is another element familiar from cloister gardens, but here it is not used in the usual way at the centre of the courtyard where the paths intersect but is instead placed to one side as a "water stone" in one of the quadrants.

More telling is the semiotic device of forming the entire cloister walkway out of letters, of words that together constitute Christian scripture. The cloister walkway as Christian philosophy wrought into ore creates a place of spiritual contemplation, of language and of communication that is enthralling for the visitor. Although reminiscent of cloister architecture, its formal articulation resembles an unusual reinterpretation of another genuine element of garden design, namely the pergola.

The message that the garden communicates is, by contrast, more straightforward for the visitor to interpret, which is appropriate for a garden that is generally well frequented by the public. The overall experience is made all the more pleasurable by the exceptionally aesthetic articulation of the garden and the stimulating interplay between its natural appearance and its artefacts.

▲ Wörtlich ein zeichenhafter Raum – eine goldglänzende Textkonstruktion aus aluminiumlegierten Segmenten rahmt den inneren Gartenhof

Literally a semantic space – a glittering golden construction of text, made of aluminium alloy segments, frames an inner courtyard

▼ Die Texte nehmen Bezug auf Natur- und Gartenmotive und führen vom Alten Testament zu Gegenwartstexten, von der Schöpfung bis zum Tod

The texts make reference to nature and gardens and span from the Old Testament to contemporary texts, and from creation to death

▼ Der Brunnen als Zitat des Kreuzgartens ist in Form eines Wassertischs aus dem Zentrum in einen der Quadranten gerückt

The fountain is cited as a traditional element of cloister gardens but not placed at the central intersection of the paths; instead it stands to one side as a "water table" in one of the quadrants

ORT	LOCATION	Gärten der Welt, Berlin-Marzahn
ENTWURF	DESIGN	relais Landschaftsarchitekten, Berlin
BAUHERR	CLIENT	Grün Berlin GmbH
PLANUNG/BAU	PLANNING/COMPLETION	2009 – 2011

WÜRDIGUNGEN | COMMENDATIONS | 2013

Grüngürtel: Impuls 2012, Köln
Green Belt: Impuls 2012, Cologne

Bereits in den 1920er Jahren wurden die ehemaligen Festungsanlagen der Stadt Köln in Parkanlagen umgewandelt sowie durch Grünflächen ergänzt. Diese Park-, Wald- und Erholungsfläche erstreckt sich heute ringförmig als Äußerer Grüngürtel auf einer Fläche von ca. 800 Hektar beiderseits des Rheins. Der Äußere Grüngürtel hat im Laufe der Jahrzehnte baulich einige Perforierungen erfahren.

Als Wiederaufnahme und Fortsetzung des Erbes aus den 1920er Jahren ist von der Stadt und dem Landschaftsarchitekturbüro WGF ein Generalplan zur Sanierung des gesamten Äußeren Grüngürtels erstellt worden. Dieser ergänzt den Masterplan für Kölns Innenstadt von Albert Speer & Partner von 2007/08.

Ziel ist es, die Nutzbarkeit des Grüngürtels für die Bürgerschaft für Freizeit und Erholung sowie die Zugänglichkeit zu verbessern. Auch sollen landschaftspflegerische Ergänzungen vorgenommen und einzelne Abschnitte weiter entwickelt werden. Das Planwerk basiert auf einer breiten Bürgerbeteiligung. Es umfasst mit dem Gesamtkonzept, einzelnen Teilräumen und sogenannten „Lupen" drei konkrete städtebaulich-freiraumplanerische Ebenen.

Mit dem neuen Planwerk ist der Äußere Grüngürtel wieder als Erholungs- und Freizeitpark für die Bewohner der angrenzenden Wohnquartiere und auch für die Gesamtstadt in das Bewusstsein gerückt. Dabei ist es gelungen, einen „Dialog" zwischen den unterschiedlichen Strukturen des Grüngürtels und den angrenzenden Siedlungs- und Verkehrsräumen herbeizuführen und hierfür jeweils eigenständige Lösungen zu finden.

In the 1920s, the former fortifications of the City of Cologne were converted into a series of parks and augmented with additional green areas. These parks, woodland and recreational areas now constitute the Outer Green Belt, a green ring on both sides of the Rhine covering an area of almost 800 hectares. Over the years building works have perforated the Outer Green Belt in several places.

To resume and continue the work started in the 1920s, the city authorities and the landscape architecture office WGF Landschaft drew up a master plan for the rehabilitation of the entire Outer Green Belt. The plan extends the master plan for Cologne city centre developed by Albert Speer & Partner in 2007–08.

The aim is to enhance the usability of the Green Belt for leisure and recreation and to improve its accessibility for the citizens of the city. Accompanying landscape rehabilitation measures are also envisaged, including the extension of individual sections. The planning framework builds on extensive contributions from the public and includes proposals for three concrete levels of urban design and urban space planning: the master plan, plans for individual subsections and so-called "loupes".

The new planning framework has raised general awareness of the potential of the Outer Green Belt as a space for leisure and recreation among the residents of the neighbouring quarters and the city as a whole. A "dialogue" has been successfully initiated between the different structures of the Green Belt and the adjacent urban and traffic spaces with a view to finding individual solutions for the respective situations.

◀ Der neue Masterplan führt Planungen fort, die in den 1920er Jahren begonnen wurden

The new master plan extends the original planning that was started in the 1920s

▶ „Lupe" auf den Rhein: In drei Ebenen – Gesamtkonzept, Teilräume und „Lupen" – erfolgt die Detaillierung der Planung

A "loupe" showing the Rhine: the master plan covers three levels of detail – the overall concept, subsection plans and "loupes"

▶ Die Planung erfolgte mit breiter Bürgerbeteiligung und in enger Abstimmung mit der Stadtverwaltung

The plan was developed in conjunction with the public and in close collaboration with the city authorities

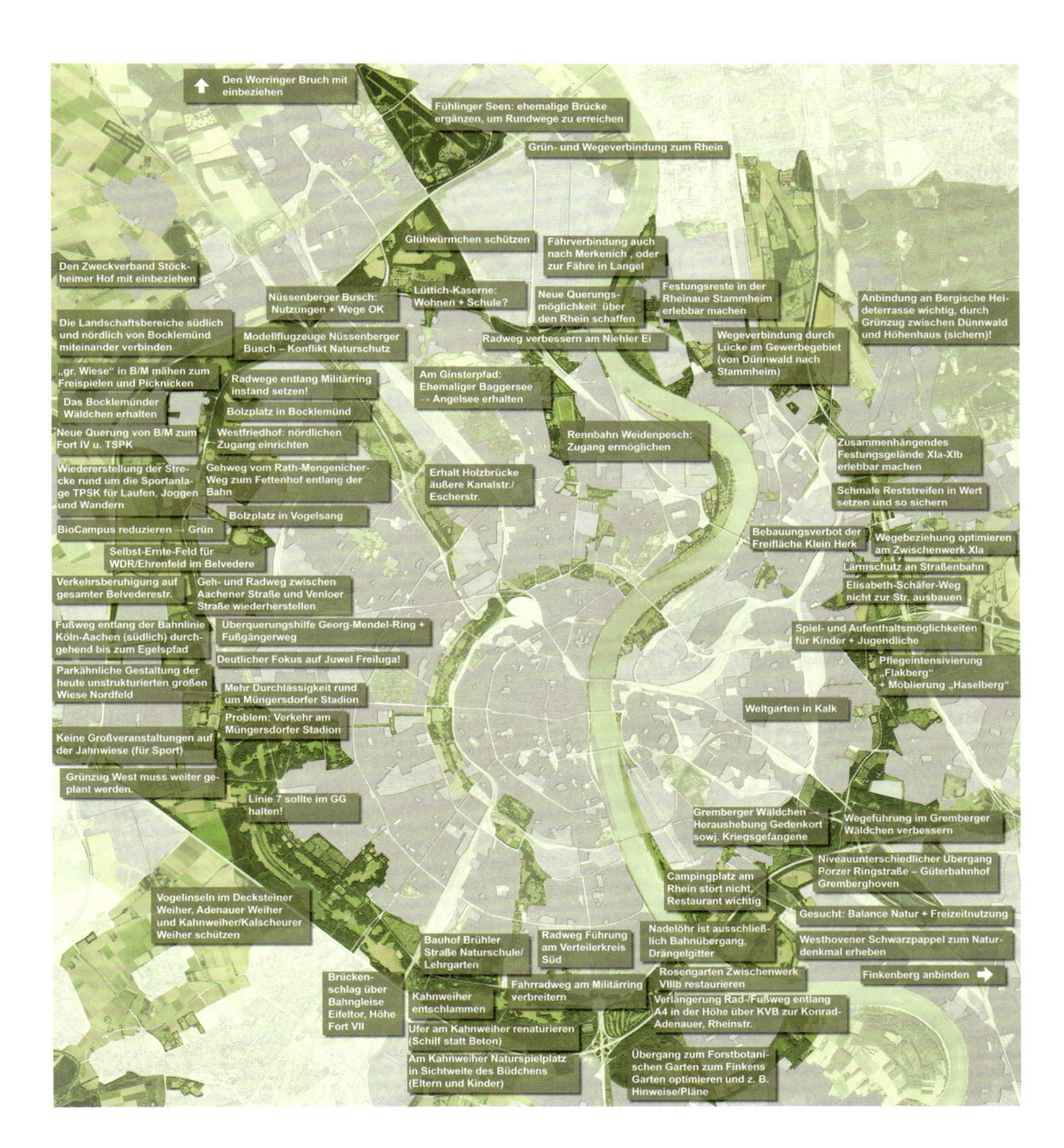

ORT	LOCATION	Äußerer Grüngürtel, Köln · Outer Green Belt, Cologne
ENTWURF	DESIGN	WGF Landschaft, Nürnberg · Nuremberg, Gerd Aufmkolk, Christoph Tauscher
BAUHERR	CLIENT	Kölner Grünstiftung, Köln · Cologne
PLANUNG/BAU	PLANNING/COMPLETION	Masterplan · Master plan 2010 – 2012

WÜRDIGUNGEN | COMMENDATIONS

WÜRDIGUNGEN | COMMENDATIONS | 2013

Elsbethenareal und Schrannenplatz, Memmingen

Elsbethenareal and Schrannenplatz, Memmingen

Schrannenplatz und Elsbethenareal in der bayrischen Kleinstadt Memmingen sind ein beispielhafter Beitrag zur nachhaltigen Stabilisierung der Innenstadt als attraktivem Ort für Wohnen, Arbeiten und Kultur.

Ausgangssituation als städtebaulicher Rahmen ist eine Folge von Straßen und unterschiedlich großen platzartigen Weitungen mit prägenden giebelständigen Bauwerken sowie der querende Stadtbach.

Der Schrannenplatz erhält seine Kohärenz durch zurückhaltendes Betonpflaster in ruhigen Formaten. Der Bach ist in den Seitenstraßen geöffnet. An der Einmündung zum Platz ist Raum für eine Rampe und schlichte Stufen, die ans Wasser heranführen, den Blick freigeben auf den Wasserlauf und eine Reihe historischer Giebel.

Auf dem Platz selbst wird der Bach nur in einem kleinen Fenster aufgedeckt, das Element Wasser aber in Form von Fontänen von allen Seiten sichtbar gemacht. Die „Bachspur", durch Öffnungen und Wasserspiele markiert, erscheint darüber hinaus veredelt durch engmaschige Metallgewebe. Bäume mit lichten Kronen werden überzeugend platziert und beleuchtet. Eine Familie unterschiedlich geformter Sitzmöbel erfüllt individuelle und kollektive Ansprüche.

Der Elsbethenhof am Theater ist teils durch Neubauten geschickt gefasst. Bänke um die erhaltenen Bäume und mobile Sitzgelegenheiten für Außengastronomie laden ein. Niedrige Leuchten und ein feinkörniger Pflasterteppich schaffen eine sympathisch-wohnliche Atmosphäre.

Das zurückhaltende, fein abgestimmte landschaftsarchitektonische Konzept und die hohe Material- und Ausführungsqualität machen diese öffentlichen Räume zu jeder Jahres- und Tageszeit interessant. Bäume und Wasser, Möblierung und Licht bringen den Betrachter geradezu in Urlaubsstimmung.

The Schrannenplatz and Elsbethenareal in the small Bavarian town of Memmingen are examples of the sustainable consolidation of the inner city as an attractive place to live, work and enjoy culture.

The urban context of the project is a succession of streets and square-like urban spaces of different sizes lined with characteristic gable-fronted buildings, as well as the stream that flows through the town.

The Schrannenplatz is given a coherent identity through the use of restrained concrete paving laid unobtrusively in different sizes. The stream flows uncovered through the side streets and where it enters the square, there is space for a ramp and a set of simple steps that lead down to the water and afford a view over the watercourse and a row of historical gables.

On the square itself, only a small window opens onto the stream, but the element of water is made visible in the form of fountains. The path of the stream is also marked with openings and water features, and by elegant floor-flush fine-mesh grating. Trees with open crowns have been placed strategically and illuminated from below, and a family of differently shaped seating arrangements cater for collective and individual seating needs.

A few well-placed new buildings lend the Elsbethenhof in front of the historical theatre a good sense of definition. Benches around the trees and create inviting situations that contribute to the pleasant, almost homely atmosphere of the square.

The restrained and balanced landscape architecture concept and its high quality of execution ensure that these are interesting public spaces at every time of day or year. Trees and water, street furniture and lighting create a light-hearted atmosphere reminiscent of being on holiday!

◀ Der Wechsel zwischen schmalen Gassen und platzartigen Aufweitungen prägt die Memminger Altstadt

The old town of Memmingen is characterised by an alternation of narrow streets and square-like urban spaces

▶ Mit Beleuchtung in Szene gesetzt: Die Stadtmöblierung vermittelt wohnzimmerähnliche Gemütlichkeit

Streetlamps as scenery: the street furniture creates a sense of home comforts outdoors

▼ Die zeitgemäße, moderne Entwurfssprache steht im reizvollen Dialog mit der historischen Bausubstanz. Bäume und Sitzelemente begleiten den Verlauf des Stadtbaches

The contemporary, modern language of the design contrasts pleasingly with the historical buildings. Trees and seating overlook the stream that flows through the town

ORT	LOCATION	Memmingen
ENTWURF	DESIGN	club L94 Landschaftsarchitekten GmbH, Köln · Cologne, Frank Flor, Jörg Homann, Götz Klose, Burkhard Wegener
BAUHERR	CLIENT	Stadt Memmingen · City of Memmingen
PLANUNG/BAU	PLANNING/COMPLETION	2010

WÜRDIGUNGEN | COMMENDATIONS | 2013

Park Phoenix West, Dortmund
Park Phoenix West, Dortmund

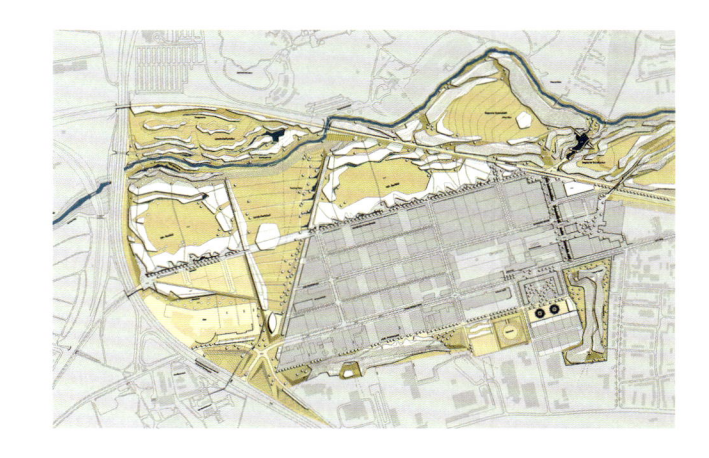

▲ Ein technologieorientierter Gewerbepark wird schrittweise eingebettet in eine sukzessive entstehende Parklandschaft

A technology-oriented business park is successively embedded in a park landscape that develops over time

Der ehemalige Stahlstandort wird als technologieorientierter Gewerbepark mit weitläufigen Freiflächen entwickelt. Das Areal ist wichtiges Bindeglied für einen regionalen Grünzug im Dortmunder Süden. Das differenzierte Parkkonzept qualifiziert den städtebaulichen Masterplan Emscher Park, ist Vorgabe für den Bau des Erschließungssystems mit einer innovativen Brückengestaltung und auch Grundlage der schrittweisen Umsetzung, Pflege und Entwicklung. Das Parknetz umgibt die Zellen, in denen sich der Technologiepark entwickelt, und stellt zusammen mit den Erschließungsalleen einen robusten Rahmen für die in Maßstab und Architekturqualität heterogene Bebauung dar.

Dieser mit geringen Finanzmitteln realisierte Entwurf eines postindustriellen Parks hat als Basis das durch Halden überformte obere Emschertal, Relikte stolzer Industriebauwerke und örtlich eingekapselte Altlasten, vielfältige Spontanvegetation sowie degradierte Flächen. Die Landschaftsarchitekten stellen besondere Orte heraus, nutzen Aussichtspunkte und schaffen neue Plätze und Promenaden; sie verknüpfen Gelände und Stadt mit einem differenzierten System von Sichten und Wegen. Neue Merkzeichen werden Relikten gegenübergestellt. Dachflächenwasser des Technologieparks wird in einer Kanalpromenade mit klaren Formen und zeitgemäßem Material gesammelt. Ein Regenrückhaltebecken, aus dem das Wasser gedrosselt an die Emscher abgegeben wird, inszeniert die beeindruckende Verkehrs- und Industriearchitektur als „geborgte Strukturen" in der Tradition des Landschaftsgartens.

Man darf gespannt sein, wie sich das Zusammenwirken von Freiraum und Bebauung, von ökologischen Faktoren und Ästhetik, von lokalen Akteuren in Planung, Bau, Nutzung und Pflege in den nächsten Jahrzehnten entwickelt.

The site of the former steelworks has been developed into a technology-oriented business park with extensive outdoor areas. The site represents an important connecting piece in a regional green belt in southern Dortmund. The differentiated park concept, elaborated in the master plan for the Emscher Park, sets out the building of a system of access routes with an innovative bridge design and serves as a basis for the successive implementation, upkeep and development of the project. The network of parks surrounds the cells in which the technology park will be established, and provides, together with the access avenues, a robust framework for the heterogeneous mix of scales and architectural qualities in the area.

The design for this post-industrial park, realised with a limited budget, is characterised by the spoil-heap landscape of the upper Emscher valley, the proud relics of its industrial past, pockets of contaminated land, a wide variety of spontaneous vegetation and degraded areas. The landscape architects highlight special locations, use viewing points and create new squares and promenades that link the site and city. New landmarks contrast with the industrial relics, and rainwater from the technology park is channelled into a canal with adjoining promenade that employs clear forms and contemporary materials. A rainwater retention pool that releases water at a controlled rate into the River Emscher is used to create a setting that, in the tradition of landscape gardens, incorporates the impressive industrial architecture and traffic infrastructure as "borrowed structures".

It will be interesting to see how the combination of outdoor areas and buildings, of ecological factors and aesthetics, and of the different local interests in the planning, building, use and upkeep of the area, will develop over the coming decades.

▲ Mit geringen Mitteln entsteht ein postindustrieller Park, der Biotope, Wegeverbindungen und Wasserflächen integriert

A post-industrial park has been realised with economical means and incorporates biotopes, pathways and bodies of water

▶ Gestaltungselemente werden kombiniert mit sichtbaren industriellen Relikten, aber auch unsichtbaren wie Kontaminationsflächen

Design elements are used not only in combination with visible industrial relics but also with invisible elements such as contaminated areas

ORT	LOCATION	Dortmund
ENTWURF	DESIGN	lohrer.hochrein landschaftsarchitekten bdla, München · Munich/Magdeburg/Perach a. Inn, Axel Lohrer
BAUHERR	CLIENT	Stadt Dortmund, vertreten durch · City of Dortmund represented by NRW.Urban GmbH & Co. KG
PLANUNG/BAU	PLANNING/COMPLETION	2007 – 2012

WÜRDIGUNGEN | COMMENDATIONS | 2013

Elisengarten, Aachen
Elisengarten, Aachen

▲ Zwischen dem Aachener Münster und der Rückseite der alten Trinkhalle spannt sich der Elisengarten als neues „städtisches Wohnzimmer" auf

The Elisengarten spans between the Aachen Cathedral and the rear façade of the old Drinking Hall, and serves as a new "urban living room"

Ein jahrelang eher beiläufig genutzter Stadtplatz wandelt sich zu einem modernen, elegant und urban anmutenden Raum. Die reiche Tradition Aachens als ein Ort der Quellen, der Bäder und des Wohlergehens wird an dieser Stelle in eindrucksvoller Weise neu entdeckt. Die alte Trinkhalle wird völlig neu eingebunden: Sie orientiert sich nun nicht mehr ausschließlich zum Straßenraum, sondern wird zum Bezugspunkt einer neu gestalteten Parkanlage, einem „grünen Wohnzimmer" mitten in der Stadt.

Ein direkt am Gebäude positioniertes Wasserbassin verstärkt diesen Ansatz und wird zur gestalterischen Klammer zwischen Architektur und Freiraum. Gleichzeitig entsteht eine wertvolle, atmosphärisch dichte Zone des Übergangs, des Nebeneinanders unterschiedlicher Raumqualitäten.

Die neu strukturierte Parkanlage greift einerseits geschichtliche Bezüge auf, setzt andererseits aber auch moderne Akzente. Wegeführung und Formkonturen zitieren bekannte Grundmotive der Gartenkultur, verleugnen jedoch nicht ihre Entstehungszeit. Ein geschickter Umgang mit vorhandener Vegetation wie auch neu positionierte Pflanzungen lassen einen zeitgenössischen Stadtgarten entstehen, der zum alltäglichen Aufenthalt einlädt. Weite Rasenflächen und flache Sitzstufen akzentuieren den Raum, der sich in kurzer Zeit zu einem beliebten Ort im Zentrum Aachens entwickelt hat.

A city square that for years has led a sideline existence has been transformed into a modern, elegant and suitably urban space. The design of the site reconnects with Aachen's rich tradition as a city of wells, baths and wellbeing in a most impressive manner. The old drinking hall, which previously related only to the road, has been reconfigured to act as the centrepiece of a newly designed park that serves as a "green living room" in the heart of the city.

A broad strip of water directly adjacent to the building reinforces this approach and serves as a mediator between the architecture and the open space of the park. At the same time it creates a valuable and atmospheric transitional zone in which different spatial qualities meet and coincide.

The new structure of the park picks up historical references while simultaneously creating decidedly modern accents. The arrangement of pathways and the delineation of contours make reference to traditional elements of garden design without pretending that they are from another time. Careful use of existing vegetation augmented with newly positioned planting results in a contemporary garden in the city that can be used for everyday activities. Extensive lawns and shallow steps that serve as benches accentuate the space which has rapidly become a popular place in the centre of Aachen.

▲ Ein leicht ansteigendes Rasenparterre mit integrierten Sitzstufen lädt zum Verweilen ein und schafft eine Balance zwischen Repräsentativität und Nutzbarkeit

A gentle incline with integral steps-cum-benches that provide places to sit on the lawn results in a space that is both representative and eminently usable

▼ Das Bassin an der Rückseite der alten Trinkhalle wurde neu angelegt und zieht das Thema des Brunnenhauses in den Außenraum

The water channel at the rear of the former pump room is new and transports the building's purpose into the outdoor space

▼ Die abendliche Lichtinszenierung unterstreicht das romantische Ambiente der Anlage

A night-time lighting scenery underlines the romantic atmosphere of the new urban situation

ORT	LOCATION	Aachen
ENTWURF	DESIGN	Lützow 7 Cornelia Müller, Jan Wehberg, Landschaftsarchitekten, Berlin
BAUHERR	CLIENT	Stadt Aachen, Stadterneuerung und Stadtgestaltung · City of Aachen, Urban Design and Renewal Department
PLANUNG/BAU	PLANNING/COMPLETION	2008–2009

WÜRDIGUNGEN | COMMENDATIONS | 2013

Drei neue Parks für Nagold
Three new parks for Nagold

▲ Der Schlossberg, zwei Flüsse und drei Parks wurden in das städtebauliche Konzept der Landesgartenschau Nagold 2012 einbezogen

The Schlossberg, two rivers and three parks have been incorporated into the urban concept for the State Garden Show 2012 in Nagold

Für die Kreisstadt Nagold in Baden-Württemberg mit ca. 22.000 Einwohnern wurden anläßlich der Landesgartenschau 2012 drei völlig neu gestaltete Parkanlagen geschaffen. Grundlage war ein vorliegendes Konzept der „Grünen Urbanität". Mit dem neu gestalteten Stadtpark Kleb und dem neuen Krautbühlpark sowie dem neuen Riedbrunnenpark entstanden insgesamt 18 Hektar neu gestalteter Grünflächen. Über einen weiteren Garten an der historischen Stadtmauer und eine Gartenterrasse am Fuße des Schlossbergs wurde auch die auf dem Schlossberg gelegene Burgruine Hohennagold in die Gesamtgestaltung einbezogen.

Die Grünräume entlang der Flüsse Nagold und Waldach bilden das neue grüne Rückgrat der Stadt, verbinden Altstadt und jüngere Innenstadtquartiere. Die als Daueranlagen konzipierten Parks binden als integrierendes und zusammenhängendes grünes Band das gesamte Stadtgebiet von Nagold ein. Es wurde eine unterschiedliche Abfolge von Grün- und Freiräumen geschaffen, die in klarer Zuordnung zu den angrenzenden Siedlungs- und Wohngebieten stehen. Die Gestaltung der Parks zeichnet sich durch eine hohe Materialqualität aus.

Mit einer neugestalteten Brückenanlage am Zusammenfluss von Nagold und Waldach und mit neuen Querverbindungen und Sichtachsen in der Stadt führen die Parks und Grünflächen zudem geschickt die unterschiedlichen Stadtteile zusammen. Das Element Wasser dient als verbindendes Thema. Neue Zugänge und Treppenanlagen am Ufer der beiden Flüsse machen diese für die Erholung nutzbar.

Die drei neuen Parkanlagen schaffen mit ihrem Charakter als Quartiersparks völlig neue Aufenthaltsqualitäten, für Bürger wie für Besucher der Stadt.

For the district town of Nagold in the state of Baden-Württemberg with 22,000 inhabitants, three new parks were created as part of the State Garden Show in 2012. Conceived as part of an existing concept for "Green Urbanism", three sites were developed – the redesigned Stadtpark Kleb in the town, the new Krautbühlpark and the new Riedbrunnenpark – providing a total of 18 hectares of designed green space. A further garden along the historical town walls and a garden terrace integrate the ruin of Hohennagold Castle on the Schlossberg into the overall design concept.

The green areas along the Nagold and Waldach rivers form a new green backbone to the town, connecting the old town with the later neighbouring quarters. Conceived for the long term, the parks serve as an integrating and continuous green band that connects all parts of the town. A succession of different green and urban spaces has been created that each relate clearly to the respective adjacent districts and residential areas. The choice of materials underlines the high quality of the design of the parks.

Through a redesigned bridge at the confluence of the Nagold and Waldach rivers and newly created connecting paths and visual axes into the town, the parks and green areas succeed in connecting the different parts of the town. Water serves as the uniting element. Tiered steps along the banks of both rivers provide new ways of accessing the river for leisure and recreation.

The three new parks serve as local centres of their respective quarters and create an entirely new quality of life for the citizens as well as for visitors to the town.

▲ Eine Treppenanlage zur Nagold macht das Wasser in der Altstadt erlebbar. Erschließung und Nutzbarkeit der Flüsse Nagold und Waldach waren Schwerpunkte im Gartenschaukonzept

Steps create a waterfront situation in the heart of the old town. Better access to and ways of experiencing the rivers Nagold and Waldach were a key aspect of the concept for the garden show.

▼ Am Fuß eines Bahnviadukts entstand der Riedbrunnenpark, der künftig als Quartierspark eines neuen Wohngebiets dienen wird

The Riedbrunnenpark was created at the foot of the railway viaduct and will function as a local green space for a new residential quarter

▼ Muschelkalk als lokales Material und Gabionen prägen die Erschließung des Schlossbergs für die Landesgartenschau

Shell limestone, a local material, and gabions serve as characteristic elements of the paths to the Schlossberg in the garden show

ORT	LOCATION	Nagold
ENTWURF	DESIGN	Stefan Fromm Landschaftsarchitekten, Dettenhausen, Stefan Fromm, Landschaftsarchitekt bdla
BAUHERR	CLIENT	Landesgartenschau Nagold 2012 GmbH
PLANUNG/BAU	PLANNING/COMPLETION	2007 – 2012

WÜRDIGUNGEN | COMMENDATIONS | 2013

Superkilen, Kopenhagen/Dänemark
Superkilen, Copenhagen/Denmark

▲ Leuchtreklamen dienen dem Kulturtransfer: Statt Werbebotschaften vermitteln sie eine globale, urbane Kultur. Die Stadtmöblierung wurde in Workshops von den multiethnischen Anwohnern selbst ausgesucht

Illuminated signage as a means of cultural expression: instead of advertising, they create a sense of global urban culture. The street furniture was selected together with the local, multi-ethnic residents in a series of design workshops

Superkilen beschreibt einen ca. 750 Meter langen, keilförmigen Stadtraum nördlich des Zentrums von Kopenhagen in einem Gebiet, das stark multi-ethnisch bevölkert ist. Die Berliner Landschaftsarchitekten Topotek 1 gewannen einen internationalen Wettbewerb zur Gestaltung des öffentlichen Freiraums in Kooperation mit der Künstlergruppe Superflex und dem Architekturbüro BIG. Die Gestaltung des Stadtraums wurde von der Stadt Kopenhagen bewusst als Aufwertungsmaßnahme für den Stadtteil initiiert und mit Beteiligung der Anwohner durchgeführt.

Drei unterschiedlich farbcodierte Abschnitte, die bestimmte Nutzungszuweisungen erhielten – Stadtplatz, Marktplatz, Park – bieten den bunt gemischten Nutzerinnen und Nutzern aus dem Quartier einen ebenso bunten „Teppich", der eine Vielzahl von Atmosphären und Nutzungsmöglichkeiten schafft.

Das Projekt entfernt sich ganz bewusst von der herkömmlichen Haltung, in der sich ein Stadtraum möglichst ruhig, homogen diszipliniert und dadurch „zeitlos" in den Kontext einzuordnen hat.

Laut, grell, fragmentiert, kontrovers und nicht mit einem Ewigkeitsanspruch versehen, zeichnet Superkilen spielerisch die Ingredienzen einer multi-ethnischen Gesellschaft nach. Der öffentliche Raum wird im wahrsten Sinne herausgestrichen als Begegnungsort, der Differenzen aufdecken und auch aushalten soll. Der Raum ist nicht nur abstrakte Bühne für ein Stadtpublikum, sondern wird zum expressionistischen Bühnenbild, das mit seinem Publikum interagiert.

Superkilen is a 750-metre-long wedge-shaped urban space north of the centre of Copenhagen in a multi-ethnic district of the city. The Berlin-based landscape architects Topotek 1 won an international competition for the design of the public space in cooperation with the artist collective Superflex and BIG architects. The redesign of the urban space was initiated by the City of Copenhagen with the express purpose of upgrading the district, and the residents were involved in its development.

Divided into three different colour-coded sections, each with a specific function – urban square, market place and park – the space offers the multi-ethnic community from the surrounding districts a similarly multi-coloured patchwork of atmospheres and possible uses.

The project consciously takes a different approach to conventional urban designs, which are typically expected to be quiet, orderly, homogeneous and to fit "timelessly" into the local context.

Superkilen is instead bold, garish, fragmented, controversial and not built to last forever, and represents a playful attempt to interpret the ingredients of a multi-ethnic society. It deliberately stands out as a place to meet that is not afraid to openly show and accommodate differences. It is not only an abstract stage for the people of the city but an expressionist stage set that interacts with its players.

▲ Eine gezielte innerstädtische Revitalisierung verfolgte die Stadt Kopenhagen mit der Gestaltung der öffentlichen Freiräume im Stadtteil Nørrebro. Entstanden ist ein bunter, universell nutzbarer Freiraum

The design of the public space represents part of a revitalisation strategy by the City of Copenhagen for the district of Nørrebro. The result is a colourful and universally usable public space

▶ Der in Schwarz gehaltene Stadtplatz schließt an den in Rot gehaltenen an. Er bietet Raum für Märkte; Palmen vermitteln die Illusion einer mediterranen Strandpromenade

The black urban square links to its counterpart in red and offers a space for holding markets. Palm trees create the impression of a Mediterranean beach promenade

ORT	LOCATION	Kopenhagen/Dänemark · Copenhagen/Denmark
ENTWURF	DESIGN	Topotek 1 Gesellschaft von Landschaftsarchitekten mbH, Berlin, Martin Rein-Cano, Lorenz Dexler, mit · with BIG – Bjarke Ingels Group und · and SUPERFLEX
BAUHERR	CLIENT	Stadt Kopenhagen · City of Copenhagen
PLANUNG/BAU	PLANNING/COMPLETION	2010 – 2012

WÜRDIGUNGEN | COMMENDATIONS | 2013

Folly Forest, Strathcona School, Winnipeg/Kanada
Folly Forest, Strathcona School, Winnipeg/Canada

Das Projekt der sukzessiven Umgestaltung eines öde asphaltierten Schulhofes in Winnipeg, Kanada, zeigt auf markante Weise, wie mit einfachsten Mitteln ein namen- und gesichtsloser Außenraum zu neuem Leben erweckt wird. Ungewöhnliche Herstellungsmethoden und der konsequente Einsatz gebrauchter Materialien ließen einen überraschend unkonventionell anmutenden Raum entstehen. Der „Tanzboden für Bäume" wurde unter aktiver Mitwirkung von Lehrern und Schülern geschaffen; die Freude am Gestalten ist dem neuen Freiraum anzumerken.

Direktheit und Aktion generieren dabei ein schlüssiges landschaftsarchitektonisches Konzept: Aufgebrochene Löcher im Asphalt werden bepflanzt, der entstehende Baumhain lässt eine völlig neue räumliche Atmosphäre entstehen. Mit wenigen Eingriffen wandelt sich der alte Schulhof zu einer abenteuerlichen Phantasiewelt. Doch trotz der sehr spontan erscheinenden Perforierung entsteht keine chaotische Trümmerlandschaft: die neuen Pflanzstellen sind sorgsam positioniert und geformt, farbige Randmarkierungen verstärken den Eindruck eines großen Sternenbildes.

Mit unbekümmerter Leichtigkeit werden vorgefundene Objekte als Möbel, Spielelemente oder auch „Ausguck für Regenwürmer" in das Konzept integriert. So entsteht ein räumliches Ergebnis, welches abseits von gestalterischen und technischen Gewohnheiten der Landschaftsarchitektur neue Perspektiven eröffnet: Als eine „Mitmacharchitektur" kann sie engagierte Menschen begeistern, ohne jedoch ins Beliebige abzugleiten und ihren gestalterischen Anspruch aufzugeben.

The project for the successive redesign of a dull, asphalted school playground in Winnipeg, Canada, is a striking demonstration of how simple means can give a nameless and faceless outdoor space a new lease of life. Unusual production methods and the consistent use of recovered materials have resulted in a surprising and unconventional space. The "dance floor for trees" was created together with the active participation of the teachers and pupils, and the fun they had shaping it shows in the end result.

Immediacy and action are here responsible for creating a coherent landscape architectural concept: broken-up sections of the asphalt have been planted and the resulting grove of trees creates an entirely new spatial atmosphere. A few small interventions are enough to transform the old school playground into an adventurous fantasy world. The very spontaneous-looking perforations have not, however, resulted in a chaotic scene of destruction: the newly planted holes have been carefully positioned and formed, and coloured edging underlines the impression of a large star-shaped figure.

With a sense of carefree nonchalance, existing objects have been refashioned as furniture, playful elements or even "peepholes for earthworms" and incorporated into the concept. The result is a spatial experience that does not employ the typical design and technical methods of landscape architecture and in the process opens up new perspectives: as a form of "hands-on architecture" it encourages interested people to get involved without drifting into arbitrariness or directionless design.

◀ ▶ Die gemeinsam mit Schülern und Lehrern vereinbarten Entwurfselemente für das Projekt Folly Forest lauteten:
1. Asphalt perforieren, 2. Bäume pflanzen, 3. Boden bedecken, 4. Gräser und Blumen aussäen, 5. Regenwürmer begrüßen

Developed together with pupils and teachers, the design concept for the Folly Forest project comprises five steps:
1. Break open the asphalt, 2. Plant trees, 3. Cover hole with soil, 4. Plant grasses and flowers, 5. Say hello to earthworms!

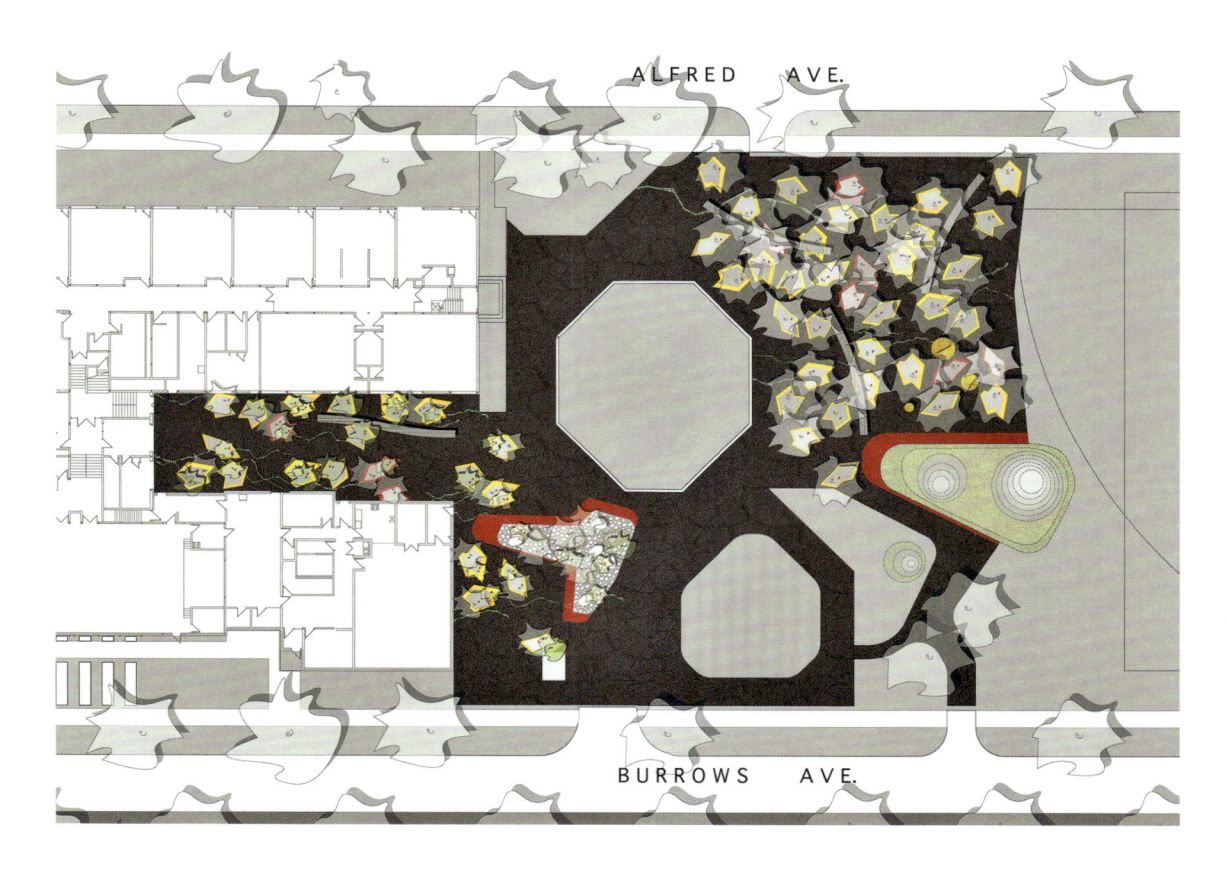

ORT	LOCATION	Winnipeg, Manitoba/Kanada · Canada
ENTWURF	DESIGN	Straub Thurmayr Landschaftsarchitekten und Stadtplaner, München · Munich/Winnipeg
		Dietmar Straub, Anna Thurmayr
BAUHERR	CLIENT	Winnipeg School Division, Strathcona School
PLANUNG/BAU	PLANNING/COMPLETION	2012

WÜRDIGUNGEN | COMMENDATIONS

SONDERPREIS INFRASTRUKTUR UND LANDSCHAFT

| 78 **Masterplan emscher:zukunft**
RMP Stephan Lenzen Landschaftsarchitekten, ASTOC Architects and Planners, Landschaft planen + bauen, Norbert Post · Hartmut Welters, Architekten und Stadtplaner GmbH
„Der Masterplan zeigt beispielhaft, wie es gelingen kann, den Umbau eines Infrastruktursystems als Motor einer integrierten räumlichen Entwicklungsplanung auf regionalem Maßstab zu nutzen."

WÜRDIGUNGEN

| 82 **Solarfeld Gänsdorf – ein wahres Märchen zur Energiewende**
Wartner & Zeitzler Landschaftsarchitekten bdla und Stadtplaner
„Beim Solarfeld Gänsdorf wird exemplarisch deutlich: Landschaftsarchitekten können den Blick der Flächeneigentümer und Investoren im Sinne einer Multifunktionalität der Anlage und Integration in das Siedlungsgefüge erweitern."

| 84 **Parkautobahn A42, Emscher Landschaftspark**
Planergruppe Oberhausen,
foundation 5+ landschaftsarchitekten
„Das Projekt versteht sich als Neuinterpretation der Rolle der Autobahn in der Industrielandschaft. Sie wird zu einem Reiseweg in die postindustrielle Kulturlandschaft."

| 86 **A281 – Zwischen Hightech, Laubenpieper und Natura 2000, Bremen**
planungsgruppe grün gmbh
„Für die unterschiedlichen Anforderungen von Mensch, Naturschutz, Landschaftsarchitektur und Verkehrsinfrastruktur hat das Projekt eine ansprechend gestaltete Lösung entwickelt."

SONDERPREIS WOHNUMFELD

| 88 **BIGyard Gartenhof, Berlin**
herrburg Landschaftsarchitekten
„Der BIGyard ist ein kleiner Hof, der durch eine clevere Gestaltung groß in Gebrauch und Wirkung wird. ... [Er] hebt sich wohltuend von der gängigen ‚paradiesischen Oase' ab ..."

WÜRDIGUNGEN

| 92 **kiezPARK FORTUNA, Berlin**
ARGE Almuth Krause, Landschaftsarchitektin, und Susanne Schnorbusch, Architektin
„Eine typische Aufgabe des Stadtumbaus Ost wurde hier vorbildlich gelöst: die Neunutzung eines aufgelassenen Schulstandortes inmitten eines Wohngebiets."

| 94 **Grünzug Centro Verde, Mannheim**
Helleckes Landschaftsarchitektur
„Entscheidend für die Qualität der gefundenen Lösung war die frühzeitige Einbindung der Landschaftsarchitektur in die städtebauliche Planung."

| 96 **Privatgarten B, Stuttgart**
Glück Landschaftsarchitektur
„Durch geschickte Nutzung der steilen Topografie, wenige, aber ausgeprägte Gestaltungsmittel und handwerklich perfekte Ausführung ist es gelungen, dem ... Garten eine adäquate Aura zu geben."

| 98 **Wohnumfeldverbesserung Wohnquartier Essener Straße, Hamburg**
Outside! Landschaftsarchitekten
„Initiiert durch die kommunale Wohnungsbaugesellschaft ist es gelungen, vielfältige Nutzungsangebote sowohl für Familien mit Kindern als auch für Ältere zu schaffen."

SPECIAL PRIZE FOR INFRASTRUCTURE AND LANDSCAPE

|78 Emscher Future master plan
RMP Stephan Lenzen Landschaftsarchitekten, ASTOC Architects and Planners, Landschaft planen + bauen, Norbert Post · Hartmut Welters, Architekten und Stadtplaner GmbH
"The master plan is a model example of how the conversion of a system of infrastructure can successfully be used as a motor for integrative spatial development planning at a regional scale."

COMMENDATIONS

|82 Gänsdorf Solar Field – A model for future renewable energy generation
Wartner & Zeitzler Landschaftsarchitekten bdla und Stadtplaner
"The solar field at Gänsdorf is an example of how landscape architects can broaden the horizon of the landowners and investors by creating a plant that is multi-functional and embedded in the existing pattern of settlement."

|84 A42 Park Motorway, Emscher Landscape Park
Planergruppe Oberhausen,
foundation 5+ landschaftsarchitekten
"The project reinterprets the role of the motorway in the industrial landscape, transforming it into a medium for experiencing a post-industrial cultural landscape."

|86 A281 – Between high-tech, allotment gardens and Natura 2000, Bremen
planungsgruppe grün gmbh
"The project has found an attractive design solution that caters for the different requirements of people, nature protection, landscape architecture and traffic infrastructure."

SPECIAL PRIZE FOR RESIDENTIAL ENVIRONMENTS

|88 BIGyard garden courtyard, Berlin
herrburg Landschaftsarchitekten
"The BIGyard is a small courtyard that employs clever design to make a big impression and be big in use – a refreshing change from the typical 'paradisiacal oasis'…"

COMMENDATIONS

|92 kiezPARK FORTUNA, Berlin
Almuth Krause, landscape architect,
and Susanne Schnorbusch, architect
"The project represents an exemplary solution to a typical urban revitalisation task in the former East German states: the reutilisation of a disused school in the heart of a housing estate."

|94 Centro Verde green corridor, Mannheim
Helleckes Landschaftsarchitektur
"The decision to incorporate the landscape architecture in the urban arrangement from an early stage has been decisive for the quality of the end result."

|96 Private garden B, Stuttgart
Glück Landschaftsarchitektur
"By skilfully exploiting the steep topography of the site and using a few simple but striking design means executed with perfect craftsmanship, the … garden has been given an appropriate aura."

|98 Residential area improvements, Essener Straße, Hamburg
Outside! Landschaftsarchitekten
"Initiated by the municipal housing association, it has been possible to create a variety of different uses for families with children as well as for older people."

SONDERPREIS INFRASTRUKTUR UND LANDSCHAFT | SPECIAL PRIZE FOR INFRASTRUCTURE AND LANDSCAPE | 2013

Masterplan emscher:zukunft
Emscher Future master plan

▶ Der Masterplan für die Emscher zwischen Dortmund und Dinslaken geht als Generationenprojekt auf die IBA Emscher Park zurück. Der Umbau eines Infrastruktursystems wird zum Motor einer integrierten Raumentwicklung im regionalen Maßstab

The master plan for the Emscher between Dortmund and Dinslaken is a project that spans generations and began with the Emscher Park International Building Exhibition. The conversion of infrastructure systems has been made a motor for integral spatial development at a regional scale

Der Umbau der Emscher von einem stinkenden Abwasserkanal hin zu einem attraktiven, ökologischen Gewässersystem ist ein Generationenprojekt, das mit der IBA Emscher Park begonnen wurde. Initiiert und finanziert durch die Emschergenossenschaft, wurde mit dem Masterplan emscher:zukunft ein für die Integration von Infrastruktur in die Landschaft beispielhafter Planungsprozess angestoßen.

In einem interdisziplinären Wettbewerb im Jahr 2003 gewann eine Strategie, die sich durch ein prägnantes Bild vermittelt: Die zukünftige Emscher soll sich gleich einem farbigen Kabelstrang entwickeln, innerhalb dessen vielfältige wasserbezogene, landschaftliche und städtebauliche Funktionen eng verwoben sind. Dieses programmatische Bild wurde im Zuge des Masterplanprozesses räumlich konkretisiert und zu einem systematischen regionalen Entwicklungs- und Handlungskonzept weiterentwickelt.

So entstand eine interaktive Planungsplattform im Dialog mit den Städten, Kreisen und Grundeigentümern entlang der Emscher. Der Umbau eines Infrastruktursystems wurde zum Motor einer integrierten räumlichen Entwicklungsplanung auf regionalem Maßstab.

Der Masterplan ersetzt keine formellen Planungsinstrumente, stellt jedoch Leitlinien für geplante Projekte auf und ist damit ein wichtiger strategischer Orientierungsrahmen. Gleichzeitig wird er kontinuierlich aktualisiert, indem rechtsgültige Planungen aufgenommen und laufend mit den übergeordneten Zielen abgeglichen werden.

Das Projekt zeigt in eindrucksvoller Weise, dass es möglich ist, durch die Zusammenarbeit zwischen verschiedenen Fachdisziplinen und einen dialogorientierten Planungsprozess einen isolierten infrastrukturellen Meideraum zu einer lebendigen Stadtlandschaft zu entwickeln.

The conversion of the Emscher system from a foul-smelling open wastewater canal into an attractive and ecological system of waterways is a project spanning several generations that first began as part of the IBA Emscher Park project. Initiated and financed by the Emscher Cooperative, the emscher:zukunft master plan marks the beginning of a model planning process for the integration of infrastructure in the landscape.

An interdisciplinary competition held in 2003 was won by a strategy described by a distinctive image: the future Emscher region should develop like a braided cable within which the diverse water-, landscape- and urban-related functions are closely interwoven. The programmatic image of the braided cable was elaborated over time into concrete spatial concepts and a systematic regional development and action concept.

The emscher:zukunft master plan is an interactive planning platform for involving and initiating dialogue with the towns, municipalities and landowners in the region of the Emscher River. The conversion of a system of infrastructure was successfully used as a motor for integrative spatial development planning at a regional scale.

The master plan does not replace formal planning instruments but elaborates guidelines for planned projects in the Emscher region and therefore serves as an important strategic framework for orientation. At the same time it is constantly being updated as new projects are awarded planning permission and are compared with the long-term aims of the project.

The master plan demonstrates most impressively that it is possible, through the collaboration of different professional disciplines and a dialogue-oriented planning process, to develop an unloved stretch of isolated infrastructure into a vibrant urban landscape.

ORT	LOCATION	Die Emscher zwischen Dortmund und Dinslaken, Nordrhein-Westfalen · The Emscher between Dortmund and Dinslaken, North Rhine-Westphalia
ENTWURF	DESIGN	RMP Stephan Lenzen Landschaftsarchitekten, Bonn, ASTOC Architects and Planners, Köln · Cologne, in Zusammenarbeit mit · in collaboration with Landschaft planen + bauen, Norbert Post · Hartmut Welters, Architekten und Stadtplaner GmbH, Dortmund
BAUHERR	CLIENT	Emschergenossenschaft Essen
PLANUNG/BAU	PLANNING/COMPLETION	2003/2006–2020

DINSLAKEN
RECKLINGHAUSEN
HERTEN
GELSENKIRCHEN
CASTROP-RAUXEL
BOTTROP
HERNE
HOLZWICKEDE
DUISBURG
OBERHAUSEN
ESSEN
DORTMUND

◀ Der Masterplan ersetzt keine formellen Planungsinstrumente, sondern stellt in einem dialogorientierten Planungsprozess Leitlinien für geplante Projekte auf. Er wird kontinuierlich fortgeschrieben

The master plan does not replace formal planning instruments but provides guidelines for planned projects as part of a dialogue-oriented planning process. It is continually being extended and updated

▲ Wasserbezogene, landschaftliche und städtebauliche Funktionen werden programmatisch verflochten und erzeugen neue Synergien. Voraussetzung für das Gelingen dieser Planung war und ist die Kooperation der unterschiedlichsten Akteure

Water-oriented, landscape and urban functions are woven together programmatically to create new synergies. A prerequisite for the success of this planning strategy was and is that the different stakeholders and users work together

▼ Vom offenen Abwasserkanal entwickelte sich die Emscher seit 2003 zu einem attraktiven, ökologischen Gewässersystem. Aus einem infrastrukturellen Meideraum wurde eine lebendige, multifuntkionale Stadtlandschaft

Since 2003, the Emscher has developed from being an open wastewater channel to an attractive ecological water system. An unloved stretch of infrastructure has been converted into a vibrant, multifunctional urban landscape

SONDERPREIS INFRASTRUKTUR UND LANDSCHAFT | SPECIAL PRIZE FOR INFRASTRUCTURE AND LANDSCAPE

WÜRDIGUNGEN | COMMENDATIONS | 2013

Solarfeld Gänsdorf – ein wahres Märchen zur Energiewende

Gänsdorf Solar Field – A model for future renewable energy generation

Anlagen und Flächen zur Gewinnung erneuerbarer Energien sind ein hochaktuelles Thema mit steigender Bedeutung in der Zukunft. Landschaftsarchitekten können den Blick der Flächeneigentümer und Investoren im Sinne einer Multifunktionalität der Anlage und Integration in das Siedlungsgefüge erweitern, den Eingriff in Natur- und Landschaftsfunktionen reduzieren, Ausgleichsmaßnahmen konzipieren und die Akzeptanz fördern.

Das Solarkraftwerk entstand auf ackerbaulichen Wirtschaftsflächen in Hofnähe. Das Netz von Flurwegen wird beibehalten, es gliedert die Einzelflächen und dient der Erschließung und Erholung. Feldhecken und Obstgehölze als wertvolle Biotopstrukturen reichern die Flur an. Das Obst kann der Verwendung zugeführt werden und es spricht nichts dagegen, innerhalb des Rahmens von Wegen, Hecken, Obstbäumen und extensiven Wiesen in Zukunft wieder zum Anbau von Nahrungsmitteln auf den fruchtbaren Böden zurückzukehren. Naturhaushalt und Landschaftsbild sind innerhalb der Solarflächen zusätzlich durch artenreiche Wiesen bereichert. Von einem öffentlichen Aussichtspunkt kann ein kritischer, aber auch durchaus positiver Blick auf das Stück „Energielandschaft" geworfen werden – eine Alternative zu intensivem Pflanzenanbau für Treibstoff- oder Biogasgewinnung.

Die Gesamtanlage ist entfernt von Ortslagen und hat Abstand zu Nachbarhöfen und archäologischen Kulturdenkmalen. Sie bleibt planerisch aber letztlich auf der Ebene des Einzelprojektes und der dafür verfügbaren Flächen. Dies zeigt sich zum Beispiel in der Nachzeichnung der Produktionsflächenkonturen durch abschirmende Feldhecken. Hier wird der nächste notwendige Schritt deutlich: das Hinausdenken und Einbinden solcher Flächen in die gesamte Landschaft als multifunktionales, vernetztes System durch alle Akteure.

Power plants and areas for harvesting energy from renewable energy sources are a topic of growing importance for the future. Landscape architects can broaden the horizon of landowners and investors by creating plants that are multi-functional, embedded in the existing pattern of settlement, that intervene less in nature and landscape, include compensation measures, and are accepted by residents and politics alike.

The solar power station has been built on an area of agricultural land in the vicinity of a farm. The network of paths between the fields has been retained and divides the individual sections of solar panels and provides pathways for access and recreation. Characteristic structural elements such as hedges and fruit trees maintain a sense of natural habitat. The fruit can be harvested and there is no reason why the land within this framework of paths, hedges, trees and grassland could not revert back to being used as fertile land for food crops at some point in the future. Extensive meadows between the solar panels contribute a rich range of species to the ecological balance and image of the landscape. From a public viewing platform, critical visitors can avail themselves of the positive potential of this kind of "energy landscape" as a viable alternative to the intensive cultivation of plants for fuel or biogas generation.

The entire complex is set apart from the nearest settlement, neighbouring farms and archaeological and cultural monuments. In planning terms, however, it only addresses the scale of a single project and the land resources available. This can be seen, for example, in the screening of the solar production plant with hedges around its perimeters. The next conceptual step would be to extend this principle to the scale of the open landscape as a multi-functional, networked system.

▲ Die Gestaltung von Energielandschaften wird ein zunehmend wichtiges Thema für die Landschaftsarchitektur. Dieses Solarfeld ist in die Flurlandschaft und -nutzung integriert – inklusive Aussichtshügel

The design of energy landscapes will become an increasingly important sector for landscape architecture. This solar field has been integrated into the pattern and usage of the landscape – and includes a viewing mound

▶ Feldhecken und Obstgehölze als Begrenzung des Solarfeldes reichern die Biotopstrukturen an, markieren aber auch die planerische Grenze des Einzelprojekts

Hedges and fruit trees as bounding elements of the solar field enrich the structure of the biotope and mark the perimeters of the project

ORT	LOCATION	Gänsdorf/Niederbayern · Lower Bavaria
ENTWURF	DESIGN	Wartner & Zeitzler Landschaftsarchitekten bdla und Stadtplaner, Landshut, Helmut Wartner und · and Rupert Zeitzler
BAUHERR	CLIENT	Q-Cells, Bitterfeld
PLANUNG/BAU	PLANNING/COMPLETION	2009

Parkautobahn A42, Emscher Landschaftspark

A42 Park Motorway, Emscher Landscape Park

▲ Markant bepflanzte „Ohrenparks" und „Parktankstellen" an den Autobahnzufahrten schaffen eine Verknüpfung zwischen den Fuß- und Radwegen des Emscher Landschaftsparks und der Autobahn

"Ear parks" with distinctive planting and "park service stations" at the motorway slip roads create a link between the footpaths and cycle paths of the Emscher Landscape Park and the motorway

Mit gestalterischen und technischen Maßnahmen wird die bestehende Autobahn A42 als Teil des Emscher Landschaftsparks in das Gefüge der Metropolregion Ruhrgebiet integriert. Ökologische und ästhetische Aspekte werden dabei gleichermaßen berücksichtigt. Die mit starkem Begleitgrün bewachsene Autobahn öffnet sich ein Stück weit und ermöglicht gezielte Blickachsen in die Stadtlandschaft. Das Begleitgrün wird abwechslungsreich gestaltet und umgebaut. Neben der Pflanzung von Leitbäumen wird die Vielfalt der Vegetation durch Auslichtung erhöht, was zu einer besseren Feinstaubbindung beiträgt und die Vielfalt der Fauna erhöht. Autobahnkreise werden als sogenannte Ohrenparks markant bepflanzt und Ausfahrten erhalten „Parktankstellen", die über Fuß- und Radwege einen Zugang in den Emscher Landschaftspark ermöglichen.

Das Projekt versteht sich als Neuinterpretation der Rolle der Autobahn in der Industrielandschaft. Sie wird zu einem Reiseweg in die postindustrielle Kulturlandschaft des Emscher Landschaftsparks. Bisherige „Unorte" des urbanen Raums werden so durch Gestaltung und Pflege in die Stadtlandschaft integriert. An der Schnittstelle zwischen Verkehrsinfrastruktur und regionalem Landschaftspark entstehen innovative Nutzungskonzepte und eine neue Form der Kulturlandschaft.

Through a combination of technical and design measures, the existing A42 motorway has been integrated in the structure of the metropolitan Ruhr conurbation as part of the Emscher Landscape Park. Ecological and aesthetic concerns are equally important aspects of the project. The motorway with its thickly planted verges will be partially opened up to reveal vistas over the urban landscape. To this end, roadside planting will be developed and augmented to make it more varied: in addition to the planting of new emblematic tree species, the variety of vegetation will be increased through thinning-out measures creating better conditions for binding fine dust particles and for increasing the diversity of the fauna. The so-called "ear-parks" at the motorway intersections will be given a distinctive planting concept and "park service stations" near the exits will enable visitors to enter the Emscher Landscape Park via footpaths and cycle paths.

The project reinterprets the role of the motorway in the industrial landscape, transforming it into a medium for experiencing the post-industrial cultural landscape of the Emscher Landscape Park. Sites that until now were "leftover spaces" in the urban realm have been reintegrated into the urban landscape through the use of design and regular maintenance. Here, where traffic infrastructure and regional landscape park meet, innovative concepts are emerging along with an entirely new form of cultural landscape.

▲ Reiseweg in die postindustrielle Kulturlandschaft: Die „Parkautobahn" A42 im Emscher Landschaftspark ist als Schnittstelle zwischen Verkehrsinfrastruktur und regionalem Landschaftspark konzipiert

A means of journeying through a post-industrial cultural landscape: the A42 "Park Motorway" in the Emscher Landscape Park is conceived as a combination of traffic infrastructure and regional landscape park

ORT	LOCATION	Emscher Landschaftspark, Ruhrgebiet · Emscher Landscape Park, Ruhr area
ENTWURF	DESIGN	Planergruppe Oberhausen, foundation 5+ landschaftsarchitekten, Kassel
BAUHERR	CLIENT	Arbeitsgemeinschaft Parkautobahn mit den Städten · Parkautobahn A42 work group with the cities Bottrop, Castrop-Rauxel, Duisburg, Dortmund, Essen, Gelsenkirchen, Herne, Herten, Moers, Oberhausen; RVR Regionalverband Ruhr, Neues Emschertal, RUHR.2010, Straßen. NRW, Ministerium für Klimaschutz, Umwelt, Landwirtschaft, Natur- und Verbraucherschutz NRW, Ministerium für Bauen und Verkehr NRW, StadtBauKultur NRW · NRW Ministry for Climate Protection, Environment, Agriculture, Nature Conservation and Consumer Protection, NRW Ministry for Construction and Transport, NRW Initiative for a better built environment
PLANUNG/BAU	PLANNING/COMPLETION	2008 –

WÜRDIGUNGEN | COMMENDATIONS | 2013

A281 – Zwischen Hightech, Laubenpieper und Natura 2000, Bremen

A281 – Between high-tech, allotment gardens and Natura 2000, Bremen

Das Projekt ist eine landschaftspflegerische Begleitplanung zum Autobahnneubau der A281 im Stadtraum Bremen. Sein Titel verdeutlicht bereits die höchst unterschiedlichen Gebietsnutzungen und -ausweisungen im Planungsraum. So verläuft der östliche Abschnitt zwischen dem Stadtteil Woltmershausen und Kleingärten, während der westliche Abschnitt entlang von Gewerbegebieten und einem Natura 2000-Schutzgebiet zu entwickeln war. Eine besondere Herausforderung sind die auf relativ kurzer Strecke auftretenden unterschiedlichen Vorprägungen.

Für die unterschiedlichen Anforderungen von Mensch, Naturschutz, Landschaftsarchitektur und Verkehrsinfrastruktur hat das Projekt eine ansprechend gestaltete Lösung entwickelt. Mit der Pusdorfer Meile wird ein zusammenhängender Parkverbund zwischen Hakenburger See und Rablinghauser Vorfluter geschaffen, auch als Ersatz für entfallende Kleingärten. Mit Hilfe von zusätzlichen Wegen und Renaturierungsmaßnahmen wird insbesondere für die Anwohner ein gesteigerter Wohn- und Erholungsnutzen erzielt. Anregungen der Bürger wurden integriert. Das Mühlenhauser Fleet verbindet die Gräben des Naturschutzgebiets Niedervieland und Stromer Feldmark. Unter Berücksichtigung der Flora-Fauna-Habitatrichtlinie (FFH) wurden die Lebensbedingungen für die FFH-relevanten Grabenfischarten wie Steinbeißer und Schlammpeitzger deutlich verbessert. Für sehr unterschiedliche Arten entsteht ein Biotopkomplex aus verschiedenen Gewässerlebensräumen.

Im Sinne umgebungsbezoger Gestaltung werden für die Region typische naturnahe Elemente wie Gewässer, Röhrichte, Auwald und Gehölze so eingesetzt, dass die mit dem Autobahnbau verbundenen neuen Elemente sich bestens in das Landschafts- und Stadtbild einfügen.

The project is a landscape upgrading measure to accompany the new A281 motorway in the region of Bremen. The project title already hints at the very different uses and declarations in the planning area. The eastern section runs between the district of Woltmershausen and allotment gardens, while the western section needed to be developed between a business park and a Natura 2000 nature protection area. A particular challenge of the site are the different prevailing situations that occur within a relatively short stretch of space.

To cater for the different requirements of people, nature protection, landscape architecture and traffic infrastructure, the project has found an attractive design solution: the new Pusdorfer Meile links together a set of parks between two bodies of water, the Hakenburger See and the Rablinghauser Vorfluter, which compensates for the loss of some of the allotment gardens. With the help of additional paths and nature restoration measures, it was possible to improve the living environment and leisure amenity value for local residents. The project design also incorporates suggestions from the public.

The Mühlenhauser Fleet connects the watercourses of the Niedervieland nature protection area and the Stromer Feldmark. In accordance with the flora-fauna-habitat (FFH) directive, it was possible to significantly improve the living conditions of freshwater fish such as the protected spined loach and weather loach. A complex of biotopes with different kinds of natural water habitats is being developed, conducive to a wide variety of species.

The project relates to its surroundings through the use of typical natural characteristics such as bodies of water, reeds, riverside coppices and woodland that help embed the elements of the new motorway in the landscape of the locality and the city.

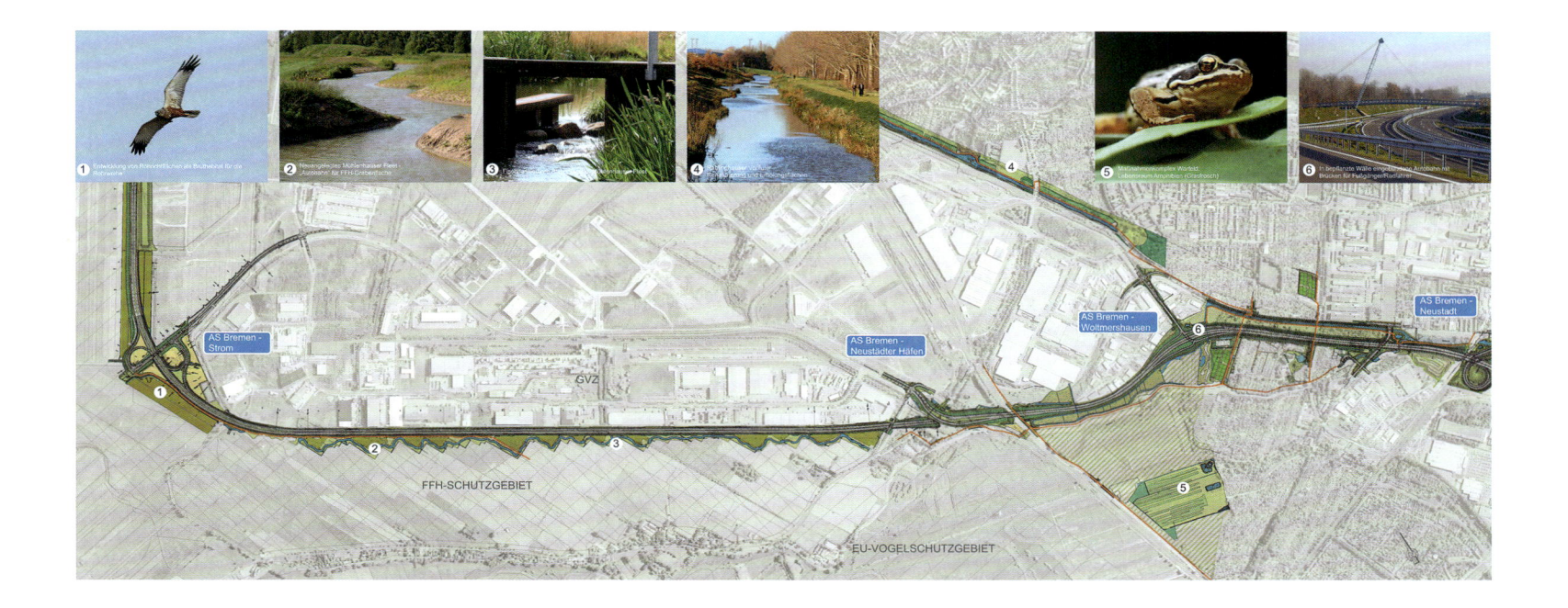

▲ Die ökologischen Ausgleichs- und Ersatzmaßnahmen wurden bereits im Vorfeld des Baus der A281 am Stadtrand von Bremen geplant und umgesetzt

The ecological compensation measures were planned and realised in advance of the construction of the A281 on the outskirts of Bremen

▼ Regionaltypische, naturnahe Elemente wie Gewässer, Röhrichte, Auwald und Gehölze prägen die mit dem Autobahnbau verbundenen Neugestaltungen

Regionally typical natural elements such as bodies of water, reeds, riverside coppices and woodland characterise the redesigned motorway environment

▼ „Autobahn für Grabenfische": Das Mühlenhausener Fleet wurde im Rahmen der Planungen verlegt und als FFH-Schutzgebiet renaturiert

"Motorway for freshwater fish": the Mühlenhausener Fleet was relocated as part of the project and restored as a Habitats Directive nature protection area

ORT	LOCATION	Bremen
ENTWURF	DESIGN	planungsgruppe grün gmbh, Bremen
BAUHERR	CLIENT	Bundesministerium für Verkehr, Bau und Stadtentwicklung, Senator für Umwelt, Bau und Verkehr Bremen · Federal Ministry of Transport, Building and Urban Development, Bremen's Senator for Environment, Construction and Transport
PLANUNG/BAU	PLANNING/COMPLETION	2004 – 2015

WÜRDIGUNGEN SONDERPREIS INFRASTRUKTUR UND LANDSCHAFT | COMMENDATIONS SPECIAL PRIZE FOR INFRASTRUCTURE AND LANDSCAPE | 87

SONDERPREIS WOHNUMFELD | SPECIAL PRIZE FOR RESIDENTIAL ENVIRONMENTS | 2013

BIGyard Gartenhof, Berlin
BIGyard garden courtyard, Berlin

▸ Eine Vielfalt von Qualitäten erhält Raum in dem eigentlich kleinen Gartenhof, der durch ein stabiles Entwurfsgerüst wohnungsnahe private und gemeinschaftliche Bereiche nischenartig integriert

The comparatively small garden courtyard accommodates a diverse range of qualities thanks to a robust design concept that incorporates private and communal areas by providing a system of niche situations

Der BIGyard ist ein kleiner Hof, der durch eine clevere Gestaltung groß in Gebrauch und Wirkung wird. Im Spannungsfeld von Privatsphäre, Ruhebedürfnis, Nutzungsdruck und Unterhalt getrauen sich die Projektverfasser, einen an sich kleinen Hof mit einer Vielzahl von Themen zu bespielen. Dies führt üblicherweise dazu, dass keine gestalterische Absicht mehr zu erkennen ist. Nicht so in diesem Fall: Ein disziplinierter Einsatz von räumlich wirksamen Elementen wie lose gestreuten Gleditsien, rohen Baumstämmen und Buckminster-Fuller-artigen Baumhäusern schafft ein stabiles Entwurfsgerüst, innerhalb dessen sich spielerisch eine Vielfalt von Qualitäten entwickeln kann.

Ein Rundweg schafft eine informelle Zonierung zwischen wohnungsnahen Bereichen und stärker bespielter Mitte. Die Bodenebene wird durch Strauch- und Staudenkissen strukturiert, was den Hof räumlich auflädt und ihn zum Garten-Hof macht. Der Mut zur Pflanze ist ein wesentliches Element der Gestaltung. Die nischenartige Mikrostruktur des Hofes im Zusammenspiel mit den eingezogenen Loggien im Erdgeschoss scheint eine gelungene Antwort auf das Bedürfnis nach räumlicher Geborgenheit innerhalb eines gut einsehbaren Hofes zu sein. Durch die Kombination von Pflanzen und artifiziellen Elementen hebt sich der Hof wohltuend von der gängigen „paradiesischen Oase" ab und erfindet eine Hofwelt, die unterschiedliche Interpretationen und unterschiedliche Nutzungsarten zulässt.

Im Wohnumfeld, dessen enges Korsett von laut postulierten Ansprüchen allzu oft zu rudimentären Entwürfen führt, leistet der BIGyard ein Bekenntnis zu einem sorgfältigen, detailgenauen und innovativen Umgang mit dem oft nebensächlich behandelten Thema.

The BIGyard is a small courtyard that employs clever design to make a big impression and be big in use. In spite of the competing demands for privacy, peace and quiet, maximisation of use and minimisation of maintenance, the project's designers boldly elected to incorporate a number of themes within a comparatively small courtyard. In most such cases this would result in the watering-down of the design intention, but here that is not this case: the disciplined use of spatially structuring elements such as loosely distributed *gleditsia* (honey locust) trees, rough-hewn tree trunks and Buckminster Fuller-inspired treehouses has created a robust framework within which a playful variety of qualities can thrive alongside one another.

A circular route creates an informal separation between areas close to the flats and the more intensively used central area. The ground is structured with cushions of shrubs and bushes, which create spaces within the courtyard and give it the character of a courtyard garden. The liberal use of plants is an essential element of its design. The niche-like microstructure of the courtyard together with the recessed loggias on the ground floor would appear to provide sufficiently for the need for sheltered areas within an otherwise not particularly private courtyard. Through its combination of plants and artificial elements, the courtyard provides a refreshing change from the typical paradisiacal "oasis", creating a courtyard environment that can accommodate different interpretations and different kinds of uses.

In a residential context in which the constraints of loudly proclaimed demands often lead to rudimentary results, the BIGyard demonstrates what a carefully considered, precisely detailed and innovative approach to this oft-neglected aspect of urban housing can achieve.

ORT	LOCATION	Berlin
ENTWURF	DESIGN	herrburg Landschaftsarchitekten, Berlin, Mareike Schönherr, Susanne Friedburg, Markus Schönherr
BAUHERR	CLIENT	Bauherrengemeinschaft Zelterstraße 5-11 GbR
PLANUNG/BAU	PLANNING/COMPLETION	2010

SONDERPREIS WOHNUMFELD | SPECIAL PRIZE FOR RESIDENTIAL ENVIRONMENTS

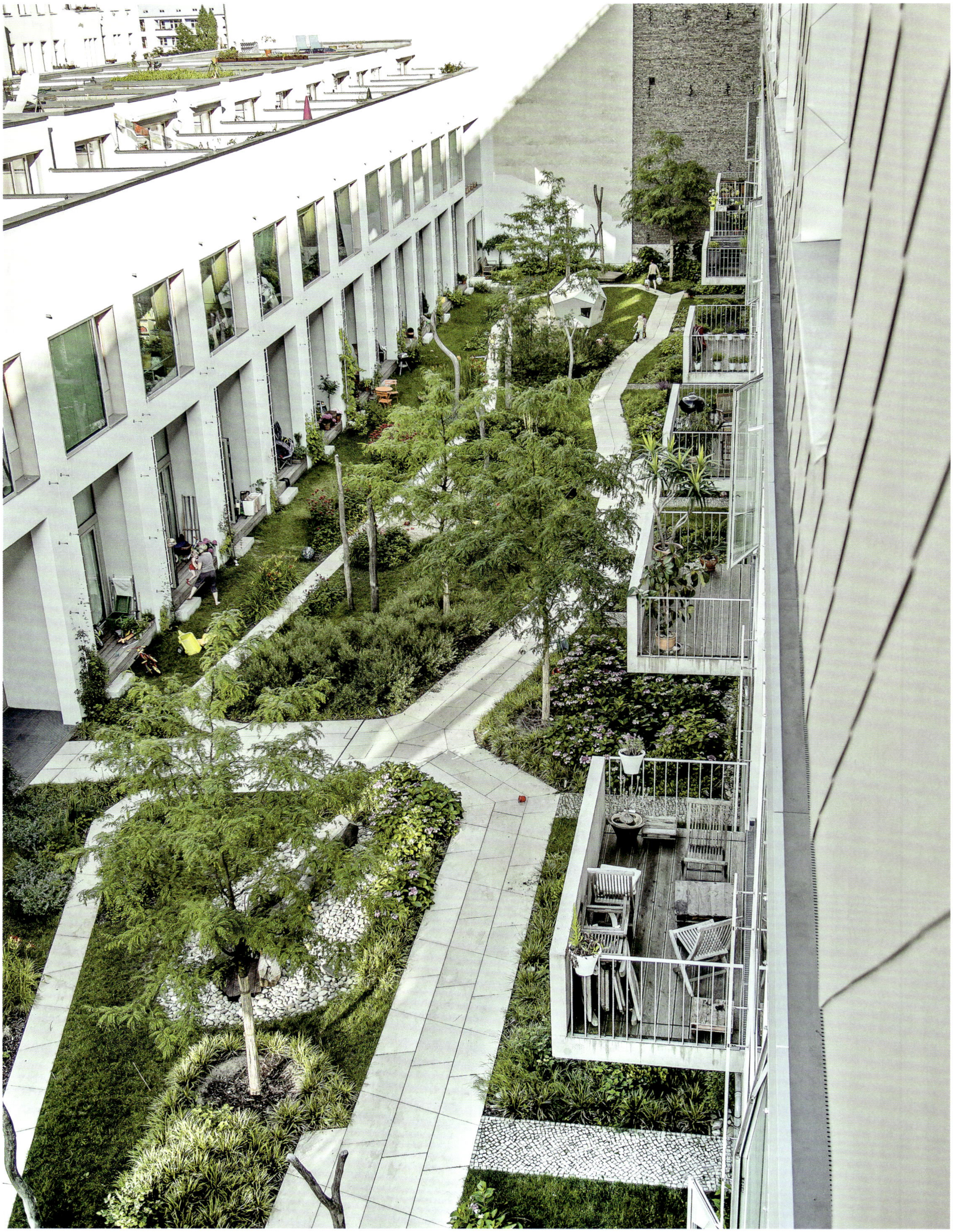

◀ Lose gestreute Gleditsien gehören zu den Elementen, die in dem Hof ein dreidimensionales Raumgerüst schaffen. Die netzförmigen Wege trennen und erschließen zugleich

Loosely arranged *gleditsia* are among the elements that lend the courtyard a sense of three-dimensional structure. The network of paths serves simultaneously to provide access and to separate areas

▶ Spielflächen und Einbauten im Hof, wie Baumhäuser und Holzplattformen, sind multifunktional geplant, so dass sie umgenutzt werden können, wenn die Kinder älter werden

Play areas and built structures in the courtyard such as tree houses and wooden decks are designed to be multifunctional so that they can be repurposed as the children grow older

▶ Der Entwurf besticht durch das Leitmotiv eines landschaftlich-weichen Gartens mit dem „Mut zur Pflanze", deren sorgfältige Verwendung zu der eigenen Gestaltsprache des Hofraums beiträgt

The design presents a compelling combination of soft landscaped garden and bold use of planting, which through its thoughtful usage contributes to the specific design quality of the courtyard space

WÜRDIGUNGEN | COMMENDATIONS | **2013**

kiezPARK FORTUNA, Berlin

kiezPARK FORTUNA, Berlin

▶ Die Fläche einer rückgebauten Schule wurde unter Einbeziehung der gesamten Nachbarschaft zu einem neuen Kiezpark. Voraussetzung des Erfolges war die Übernahme der Fläche durch die Wohnungsgenossenschaft

The site of a disused school has been reclaimed for use as a neighbourhood park, designed in collaboration with the residents. A key factor was the willingness of the housing association to take over responsibility for the site

Eine typische Aufgabe des Stadtumbaus Ost wurde hier vorbildlich gelöst: die Neunutzung eines aufgelassenen Schulstandortes inmitten eines Wohngebiets.

Die rund 27.000 Quadratmeter große Fläche wurde als „Ort des Alltags und der Begegnung", als aktiv zu nutzende und öffentlich zugängliche neue Quartiersmitte entwickelt. Die Gestaltung der Kernfläche von 11.000 Quadratmetern als Kiezpark wurde von Anwohnern, Vereinen, sozialen Trägern und Eigentümern durch einen kontinuierlich tagenden und transparenten Stammtisch begleitet und in themenbezogenen Workshops mitgestaltet. Es entstanden eine Streuobstwiese, Inseln mit Frühlingsblühern, Kräuter- und Staudenbeete, Wiesenflächen, ein Steingarten und ein Wasserspielplatz. Die Mitte des Parks ist geprägt von einem Bachlauf mit Teich, einem Platz unter einer Pergola und einem „Gartenzimmer". Ein Weg begleitet die Pergola durch den Park und eröffnet immer wieder neue Ansichten der einzelnen Elemente der Grünanlage.

Entscheidend für den Erfolg des Vorhabens war die Bereitschaft der Wohnungsgenossenschaft, die brachgefallene Fläche vom Land Berlin zu übernehmen, gemeinsam mit Landschaftsarchitekten hochwertig zu gestalten und nicht nur für die eigene Nachbarschaft, sondern für die Quartiersöffentlichkeit zugänglich zu machen. Durch die genossenschaftliche Trägerschaft dürfte auch die nachhaltige Nutzung und Pflege des Parks garantiert sein.

Der Park erhielt eine Auszeichnung durch den Rat für Nachhaltigkeit als Projekt 2013.

The project represents an exemplary solution to a typical urban revitalisation task in the former East German states: the reutilisation of a disused school in the heart of a housing estate.

Extending over an area of nearly 27,000 square metres, the site was to serve as "a meeting place for everyday use" and as an actively usable, publicly accessible new centre for the surrounding quarter. The design of the central 11,000-square-metre-large section of the site as a neighbourhood park was undertaken together with local residents, community associations, social agencies and owners in a series of workshops and a roundtable that met regularly over the course of the project. The park contains an orchard, islands with spring flowers, herbaceous plant and shrub beds, lawns, a stone garden and a water playground. A stream runs through the centre of the park feeding a pond where there is also a square beneath a pergola and a "garden room". A path alongside the pergola runs the length of the park and provides ever-changing views of the individual elements of the green area.

A key factor for the success of the project was the willingness of the housing cooperative to take over responsibility for this wasteland area from the State of Berlin, to create a high-quality design together with the landscape architects and to make it accessible not just to the residents in the cooperative's buildings but to the quarter as a whole. The cooperative's responsibility for the site will most likely also guarantee the long-term use and upkeep of the park.

The park was named an exemplary project by the German Council for Sustainable Development in 2013.

▸ Die hölzerne Pergola begleitet den Weg durch den vielfältig gestalteten Park mit immer wieder neuen Ansichten und Nutzungsmöglichkeiten

A wooden pergola marks the path through the park, providing ever-changing vistas and a range of functions in the varied character of the park

ORT	LOCATION	Berlin-Marzahn
ENTWURF	DESIGN	ARGE Almuth Krause, Landschaftsarchitektin, und Susanne Schnorbusch, Architektin · Almuth Krause, landscape architect, and Susanne Schnorbusch, architect, Berlin
BAUHERR	CLIENT	FORTUNA Wohnungsunternehmen eG
PLANUNG/BAU	PLANNING/COMPLETION	2010 – 2012

WÜRDIGUNGEN | COMMENDATIONS | 2013

Grünzug Centro Verde, Mannheim
Centro Verde green corridor, Mannheim

▸ Als „Vorleistung" zur Adressbildung des Neubaugebietes entstand der langgestreckte Grünzug Centro Verde mit Baumhainen und großzügigen Wiesenflächen

The green corridor – the Centro Verde – was completed in advance of the new housing scheme to define the vacant site as a distinctive place, and provides expansive lawns, vegetation and groves of trees

▸ Das Konzept zur Erhöhung der Lagequalität auf dem Gelände einer ehemaligen Kaserne ist für die Investoren aufgegangen und strahlt auch auf die umliegenden Nachbarschaften aus

The concept for improving the quality of the location on the site of a former military barracks has not only been successful in attracting buyers but has also benefited the entire neighbourhood

Der Grünzug Centro Verde stellt das Herz eines neuen Wohngebiets auf dem Gelände einer ehemaligen Kaserne im Nordosten von Mannheim dar. Der Bauherr hat den Grünzug als Mittel der Adressbildung eingesetzt und war bereit, trotz des damit verbundenen finanziellen Risikos die Realisierung zeitlich dem Hochbau vorzuziehen. Durch den Park ist eine neue Lagequalität entstanden, die vorher für potenzielle Käufer und Investoren nicht vorstellbar war und die auch auf die bereits bestehenden Nachbarschaften ausstrahlt.

Der lineare Grünzug ist als großzügiges Wiesenband mit eitlichen Fassungen aus Weißbeton gestaltet. Die Wiesenfläche ist mit perspektivisch gestaffelten Kiefern und Himalaja-Birken bestanden. Flächige Pflanzungen aus Strauchweiden und Stauden begrenzen die Seiten des Parks. Die Endpunkte der Anlage bilden Baumhaine aus Vogelkirschen, die einmal als Spielbereich, einmal als erhöhte Aussichtsplattform ausformuliert sind.

Entscheidend für die Qualität der gefundenen Lösung war die frühzeitige Einbindung der Landschaftsarchitektur in die städtebauliche Planung – ein gutes Beispiel dafür, wie die Freiraumgestaltung dem Hochbau vorangehen kann.

The Centro Verde green corridor represents the heart of a new housing scheme on the site of a former military barracks in northeast Mannheim. The client saw the green corridor as a key location factor for the development and was willing, despite the financial risk involved, to embark on its development ahead of the construction of the houses. The park gives the location a sense of place that would not otherwise have been tangible for potential buyers and investors and that radiates beyond the adjoining buildings into the neighbourhood behind.

The linear corridor takes the form of a broad band of grassland framed at its edges by low walls of white concrete. The lawns are planted with Himalayan pine and birch trees in a staggered, perspective arrangement. Ground cover in the form of willow shrubs and bushes give definition to the sides of the corridor, and at each end of the strip is a rowanberry grove, one enclosing a play area, the other serving as a raised viewing platform.

The decision to incorporate the landscape architecture in the urban arrangement from an early stage has been decisive for the quality of the end result and is a good example of how the design of outdoor spaces can precede the architecture around it.

ORT	LOCATION	Mannheim, Neckarstadt-Ost
ENTWURF	DESIGN	Helleckes Landschaftsarchitektur, Karlsruhe, Stefan Helleckes, Landschaftsarchitekt bdla
BAUHERR	CLIENT	GBG-Mannheimer Wohnungsbaugesellschaft mbH
PLANUNG/BAU	PLANNING/COMPLETION	2009 – 2011

WÜRDIGUNGEN | COMMENDATIONS | 2013

Privatgarten B, Stuttgart
Private garden B, Stuttgart

▶ Mit höchster Ausführungsqualität besticht dieser Hausgarten. Der Bodenbelag aus Muschelkalk setzt sich im Innern des Hauses fort

Executed to the highest quality, this garden impresses at all levels. The surfacing of shell limestone continues into the interior of the house

▶ Der Höhenunterschied des Grundstücks von 12 Metern wurde für die Staffelung in verschiedene Terrassen mit Sitzplätzen, Pflanzflächen und Wasserspielen genutzt, Wasser dient als verbindendes Element

The significant height difference of the site – 12 metres – has been bridged using a series of different terraces with seating areas, plant beds and water features. Water serves as the uniting element

Der extreme Zuschnitt eines privaten Wohngrundstücks mit zwölf Metern Höhenunterschied führte bei der Gliederung des Gartens zu einem hohen Anteil an architektonischen Elementen, an Mauern, Treppen und unterschiedlichen Ebenen mit dem Ziel einer engen Symbiose von Garten und Architektur. Die architektonische Sprache wurde gewissermaßen mit den Mitteln der Gartengestaltung weiter gesprochen.

Natursteinmauern bilden die Sockelzonen und erden die mit Weißbeton ausgeführten Treppen- und Terrassenelemente. Der steile Hang wird mit verschiedenen Ebenen, vom unteren Pool mit Liegefläche bis zum abendlich besonnten Sitzplatz am höchsten Punkt des Grundstücks, mit Pflanzbeeten und Rasenterrassen genutzt, um interessante und vielfältige Aufenthalts- und Sitzmöglichkeiten zu bieten. Die Muschelkalkbeläge ziehen sich ins Innere des Hauses hinein und verbinden Innen und Außen zu einem gesamtheitlichen Wohn- und Lebensraum.

Die rückwärtige Stützmauer wurde mit eleganten Kragstufentreppen und einer oberen Holzlamellenwand zum Blickfang. Dazu trägt auch das Wasser bei, das, eine reliefierte Wand hinabrinnend, den über die ganze Breite des Grundstücks reichenden Wassergraben in Bewegung bringt.

Durch geschickte Nutzung der steilen Topografie, wenige, aber ausgeprägte Gestaltungsmittel und handwerklich perfekte Ausführung ist es gelungen, dem ambitionierten Haus mit dem Garten eine adäquate Aura zu geben.

The steeply inclined private plot with a height difference of twelve metres made it necessary to structure the garden with a large number of architectonic elements such as walls, steps and different levels. The design strives to achieve a symbiosis of house and garden. As such, the language of the architecture is continued in the landscaping of the garden.

Stone masonry has been used for the plinth zone, rooting the stairs and terracing of white concrete in the ground. The sloping site is divided into different levels with a pool and lounging area at the bottom and a seating area in the evening sun at the highest point of the plot. Plant beds and lawn terracing are used to create interesting and varied places to sit and enjoy the garden. The shell limestone paving continues into the interior of the house, connecting the indoor and outdoor areas to form a continuous living space.

Special attention has been given to the retaining walls at the rear of the house: the elegant cantilevered steps and slatted wood wall at the top transform them into an attractive, eye-catching elevation. This impression is underlined by the use of water as a further design element: trickling down over a contoured section of wall, it sets water in motion along a linear pool of water that extends the entire width of the plot.

By skilfully exploiting the steep topography of the site and using a few simple but striking design means executed with perfect craftsmanship, it has been possible to create a garden that complements the bold design and aura of the house.

ORT	LOCATION	Stuttgart
ENTWURF	DESIGN	Glück Landschaftsarchitektur, Stuttgart, Michael Glück
BAUHERR	CLIENT	Jutta und · and Dieter Blocher
PLANUNG/BAU	PLANNING/COMPLETION	2009 – 2010

WÜRDIGUNGEN SONDERPREIS WOHNUMFELD | COMMENDATIONS SPECIAL PRIZE FOR RESIDENTIAL ENVIRONMENTS

WÜRDIGUNGEN | COMMENDATIONS | 2013

Wohnumfeldverbesserung Wohnquartier Essener Straße, Hamburg
Residential area improvements, Essener Strasse, Hamburg

Eine „Kunstachse" durchzieht das Quartier. Die Mosaike dafür wurden zusammen mit Schulen und Anwohnern entworfen und realisiert

An "art axis" runs through the quarter and incorporates mosaics designed and realised by local schoolchildren and residents

Das Wohnumfeld des Anfang der 1980er Jahre errichteten, ca. 75 Hektar umfassenden Quartiers Essener Straße in Hamburg-Langenhorn mit einem überdurchschnittlich hohen Anteil von Kindern, Jugendlichen und Migranten war nach 30 Jahren erneuerungsbedürftig. Unter intensiver Anwohnerbeteiligung wurden Freiflächen erneuert und dabei mit Spielplätzen, Mietergärten und neu gestalteten Stellplätzen versehen. Es wurden separate Fußwegeverbindungen geschaffen, so dass man das Quartier ungestört vom motorisierten Verkehr durchqueren kann.

Initiiert durch die kommunale Wohnungsbaugesellschaft ist es gelungen, vielfältige Nutzungsangebote sowohl für Familien mit Kindern als auch für Ältere zu schaffen. Jugendliche wurden nicht nur in die Planung einbezogen, sondern haben selbst aktiv an einer Jugendfreizeitfläche mit Pavillon mitgebaut.

Hervorzuheben ist die „Kunstachse" als identitätsstiftendes Element, die gemeinsam mit Schulen und Anwohnern entworfen und realisiert wurde – ein bemerkenswerter Kontrast zu der mancherorts beobachtbaren Vernachlässigung und Verwahrlosung von Kunstobjekten im Wohnumfeld.

The residential environment of the 75-hectare-large quarter built in the 1980s along the Essener Strasse in Hamburg-Langenhorn has an above-average proportion of children, young people and migrants and, after almost 30 years of use, was in need of renewal. In conjunction with the residents, a design for the renovation of the outdoor areas was developed, including playing areas, residents' gardens and redesigned car parking. Separate footpaths were created so that one can cross the quarter undisturbed by motorised traffic.

Initiated by the municipal housing association, it has been possible to create a variety of different uses for families with children as well as for older people. Teenagers were not only invited to take part in the planning process but also actively contributed to the building of a youth recreation area with pavilion.

A special feature is the "art axis", designed and realised jointly by schoolchildren and residents as an element that helps to create a sense of identity – an idea that contrasts markedly with the neglect and dilapidation of art objects seen in other residential projects.

▲ Die Jugendfreizeitfläche mit Pavillon entstand in gemeinschaftlicher Arbeit mit Jugendlichen aus dem Quartier. Initiator des Projekts ist eine kommunale Wohnungsbaugesellschaft

The youth recreation area with pavilion was built together with young people from the quarter. The project was initiated by the municipal housing association

▶ Dank einer intensiven Beteiligung der Anwohner bleibt Vandalismus in dem neu gestalteten Wohnumfeld aus

By actively involving local residents, the newly created outdoor amenities have not suffered from the kind of vandalism seen elsewhere

ORT	LOCATION	Hamburg-Langenhorn
ENTWURF	DESIGN	Outside! Landschaftsarchitekten, Hamburg, Gottfried Neder, Gerd Grunau GbR
BAUHERR	CLIENT	SAGA Siedlungs-Aktiengesellschaft Hamburg
PLANUNG/BAU	PLANNING/COMPLETION	2007 – 2012

PETER-JOSEPH-LENNÉ-PREIS | PETER JOSEPH LENNÉ PRIZE | 2012

Strategie Stadtlandschaft – natürlich urban produktiv
Urban Landscape Strategy – natural urban productive

Mit der Auslobung des Lenné-Preises bekennt sich die Stadt Berlin zu ihrem „grünen Erbe" und fördert mit diesem Nachwuchswettbewerb nicht nur die Profession der Landschaftsarchitektur, sondern auch die aktuelle Diskussion um die Gestaltung der für die Stadt so wichtigen Grün- und Freiräume.

Das urbane Grün in Berlin ist eine wertvolle Ressource. Es erhöht die Lebensqualität für die Berlinerinnen und Berliner genauso wie für Gäste aus aller Welt. Das vielfältige Grün ist Reichtum ebenso wie Wirtschaftsfaktor. Und es bringt Verpflichtungen mit sich: Es ist eine Herausforderung, das Berliner Grün zu sichern und auszubauen. Dieser Aufgabe hat sich der Berliner Senat mit der „Strategie Stadtlandschaft Berlin" verpflichtet.

PLÄNE FÜR DIE ZUKUNFT

Diese grundlegende strategische Auseinandersetzung mit der Stadtlandschaft wird bewusst als integraler Teil der Stadtentwicklung aufgefasst. Berlin stellt sich den neuen Herausforderungen mit einem systematischen und umfassenden Ansatz. Der Berliner Senat hat drei neue strategische Konzepte beschlossen, die sich ergänzen und eng verzahnt mit dem „Grün" als wesentlichem Faktor einer nachhaltigen Stadtentwicklung befassen: der Stadtentwicklungsplan Klima, die Berliner Strategie zur biologischen Vielfalt und die Strategie Stadtlandschaft.

KONZEPT DER STRATEGIE STADTLANDSCHAFT

Die Strategie Stadtlandschaft ist auf die großen zukünftigen Aufgaben der Stadtentwicklung ausgerichtet. Im Mittelpunkt stehen die Themen Klimawandel und ressourceneffiziente Stadt, demografischer Wandel und kulturelle Vielfalt. Neue gesellschaftliche Trends, wie die Do-it-yourself-Kultur, die Verknüpfung von urbanen und ländlichen

von · by Michael Müller The awarding of the Lenné Prize underlines the City of Berlin's commitment to its "green heritage", promoting not only young professionals in the field of landscape architecture but also furthering current debate on the design of the green and urban spaces that are so vital for our cities.

Urban green is a valuable resource in Berlin. It improves the quality of life for Berlin's residents as well as for international guests, and the diverse kinds of green spaces are both an asset as well as an economic factor. This, however, comes with the obligation to protect and consolidate the green spaces in the city. The Berlin Senate has committed itself to this task through its "Berlin Urban Landscape Strategy".

PLANS FOR THE FUTURE

A fundamental strategic review of the urban landscape is seen as being integral to the development of the city. Berlin has taken a systematic and comprehensive approach to tackling the new challenges. Three new strategic concepts have been agreed that complement one another and regard urban green as a key factor for sustainable urban development: the Urban Development Plan on Climate; the Biodiversity Strategy; and the Urban Landscape Strategy.

THE CONCEPT OF THE URBAN LANDSCAPE STRATEGY

The Urban Landscape Strategy aims to address the most important urban development issues facing the city in the future. Key issues include climate change and a better use of resources, demographic change and cultural diversity. New social trends, such as the do-it-yourself culture, the emergence of urban-rural lifestyles and changing patterns of mobility are being incorporated into the strategy.

The Urban Landscape Strategy develops the city's existing potential along the lines of three primary themes: "Beautiful

Lebensstilen und eine veränderte Mobilität werden in die Strategie Stadtlandschaft aufgenommen.

Die Strategie Stadtlandschaft entwickelt bestehende Stärken mit den drei Leitbildthemen „Schöne Stadt", „Produktive Landschaft" und „Urbane Natur" weiter. Ein Netz aus bestehenden Grünflächen und als öffentliche Freiräume nutzbaren Straßen wird zum Grundgerüst der lebenswerten Stadt. Die „Schöne Stadt" zielt dabei auch auf eine Qualifizierung historischer und aktueller Freiraumarchitektur. Ein räumlicher Schwerpunkt liegt in bioklimatisch belasteten und sozial benachteiligten Gebieten. Die Berliner Stadtnatur ist auch ein ökonomisch und sozial produktiver Raum. „Produktive Landschaft" verbindet Kleingärten, Landwirtschaft und Subsistenzwirtschaft (Selbstversorgung) mit der Do-it-yourself-Kultur von Zwischennutzern, Raumpionieren, Unternehmern und einem ökologisch motivierten Lebensstil. Aktives Mitgestalten stärkt bürgerschaftliches Engagement, erhöht die Verantwortung für das städtische Grün und schafft neue Entfaltungsräume.

„Urbane Natur" steht für ein Naturerleben mitten in der Stadt und zielt gleichzeitig auf die Förderung der biologischen Vielfalt, Versorgung mit sauberem Trinkwasser und kühler Luft.

UMSETZUNG DER STRATEGIE STADTLANDSCHAFT

Zur Umsetzung der Strategie Stadtlandschaft gilt es, den Wert der Grün- und Freiräume deutlicher herauszustellen. Voraussetzung dafür ist eine umfassende Kommunikation, in deren Zentrum modellhafte Referenzprojekte stehen, wie der Große Tiergarten, die Parklandschaft Tempelhof oder das Grüne Band entlang der ehemaligen Berliner Mauer. Sie füllen das Leitbild mit Leben, machen es anschaulich und weisen als gute Beispiele den Weg in die Zukunft, damit das Grün der Stadt weiterhin Berlin zu einer lebens- und liebenswerten Metropole macht.

City", "Productive Landscapes" and "Urban Nature". Existing green areas in the city and publicly usable streetspaces will be connected to form a network of liveable outdoor spaces in the city. The "Beautiful City" theme aims to improve the quality of the city's historical and contemporary landscape architecture. A particular area of focus is bioclimatically polluted and socially disadvantaged areas. Berlin's urban nature is also an economic and socially productive space. The "Productive Landscapes" theme connects allotment gardens, urban agriculture and subsistence farming initiatives with the do-it-yourself culture of temporary uses, urban pioneers, businesses and ecologically oriented lifestyles. The ability to contribute to shaping one's environment fosters active citizenship, encourages people to assume responsibility for urban spaces and creates new opportunities for creative outlets. Finally, the "Urban Nature" theme concerns the experience of nature in the heart of city and aims to improve biological diversity, better provision of clean drinking water and cool air in the city.

IMPLEMENTING OF THE URBAN LANDSCAPE STRATEGY

To implement the Urban Landscape Strategy, it is necessary to raise awareness of the value of open and green spaces in the city. A comprehensive communication strategy is envisaged that will profile exemplary case study projects such as the Grosse Tiergarten, the Tempelhof Park Landscape or the Green Band along the route of the former Berlin Wall. They breathe life into the vision, communicate its intention and provide best-practice examples for the future so that green spaces in the city will continue to contribute to making Berlin a liveable and lovable metropolis.

Peter-Joseph-Lenné-Preis 2012
Peter Joseph Lenné Prize 2012

Der Peter-Joseph-Lenné-Preis ist auch 2012, in seinem 47. Jahr, der größte internationale Nachwuchswettbewerb der Landschaftsarchitektur. 90 Arbeiten aus neun Ländern wurden eingereicht, darunter Deutschland, Spanien, Bulgarien, Italien, Polen, Schweiz, Frankreich sowie die USA und Australien. Studenten und Absolventen internationaler Hochschulen sowie praktizierende Landschaftsarchitekten, Hochbauarchitekten, Stadtplaner und Designer nahmen am Wettbewerb teil. Gefragt wurde nach einer interdisziplinären Bearbeitung städtebaulicher, landschaftsplanerischer und landschaftsarchitektonischer Aspekte in zwei beispielhaften Aufgaben.

Für die Wettbewerbs-Jury stand die Frage nach einem schlüssigen und relevanten Gesamtkonzept im Vordergrund. „Die Qualitäten aller Arbeiten, vor allem in der Analyse, sind sehr hoch", sagte Jury-Vorsitzende Professor Gabriele Kiefer, Institut für Landschaftsarchitektur an der Technischen Universität Braunschweig. Professor Günther Vogt, Institut für Landschaftsarchitektur an der Eidgenössischen Technischen Hochschule Zürich, hob die Bereitschaft hervor, neben Studium und Beruf diesen spannenden Wettstreit anzunehmen. Stephan Felber, Leiter der Sektion Siedlungs- und Freiraumentwicklung im Departement Bau, Verkehr und Umwelt im schweizerischen Kanton Aargau, war dankbar für das intensive Interesse an der Aufgabe „Landschaftspark Hochrhein" und zeigte sich „von der Qualität der Darstellungen und der grafischen Vermittlung der Inhalte" beeindruckt. Annina Gräfin Fugger-Babenhausen, freie Landschaftsarchitektin und Vertreterin des Garden Club of Bavaria, äußerte sich begeistert „von den zahlreichen guten Ansätzen und Ideen zur Bearbeitung der Aufgaben".

von · by Christoph Rosenkranz

In 2012, in its 47th year of existence, the Peter Joseph Lenné Prize still remains the largest international prize for young professionals in the field of landscape architecture. A total of 90 entries were submitted from nine countries: Germany, Spain, Bulgaria, Italy, Poland, Switzerland and France as well as the USA and Australia. Students and graduates of international universities, as well as practicing landscape architects, architects, urban designers and designers developed interdisciplinary approaches to urban design, landscape planning and landscape architecture challenges for two exemplary projects.

For the competition jury, the most important criterion was evidence of a coherent and relevant general concept. "Overall, the quality of the submissions, and especially the analytical studies, was very high," remarked Professor Gabriele Kiefer from the Institute for Landscape Architecture at Braunschweig Technical University, who headed the competition jury. Professor Günther Vogt from the Institute for Landscape Architecture at the Swiss Federal Institute of Technology (ETH) Zurich was impressed by the willingness of participants to take on such fascinating projects alongside their regular studies and work. Stephan Felber, Head of Urban and Regional Planning at the Department for Building, Transport and the Environment in the Swiss Canton of Aargau, appreciated the significant interest shown in the Upper Rhine project and was impressed by "the quality of the presentations and graphic communication of the ideas". And Annina Gräfin Fugger-Babenhausen, a freelance landscape architect and representative of the Garden Club of Bavaria, was glad to see such a "large number of good ideas and approaches to tackling the project tasks".

EINSCHÄTZUNG DER JURY ZUM LENNÉ-PREIS

Zunehmend wurden stark künstlerische und konzeptionelle Lösungsvorschläge unterbreitet. So dienen Strukturvorlagen wie Bodenbeläge oder Grafiken als Chiffre, einen Ort zu transformieren. Dabei weicht die Gestaltung von klassischen freiraumplanerischen Themen ab und beschränkt sich auf die überspitzte Darstellung einzelner Oberflächentexturen.

Die Gestaltungsvorschläge zahlreicher Arbeiten folgten keinem festgelegten Leitmotiv, wenngleich die Komplexität der Wettbewerbsgebiete intelligent analysiert und plakativ dargestellt wurden. Die gewonnenen Ergebnisse in ein schlüssiges landschaftsarchitektonisches Konzept zu überführen, stellte sich allgemein als schwierig dar: Detaillierte Auseinandersetzungen mit dem Ort und seinen Eigenheiten fehlten vielen Arbeiten. Zahlreiche Arbeiten nutzten einerseits unterschiedlichste konzeptionelle Ansätze, andererseits waren diese von sich wiederholenden Formalismen geprägt. Räumliche Neukonzeptionen wurden vernachlässigt. „Eine negativ auffallende Tendenz ist der weitgehende Verzicht auf die Kraft der Pflanzen zur räumlichen und gestalterischen Inszenierung", urteilte die Jury. Ebenso empfahl die Jury, die Komplexität der Aufgabenstellung für die kommenden Auslobungen zu überdenken.

Die Anzahl der Arbeiten, die ökologische Belange wie die Aufbereitung von Regenwasser oder die Erhöhung der Wasserqualität durch Pflanzenfilter mit gestalterischen Herausforderungen verbinden, nahm zu. Neue Forschungsergebnisse zu Klimafolgen wurden bei der Pflanzenwahl berücksichtigt. Nachhaltige und an den Ort angepasste Gestaltungen nehmen mit jedem neuen Jahrgang zu.

THE JURY'S ASSESSMENT OF THE LENNÉ PRIZE

Overall, a trend towards decidedly artistic and conceptual proposals can be observed. Structural patterns such as floor surfacing or graphics are being used as a means to transform a place. In the process the designs often diverge from the classical topics of landscape design, focussing instead on an exaggerated presentation of individual surface textures.

The design proposals contained in a large number of the submissions did not follow a specific leitmotif or guiding principle, although the complexity and multiple facets of the competition area were analysed intelligently and presented effectively. In general, however, entrants had difficulty in translating their findings into a coherent landscape design concept: the majority of the submissions lacked a detailed examination of the place and its particular qualities. Many projects made use of quite different conceptual approaches but then subjected them to repeating formalist treatment. Attempts to reconceive spaces were lacking. "A negative trend," according to the jury, "is a general neglect of the potential of plants to create spatial and visual situations." The jury also recommended that the complexity of the tasks for the coming award be reconsidered.

The number of projects that managed to incorporate ecological concerns, such as rainwater purification or improved water quality through the use of plant filters, into their design approach has increased. Similarly, new research findings on the consequences of climate change for locations and plants were also taken into consideration. Sustainability concerns and location-specific design approaches have increased with each year.

[Rhîn]flections   Ein Grenzfluss als Spiegel der Kulturen

140588

Der Rhein als Spiegelachse

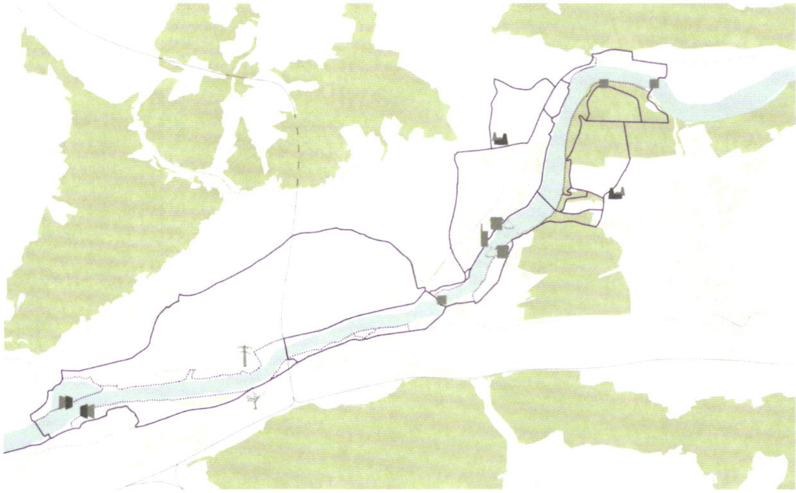

Großer Rundweg mit acht Refelxionen im Maßstab 1:25000

In dem Konzept [Rhîn]flexions fungiert der Rhein als Spiegelachse, die eine trennende und gleichzeitig verbindene Funktion hat. Das Spiegelbild kommuniziert mit den Uferseiten auf deutscher und schweizer Seite und schafft eine Beziehung zwischen ihnen. Kulturelle Besonderheiten werden über die Spiegelachse hinweg ausgetauscht oder über Spiegelflächen reflektiert.

Fußgänger und Radfahrer werden auf dem ausformulierten Rundweg an acht Spiegelungen vorbeigeführt, die je nach Variantenwahl besichtigt werden können. Die gepunktete Linie auf der Wegekarte stellt eine Verlangsamung dar. Hier müssen Radfahrer teilweise absteigen und ihr Fahrrad aufgrund des Reliefs schieben. Durch die Entschleunigung und die notwendige körperliche Betätigung bietet sich die Möglichkeit der Wahrnehmungsveränderung.

Das Projekt kommuniziert über zwei Arten der Reflexionen: Verspiegelte Elemente und einer realen gebauten Spiegelung. Die Spiegelflächen haben verschiedene Ausprägungen: an der nord-östlichsten Station, dem Wasserkraftwerk Ryburg-Schwörstadt, wird dessen Fassade verspiegelt und schafft so den Austausch zwischen deutschem und dem schweizer Ufer. Ebenso bei dem Turm der alten Brauerei: auch hier spiegelt sich das gegenüberliegende Ufer in der Fassade.

Ein weiterer Spiegelkubus befindet sich im Buchenwald am Rande des Stausees und ist rundum verspiegelt. Er geht so eine Verbindung mit dem für die Region typischen Buchenwald ein. Ein ähnliches Prinzip wird auf der Steinernen Brücke in Rheinfelden angewandt: Hier spiegelt ein Spiegelkubus, welcher sich mitten auf der Spiegelachse, dem Rhein befindet, im bestimmten Winkel das jeweilige Ufer wieder. So erlebt der Besucher eine Wahrnehmungstäuschung, die ihn zum Reflektieren anregt.

Kurz vor dem Wasserkraftwerk August-Wyhlen befindet sich ein Landausläufer, auf dem zwei Spiegelwände installiert sind, durch die man hindurchgehen kann. Dieses Phänomen findet sich auch direkt gegenüber auf der schweizer Seite wieder.

Die reale Spiegelung reflektiert kulturelle Merkmale der zwei Länder auf die gegenüberliegende Uferseite. Hier stellt der Rhein ebenfalls die Spiegelachse dar. Eine Besonderheit sind die Salinentürme auf der schweizer Seite, nahe der Stadt Möhlin. Sie werden als Aussichtstürme neu interpretiert und auf die deutsche Seite im gleichen Abstand zur Spiegelachse reflektiert. Dies passiert auch mit einem für die Region typischen Fischernetz in Rheinfelden: Dieses wird, nachdem es auf die gegenüberliegende Uferseite gespiegelt wird, zu einer Schaukel oder Hängematte umfunktioniert. Durch den Perspektivwechsel und das längere Verweilen an einem Ort wird die Wahrnehmung der umgebenden Landschaft verändert.

Stromabwärts werden Strommasten, die bereits mehrfach das Landschaftsbild auf deutscher Seite prägen, an der Spiegelachse gespiegelt und treten als natürliche Nachahmung dieses Landschaftsmerkmals auf der schweizer Seite in Erscheinung. Der eiserne Strom-Mast wird zum Strom-Baum.

Durch das wiederholte Auftreten der Elemente in der Landschaft auf den beiden Rheinseiten wird der Besucher auf das Thema der Spiegelungen zwischen Deutschland und der Schweiz sensibilisiert.

Durch die Spiegelungen kommt das gegenüberliegende Ufer näher an den Besucher heran und der Rhein als Spiegelachse fungiert nicht mehr als trennendes, sondern als kommunizierendes Element.

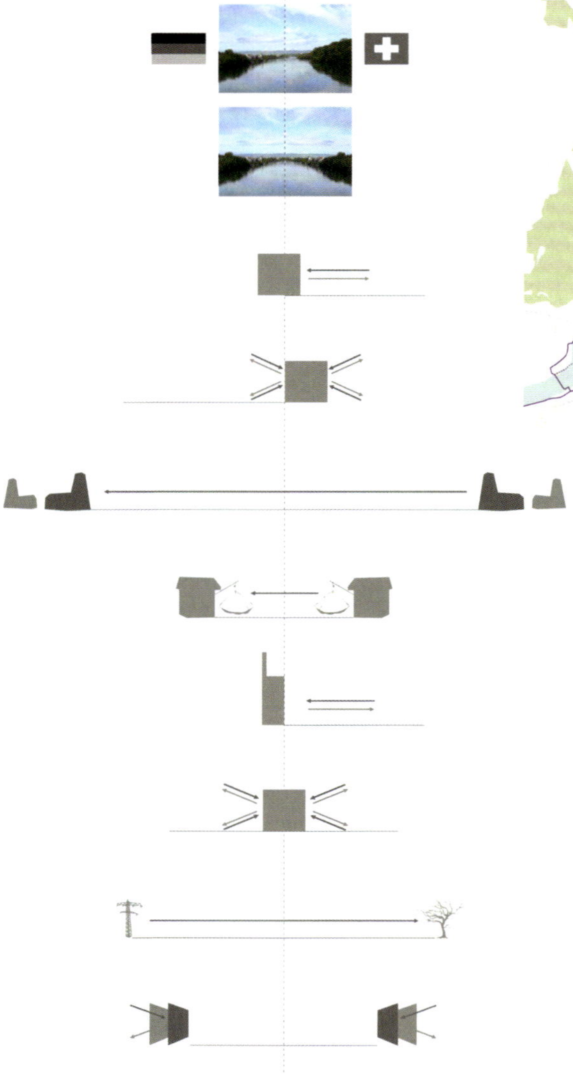

Acht Reflexionen spiegeln sich an der Spiegelachse, dem Rhein

Die gespiegelten Salinentürme auf deutscher Seite bieten den Besuchern neue Aussichtspunkte

◀ ▶ Peter-Joseph-Lenné-Preis: Der Rhein wird zur Spiegelachse zweier Kulturen. Gespiegelt werden in der Horizontalen die Landschaft, in der Vertikalen unter anderem Gebäude als Land-Art-Objekte. Als kraftvolle, poetische und zeitgenössische Interpretation verdeutlicht das Thema Spiegelung die unterschiedlichen Maßstäbe im Landschaftsraum Hochrhein. Isabel Maier-Harth aus Freising und Dennis Pytlik aus München wurden mit dem Peter-Joseph-Lenné-Preis ausgezeichnet

The Rhine is transformed into an axis of reflection for two cultures. In the horizontal axis, the landscape is reflected, while in the vertical axis buildings and other elements function as reflectors and Land Art objects. This powerful, poetic and contemporary interpretation employs the device of reflection to reveal the different scales of the landscape of the Upper Rhine. Isabel Maier-Harth from Freising and Dennis Pytlik from Munich were awarded the Peter Joseph Lenné Prize for their project

GROSSER RUNDWEG IM LANDSCHAFTSPARK HOCHRHEIN – TRINATIONALE AGGLOMERATION BASEL

Die Metropolregion Basel ist Lebens- und Wirtschaftsraum in der Nordschweiz und geprägt durch die Grenzlage zu Deutschland und Frankreich. Die Region hat 830.000 Einwohner und täglich 50.000 Grenzgänger.

Bestandteil der Entwicklung der Metropolregion ist eine staatsübergreifende gemeinsame Stadt-, Regional- und Landschaftsplanung. Der Landschaftspark Hochrhein erstreckt sich über die schweizerische und deutsche Seite des Rheintals. Kleine und mittelgroße Städte, landwirtschaftliche Flächen, die Nutzung von Wasserkraft und ein hohes Naturpotenzial charakterisieren diesen mosaikartigen Wohn- und Erholungsraum, geprägt durch Rheinuferwälder, Bachtäler, Weiden, Äcker und Obstbaumwiesen. Eine Besonderheit sind die kulturgeschichtlichen Zeugnisse der römischen Antike. Die Sicherung dieses Landschaftsraums ist Ziel einer kooperativen Planung.

Wettbewerbsaufgabe war es, attraktive Wegeverbindungen durch gestalterische Akzentuierungen zu einem großen Rundweg von Basel bis Möhlin zu vernetzen. Attraktive landschaftliche Szenarien, touristische Sehenswürdigkeiten, industriekulturelle Attraktionen, zeitgenössische Architekturen und siedlungstypische Merkmale galt es in den Rundweg einzubeziehen. Für neue Rheinübergänge sollten Vorschläge gemacht werden.

Die komplexe Aufgabenstellung wurde in den meisten Arbeiten sehr genau analysiert, um wichtige Potenziale für

LARGE LOOP IN THE UPPER RHINE LANDSCAPE PARK PROJECT – BASEL EAST TRINATIONAL CONURBATION

The metropolitan region of Basel in northern Switzerland adjoins both Germany and France and is a conurbation where many people live and work. The region's population is 830,000 of which 50,000 cross the border each day.

The development of the metropolitan region is governed by a joint cross-border urban, regional and landscape development policy, and the Upper Rhine Country Park is of special relevance in this respect as it extends across both the Swiss and German sides of the Rhine valley. The area is characterised by a mosaic of small and medium-sized towns, agricultural land, hydroelectric facilities and natural resources including riverside woodland, stream valleys, meadows, fields and orchards. Historical remains from Roman times are a further cultural feature of the area. The objective of the collaborative planning project is to develop a landscape conservation concept for the region.

The competition task was to structure an attractive network of paths through the accentuation of key points to form a large loop between Basel and Möhlin. The loop should incorporate attractive landscape scenarios, tourist attractions, industrial heritage sites, contemporary architecture and typical aspects of the residential areas into the concept. In addition, new proposals for crossing the Rhine should be presented.

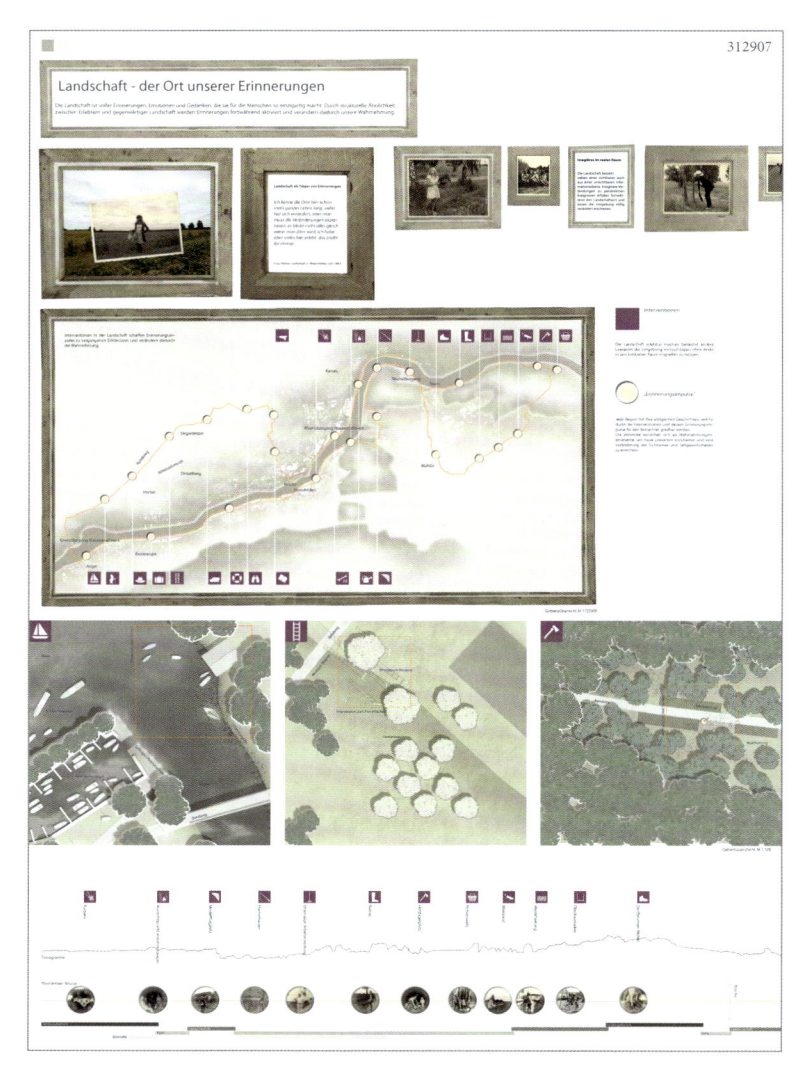

die landschaftsplanerische Ausgestaltung eines Rundweges durch den Hochrheinpark zu identifizieren.

DIE PREISTRÄGER

Isabel Maier-Harth aus Freising und Dennis Pytlik aus München wurden für ihren Entwurf *[Rhîn]flections* mit dem Peter-Joseph-Lenné-Preis ausgezeichnet.

Der Rhein, der den Landschaftsraum im Landschaftspark Hochrhein bestimmt, wird vom Grenzfluss zur Spiegelachse zweier Kulturen. Das in der Gartenkunstgeschichte bekannte Gestaltungselement der Spiegelung wird hier nicht nur als horizontale, also landschaftliche Spiegelung aufgenommen, sondern auch vertikal eingesetzt. In Spiegeln an Gebäuden und Spiegeln als Land-Art-Objekten halten sich die Rheinnachbarn den Spiegel im landschaftlichen Maßstab vor. Diese Idee unterstützt eine kraftvolle, poetische und zeitgenössische Interpretation des Landschaftsraums Hochrhein.

Almost all the submitted projects undertook a detailed and precise analysis of the complex task in order to identify the areas of greatest potential for the landscape design of the circular route through the Upper Rhine Landscape Park.

THE AWARD WINNERS

The Peter Joseph Lenné Prize was awarded to Isabel Maier-Harth from Freising and Dennis Pytlik from Munich for their project *[Rhîn]flections*.

The project takes the Rhine as the defining aspect of the landscape in the Upper Rhine Landscape Park and reconfigures it: what was formerly a boundary between two nations is made an axis of reflection for the two cultures. The mirror is a well-known device in the history of garden design and is used here not just horizontally as a means of reflecting the landscape, but also vertically. Mirrors mounted on buildings and mirrors as Land Art

Peter-Joseph-Lenné-Anerkennung: Gespielt wird mit der Wahrnehmung der Landschaft, dem Verhältnis zwischen Bild als Landschaft und Erinnerung als Raum. Dabei liegt der Fokus auf der Schönheit und den Nutzungsmöglichkeiten der Kulturlandschaft als Nutz-, Lebens- und Erholungsraum, akzentuiert durch künstlerische Installationen. Elisabeth Thiel aus Petershausen wurde mit einer Peter-Joseph-Lenné-Anerkennung ausgezeichnet

Peter Joseph Lenné Award: The project plays with our perception of landscape and the relationship between our image of the landscape and our memory of the space. The focus lies on the beauty and ways of using the cultural landscape as a functional space, living environment and place of recreation, accentuated by art installations. Elisabeth Thiel from Petershausen was awarded the Peter Joseph Lenné Award for her project

Elisabeth Thiel aus Petershausen wurde für ihre Arbeit *Landschaft – der Ort unserer Erinnerungen* mit einer Peter-Joseph-Lenné-Anerkennung ausgezeichnet.

Ist das Rheintal mehr Bild als Landschaft, mehr Erinnerung als Raum? Im Spiel mit der Bildhaftigkeit unserer Landschaftswahrnehmung wurden die Übergänge charakteristischer Landschaftsräume und die prägende Topografie sehr genau herausgearbeitet. In den Rundweg sind Attraktionen integriert, die durch ihre vielseitigen Funktionen die Wahrnehmung der Landschaft als Nutz-, Lebens- und Erholungsraum verstärken. Kunstinstallationen markieren diese besonderen Orte.

Die Arbeit *grenzenlos* von Isabella de Andrade Adauto Costa aus Freising und Jun Yang aus München erhielt ebenfalls eine Peter-Joseph-Lenné-Anerkennung.

Zahlreiche Attraktionen des städtisch sowie land- und forstwirtschaftlich geprägten Landschaftsraums werden durch ein weitgreifendes Wegenetz erlebbar. Auf größere bauliche Maßnahmen wird verzichtet und stattdessen eine sich wiederholende Möblierung in Form von Bänken, Schaukeln, Pavillons, Plattformen, Türmen und Stegen eingesetzt. So entsteht ein identitätsstiftendes Moment, das als Marke im Landschaftspark beiderseits des Flusses die gleichen Zeichen setzt. Die genaue Analyse des Raums wird durch die sensible Platzierung dieser Raumausstattung unterstrichen.

objects allow the neighbouring countries to, as it were, hold up a mirror to each other at the scale of the landscape. The idea represents a powerful, poetic and most contemporary interpretation of the landscape of the Upper Rhine.

A commendation, the Peter Joseph Lenné Award, was awarded to Elisabeth Thiel from Petershausen for her project *Landschaft – der Ort unserer Erinnerung* (Landscape – The Place of Our Memories).

Is the Rhine Valley more image than landscape, more memory than space? By playing with the imagery that influences our perception of the landscape, the project carefully elaborates the transitions between characteristic landscapes and their defining topography. The designer incorporates attractions into the loop that, through their diverse functions, heighten our perception of the landscape as a functional space, a living environment and a place of recreation. Art installations mark these special places.

Isabella de Andrade Adauto Costa from Freising and Jun Yang from Munich were also commended, and received the Peter Joseph Lenné Award for their project *grenzenlos* (boundless).

The project introduces an extensive network of paths that make it possible to experience the numerous attractions of the local landscape and its urban areas, agricultural land and woodland. The project refrains from making large built interventions, instead conceiving of a system of recurring furniture elements in the form of benches, swings, pavilions, platforms, towers and walkways. The vocabulary of these elements is employed throughout the country park on both sides of the river, lending the park a common identity. The sensitive placement of these elements underlines the precise spatial analysis on which the concept is based.

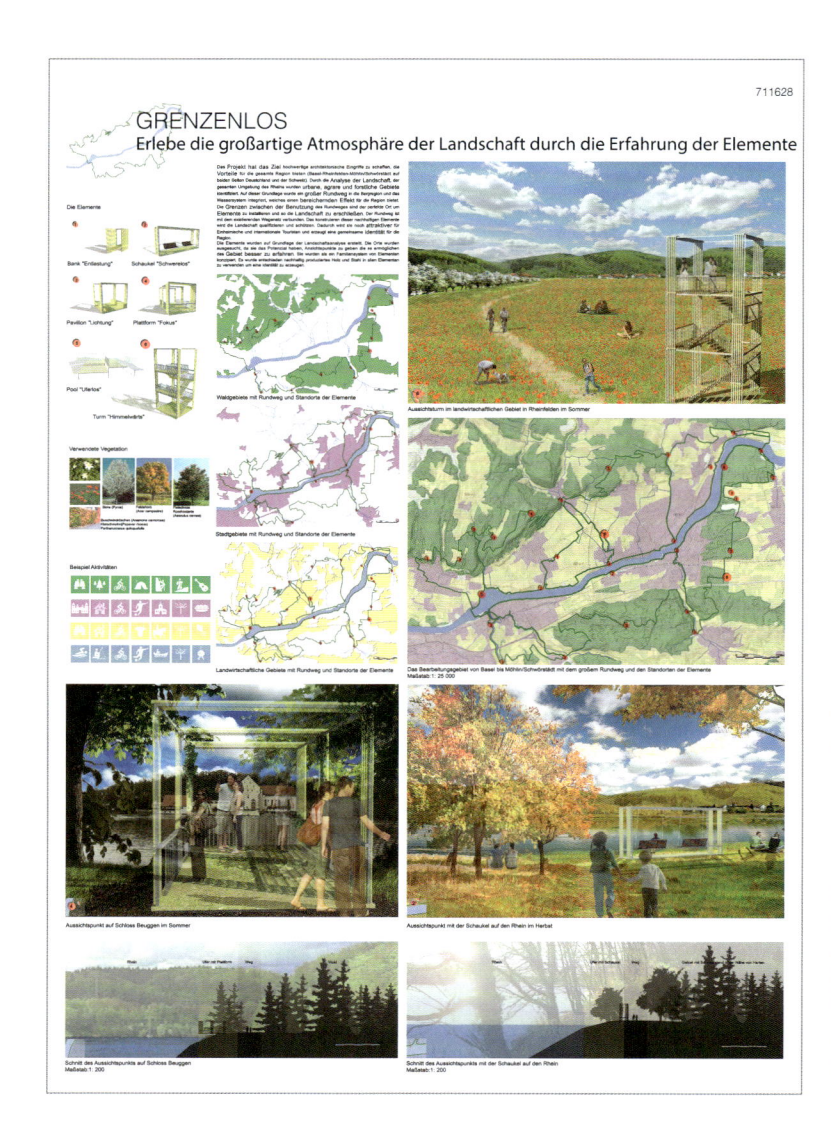

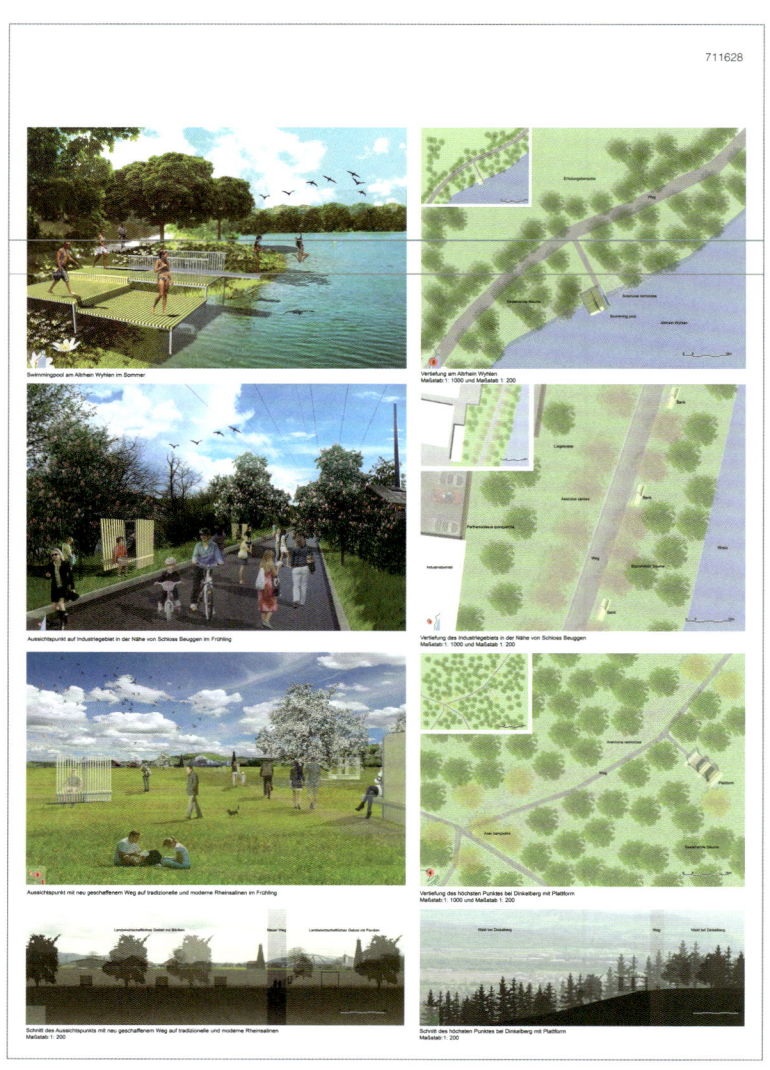

▲ Peter-Joseph-Lenné-Anerkennung für Landschaftspark Hochrhein: Der neue Rundweg führt durch städtisch sowie land- und forstwirtschaftlich geprägte Landschaftsräume. Vorgeschlagen wird ein identitätsstiftendes Leitsystem durch sich wiederholende Elemente beiderseits des Rheins: Bänke, Schaukeln, Pavillons, Plattformen, Türme und Stege laden an exponierten Stellen ein, das naturräumliche Potenzial des Landschaftsparks zu erkunden. Isabella de Andrade Adauto Costa aus Freising und Jun Yang aus München wurden mit einer Peter-Joseph-Lenné-Anerkennung ausgezeichnet

Peter Joseph Lenné Award for Upper Rhine Landscape Park: The new loop winds its way through urban, agricultural and wooded sections of the landscape. A system of repeating elements is conceived to give both sides of the Rhine a common identity: benches, swings, pavilions, platforms, towers and walkways are positioned at key points and invite one to explore the natural qualities and potential of the country park. Isabella de Andrade Adauto Costa from Freising and Jun Yang from Munich were awarded the Peter Joseph Lenné Award for their project

▶ Peter-Joseph-Lenné-Anerkennung für An der Urania: Die Arbeit bezieht sich mit dem landschaftsgestalterischen Element des Kiefernwalds auf die märkische Landschaft. So entsteht ein eigenständiger Raum im Stadtgefüge mit überraschendem Charakteristikum. Die mit Obstbäumen bestandene Wiese am Lützowplatz ermöglicht den direkten Zugang zum Landwehrkanal. Hagen Schmidt aus Berlin wurde ausgezeichnet mit einer Peter-Joseph-Lenné-Anerkennung ausgezeichnet

Peter Joseph Lenné Award for An der Urania: The project draws its inspiration from the landscape potential of the pine forest typical of the landscape of the Brandenburg Marches near Berlin. The result is a distinctive space in the city with a surprising character of its own. The grass lawn of the Lützowplatz is planted with fruit trees and provides direct access to the Landwehr Canal. Hagen Schmidt from Berlin was awarded the Peter Joseph Lenné Award for his project

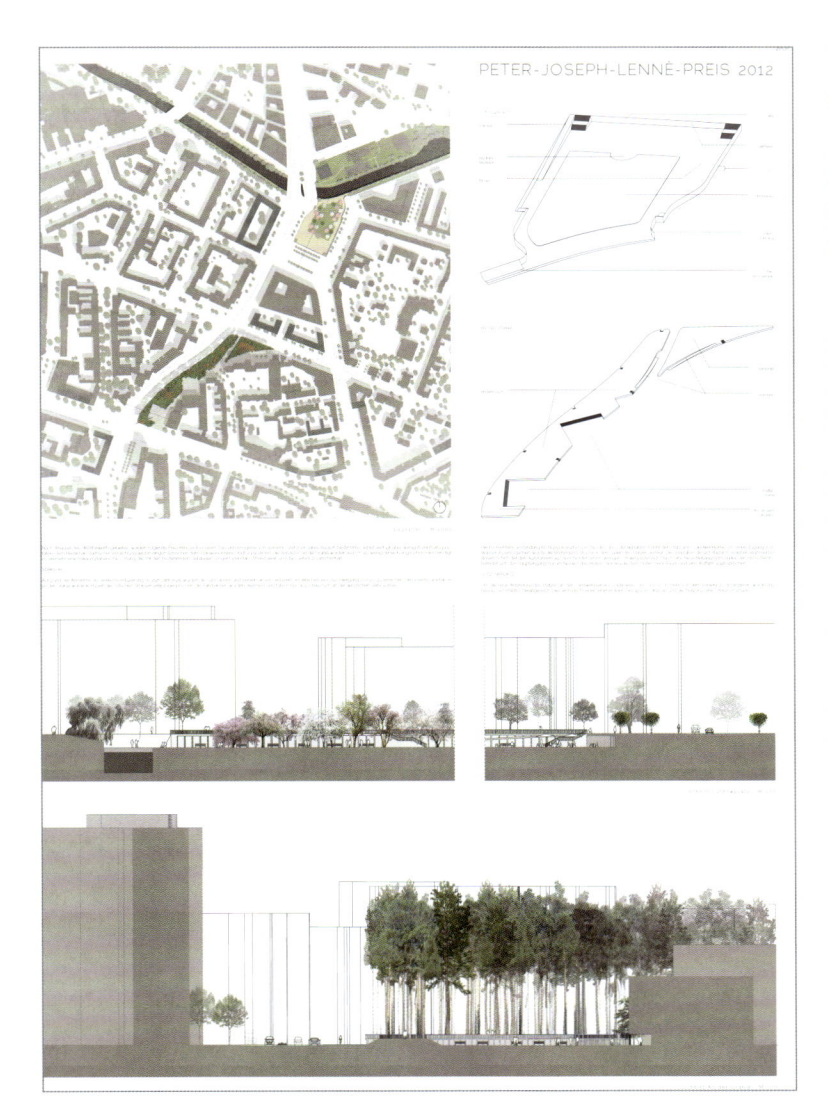

AN DER URANIA – AUFWERTUNG EINES STÄDTISCHEN TRANSITRAUMS IM ZENTRUM BERLINS

Das Bearbeitungsgebiet in der Berliner Innenstadt ist in der City West entlang des Straßenzugs An der Urania gelegen. Geprägt vom Städtebau der autogerechten Stadt, ist dort in den 1960er und 1970er Jahren nach amerikanischem Vorbild ein Areal entstanden, in dem mehrspurige Verkehrstrassen, Begleitgrün, eine offene Bauweise und Hochhäuser das Stadtbild bestimmen. Die wenig attraktiven Freiräume am Lützowplatz und der Mittelstreifen des Straßenzugs haben eine nur geringe Aufenthaltsqualität. Die Straße am Lützowplatz wirkt als Barriere. Zusätzlich belasten Lärm und Staub das Areal.

Ausgangspunkt für die städtebauliche und freiräumliche Neugestaltung des Gebiets ist die Reduzierung überdimensionierter Straßenräume. Das Bauhaus-Archiv und das Veranstaltungszentrum Urania sollen als kulturelle und architektonische Höhepunkte angemessen in das

AN DER URANIA – STRUCTURAL UPGRADING OF AN INNER-CITY TRANSIT SPACE IN THE HEART OF BERLIN

The project site lies in the City West area in the heart of Berlin, along a stretch of road named "An der Urania". The area was developed in the 1960s and 1970s according to car-centred planning principles, and multi-lane roads, grass verges and open spaces with high-rise buildings dominate the townscape. The few urban spaces – an unattractive open area at the Lützowplatz and the central reservation of the road – are uninviting places with little in the way of urban qualities. The road on the Lützowplatz creates a barrier and the site is dominated by the noise and dust of traffic.

The starting point for the redesign of the urban configuration of the area and its open spaces is a reduction of the over-sized dimensions of the street space. The Bauhaus Archives and the Urania Cultural Centre, as the

Urban Picturesque

181294

Städtebauliches Konzept

In dem übergeordneten, städtebaulichen Konzept ist der Fokus zum einen auf die Entlastung und Anpassung der Verkehrswege der Schillerstraße, An der Urania, Martin-Luther-Straße, Kurfürstenstraße, Lietzenburger Straße, Bayreuther Straße und zum anderen auf die neue, städtebauliche Strukturierung des Gebiets gerichtet. Von einer Anpassung der Kleiststraße wurde abgesehen, da diese mitunter ein Teil des historischen Generalzuges bildet. Die Entlastung der Verkehrswege wird durch die Verkleinerung bzw. Verjüngung der oben genannten Straßen erreicht. Der hierdurch gewonnene Flächenzuwachs wird für zusätzlichen Wohn- und Nutzraum sowie für zusätzlichen Erholungsraum genutzt. Durch die städtebauliche Neustrukturierung an den Straßen An der Urania, Kurfürstenstraße, Lietzenburger Straße und der Martin-Luther-Straße entstehen unter anderem für das Quartier interessante und vielseitig nutzbare Räume, wie z. B. Plätze (siehe Kreuzung An der Urania - Lietzenburger Straße / Kleiststraße), grüne Zwischenräume / Pufferzonen (siehe An der Urania, Grünverbindung zwischen Schillerstraße und Einemstraße) oder passageartige Räume (siehe Lietzenburger Straße / Bayreuther Straße und zwischen Neubau- und Bestandsgebäude An der Urania). Für die geplanten Gebäude ist eine Mischnutzung, wie beispielsweise Wohnen, Gewerbe oder Kultur (Erweiterung Urania-Gebäude) vorgesehen. Neben der Optimierung der oben genannten Verkehrswege, wurde auch die Grünstruktur der Straßenräume verbessert oder ergänzt.

The Urban Picturesque

Ein zentrales Element des Entwurfs ist das Erleben und Erfahren urbanen Umfelds durch den pittoresken Blick auf die Umgebung - über das Medium des Pittoresken. Der Begriff des Pittoresken stammt aus dem 18. Jahrhundert und ist ein Synonym für das Bildhafte oder das Malerische. Es beschreibt einen Prozess aus der künstlichen Darstellung und der Gestaltung der Landschaft. Inspiriert wurde diese Art von ästhetischer Bewegung durch die Landschaftsmalerei des 17. Jahrhunderts, den Werken von Claude Lorrain sowie weiteren, bedeutsamen Künstlern. Ein beliebtes Handwerkzeug für die Sympathisanten der pittoresken Bewegung war das „Claude Glas", welches nach dem Künstler benannt wurde und im Englischen auch als „Black Mirror" bekannt ist. Das Claude Glas ähnelt einem konvex geformten, eingefärbten Spiegel, der das betrachtete Sujet abstrahiert und somit vereinfacht wiedergibt. Durch die verschiedenen Einfärbungen des Glases können unterschiedliche Stimmungen erzeugt werden (z. B. Kälte oder Wärme). Durch das Betrachten des Sujets mit dem Claude Glas wird der Betrachter an das Motiv herangeholt und erhält somit Spielraum für individuelle Interpretation der Szenerie. Das in dem Entwurf vor Ort installierte Claude Glas setzt sich wie folgt zusammen: Das erste Bauteil ist der fest im Boden installierte Sockel mit Informationen über die Pittoreske sowie über den Namensgeber des Claude Glases, Claude Lorrain. Zusätzlich können von den Besuchern digitale Informationen über den Standort sowie kurze Audio-Informationen über am Sockel abgebildeten QR-Code abgerufen werden. Das zweite Bauteil ist der um 360° frei drehbare Aufsatz. Mit ihm kann der Besucher sein Motiv frei wählen oder beliebig zwischen den Szenarien wechseln. Die vier an Aufsatz fest installierten Claude Gläser fungieren zwischen dem Sujet und dem Betrachter als eine Art Übermittlungsmedium. Die Herkulesbrücke eignet sich hervorragend für die Installation eines Claude Glases, da sie direkt am Kreuzungspunkt zweier Sichtachsen (Nollendorfplatz - Großer Stern und Landwehrkanal - Potsdamer Platz / Fernsehturm). Neben der permanenten Installation auf der Herkulesbrücke kann das Claude Glas stadtweit an geeigneten Orten aufgestellt werden.

Dadurch würde ein stadtweites Netzwerk aus Claude Gläsern entstehen, welche für neue, räumliche Verbindungen der einzelnen Bezirke sorgen könnten.

Entwurf Lützowplatz

Der äußere Bereich bildet den Übergang zwischen der urbanen und der grünen Struktur. Dieser Bereich definiert eine klare Trennung zwischen dem Verkehrsbereich und dem Aufenthaltsbereich, soll diese jedoch nicht voneinander abgrenzen. Mittels Strauchpflanzungen soll der Aufenthaltsbereich von der Straße Lützowplatz separiert werden.

Ein besonderes Merkmal des Entwurfs ist die östlich des Platzes befindliche, ca. 70 m lange Bank, welche sowohl der Lützowstraße als auch des Lützowplatzes zugewandt ist und diese miteinander verbindet. Des Weiteren befinden sich vereinzelt auf der Fläche verteilte Holzdecks zum Sitzen und Verweilen.

Der zweite Bereich des Entwurfs ist geprägt durch eine großzügig angelegte Rasenfläche, welche durch den querenden Fußweg in zwei Flächen geteilt wird. Die Rasenfläche verfügt über unterschiedliche Topographien. Der höchste Punkt der Rasenfläche befindet sich im Südwesten und beträgt ca. 0,75 m über dem Gehwegniveau. Hierdurch soll die direkte Sicht auf den Lützowplatz abgeschwächt werden. Der bereits oben erwähnte Querungsweg nimmt die historische Sichtachse zwischen der Einemstraße und dem Nollendorfplatz zum Großen Stern und dem Tiergarten wieder auf.

Entwurf Lützowufer

Ziel des Entwurfs für das Lützowufer ist die Ausbildung von großzügigen Promenadenwegen entlang des Landwehrkanals, durch die eine Stärkung der Uferbereiche als wichtige Grünverbindung bewirkt werden soll. Der Entwurf gliedert sich in jeweils vier verschiedene Uferbereiche.

Der südöstliche Uferbereich wird durch einen Höhenunterschied von ungefähr einem Meter von dem Gehweg zum Promenadenweg klar definiert. Dieser wird durch eine Stützmauer abgefangen, welche zugleich als durchgehendes Sitzelement im Bereich des Ufers dient.

Der nordöstliche Uferbereich erstreckt sich entlang des Bauhausarchives. Dieser ist durch einen breiten Promenadenweg entlang des Ufers gefasst. Auf der Höhe des Bauhausarchives erstreckt sich eine großzügig angelegte Treppenanlage, die das Sitzen am Wasser ermöglicht. Die an der Bucht befindlichen Rasenflächen sind durch eine Sitzmauer gefasst.

Der nordwestliche, höher gelegene Uferbereich ist durch die Bebauung des Tiergartendreiecks, sowie des Konrad-Adenauer-Hauses geprägt. Ein breiter Promenadenweg erstreckt sich entlang des Ufers und wird durch eine Heckenpflanzung von der angrenzenden Straße separiert. Das nördliche Ufer bietet dem Besucher einen promenadenartigen Raum zum Aufenthalt und zum Durchqueren.

Der südwestlich, tiefer gelegene Uferbereich bietet dem Besucher die Möglichkeit durch die großzügig angelegten Treppenanlagen bis an das Wasser des Landwehrkanals heranzutreten. Zwischen den Treppenanlagen befinden sich Filterbereiche, welche mit geeigneten Wasserpflanzen angelegt sind und neben dem technischen Aspekt auch einen ästhetischen Wert aufweisen. Als ein Puffer zwischen der vorhandenen Straße Lützowufer und den Uferbereichen dient ein Promenadenweg mit integriertem Altbaumbestand.

Aussagen zur Vegetation

Sowohl bei dem Entwurf des Lützowplatzes als auch bei dem Entwurf der Uferbereiche wurde großer Wert auf die Erhaltung und Ergänzung des vorhandenen Baumbestands gelegt.

Durch die neu geplanten Straßenbäume an den Straßen An der Urania, Lützowplatz, Schillerstraße, Einemstraße, Kurfürstenstraße, Lietzenburger Straße sowie an der Martin-Luther-Straße wird die Grünstruktur des Gebietes ergänzt und somit aufgewertet. Die Artenauswahl soll auch an dem in der Umgebung befindlichen Baumbestand orientieren (z. B. Platanus cf., Tilia cf.). Die Artenauswahl erfolgte anhand der Gegebenheiten des Standortes.

Neben der Erhaltung des vorhandenen Baumbestands ist auch ein Hauptaugenmerk auf die Bepflanzung der Uferzonen gelegt worden. Die zur Reinigung dienenden Filterschichten verfügen über eine spezielle Bepflanzung. Diese wird im nachstehenden Text über das Filtersystem des Landwehrkanals näher beschrieben.

110

◀ ▶ Peter-Joseph-Lenné-Preis: Am Lützowplatz entsteht ein stimmungsvoller Ort, der die historische städtebauliche Prägung der Lenné'schen Planung aufgreift, einen neuen Zugang zum Landwehrkanal schafft und somit das Verweilen am Wasser ermöglicht. Die städtebauliche Nachverdichtung reagiert sensibel auf vorhandene Platzqualitäten und erhöht durch abwechslungsreiche Raumfolgen die Aufenthaltsqualität. Zur Reinigung des Wassers wird eine Pflanzenfilteranlage vorgeschlagen. Lasse Malzahn und Lucas Rauch, beide aus Berlin, wurden mit dem Peter-Joseph-Lenné-Preis ausgezeichnet

Peter Joseph Lenné Prize: A new atmospheric place has been created around the Lützowplatz that picks up the historical principles of Lenné's plan and provides access to the Landwehr Canal, creating a pleasant waterside situation. Urban densification measures respond sensibly to the existing urban spaces, and enrich the urban experience by creating a succession of spaces with different characters. Plant filters are proposed for water purification. Lasse Malzahn and Lucas Rauch, both from Berlin, were awarded the Peter Joseph Lenné Prize for their project

städtebauliche Konzept eingebunden werden. Die Neugestaltung soll dem Ziel folgen, den Straßenraum für den zunehmenden Fußgänger- und Radverkehr zurückzugewinnen und die derzeitige Trennwirkung der Straße am Lützowplatz aufzuheben.

Aufgabe war es, ein freiraumarchitektonisches gestalterisches Gesamtkonzept zu entwerfen und dieses mit angrenzenden Quartieren und Straßenzügen sowie vorhandenen Grünanlagen zu verflechten. Die stadträumliche Funktion als Tor zur City West ist wesentlicher Bestandteil eines schlüssigen städtebaulichen Konzepts.

DIE PREISTRÄGER

Lasse Malzahn und Lucas Rauch, beide aus Berlin, wurden für ihre Arbeit *Urban Picturesque* mit dem Peter-Joseph-Lenné-Preis ausgezeichnet.

Der Entwurf schlägt eine Urbanisierungsstrategie vor, die anstelle der bisherigen autogerechten Stadt einen atmosphärisch und räumlich dichten Stadtteil erzeugt. Dieser Stadtteil ist, ganz im Sinne Lennés, durch ein Freiraumsystem gegliedert. Straßenräume, Promenaden und Stadtplätze unterschiedlichen Charakters sowie ein Quartierspark und der Landwehrkanal bieten in abwechslungsreichen Raumfolgen eine neue Aufenthaltsqualität. Auch der Lützowplatz ist neu strukturiert. Durch die Neugestaltung der Uferbereiche des Landwehrkanals wird einer Lenné'schen Planung besonderer Respekt erwiesen. Der Promenadenweg südlich des Landwehrkanals lädt zum

two most important cultural and architectural points of interests, need to be adequately integrated into the urban concept. The redesign should aim to upgrade the streetspace to make it usable for pedestrians and cyclists and to reconfigure the Lützowplatz so as to remove the road's barrier function.

The task of the project was to develop an overall design concept for the urban area and to reconnect it with the neighbouring districts, thoroughfares and existing green spaces. A central aspect of the project is the coherent reformulation of the urban space as a gateway to the City West area of Berlin.

THE AWARD WINNERS

Lasse Malzahn and Lucas Rauch, both from Berlin, were awarded the Peter Joseph Lenné Prize for their project *Urban Picturesque*.

The design proposes an urbanisation strategy that converts the prevailing car-centred townscape into an atmospheric and more densely spatially articulated urban district. The design follows the model set down by Lenné himself, structuring the district using a system of open spaces. Street spaces, promenades and urban squares with different characters, as well as a district park and the Landwehr Canal, provide a succession of spaces with different urban qualities. The Lützowplatz is also restructured. The project pays particular respect to Lenné's planning principles through its redesign of the

PETER-JOSEPH-LENNÉ PREIS 2012 /// BERLIN . STRASSENZUG AN DER URANIA UND ANGRENZENDER STADTRAUM /// BEGREEN   512540

01 PLANUNGSRAUM
Durch die prognostizierte Abnahme des motorisierten Individualverkehrs entsteht entlang der Urania ein neuer Raum, der durch seine Lage und Größe großes Potenzial aufweist um zu einem attraktiven innerstädtischen Freiraum entwickelt werden zu können.

02 NEUE QUARTIERE
Der Verkehrsraum wird auf einer Seite gebündelt. Die dadurch entstehende Fläche wird den jeweils angrenzenden Quartieren zugesprochen. Der Transitraum wird zu einem vielseitig nutzbaren Aufenthaltsraum für Bewohner, Besucher und Berufstätige.

03 GRÜNES BAND
Mit einem hohen Anteil an Grünflächen soll ein Kontrast zum angrenzenden stark versiegelten Stadtraum entstehen und gleichzeitig eine Brücke zu bestehenden Grünflächen geschlagen werden. So entsteht ein neues grünes Entrée für die City West, das Besucher und Bewohner empfängt und für den Stadtteil identitätsstiftend ist.

04 VERBINDUNGEN
Der 1km Meter lange Grünzug wird durch eine Vielzahl an Querungen, die die bestehenden Trampelpfade aufgreifen, in einzelne Grünflächen gegliedert. Dadurch wird eine große Durchlässigkeit gewährleistet, um die angrenzenden Quartiere miteinander zu verbinden.

05 ERHÖHUNG
Die einzelnen grünen Felder werden um 45cm erhöht, dadurch entstehen vielseitige Anlagerungsmöglichkeiten. In der Aufkantung ist eine indirekte Beleuchtung integriert, die auch nachts den repräsentativen Aspekt dieses zentralen Ortes betont.

06 BODEN / BELÄGE
Die einzelnen Grünflächen werden mit zwei verschiedenen Vegetationsgesellschaften versehen: Blumenwiesen, die stadtökologischen Zielen folgt und Nutzwiesenbereiche, die vielseitige Funktionen übernehmen. Die Bodenbeläge der Wege- und Platzflächen, die sich durch den Grünzug ziehen werden mit den Berlin typischen Bodenbelägen gestaltet. Die Berliner Platte und der Kleinpflasterstein.

07 GEBÄUDE
An zentralen Bereichen werden die Rasenflächen aufgeklappt um Gebäude zu integrieren, die belebend für den Grünzug und Stadtteil sind (z.B. Cafes, Büros, Dienstleistung, usw.). Diese Gebäude sind so gestaltet, dass der Grünraum bis zur Dachfläche führt. Neben den Gebäuden akzentuieren die bestehenden Kunstinstallationen den Grünzug.

08 BÄUME
Die bestehenden Bäume werden nach Möglichkeit erhalten. Um den gesamten Freiraum stärker als Einheit wahrzunehmen wird die Robinie als Leitbaum eingesetzt und ergänzend gepflanzt. Das hellgrüngelbe Laub steht im Kontrast zur Bestandsvegetation und erzielt eine hohe Fernwirkung. Die Baumreihe auf dem Lützowplatz besteht ebenfalls aus Robinien auf sich leitet den Blick über die Platzfläche der Landwehrbrücke.

GESAMTKONZEPTION M1:2000

Legende:
- Großer Tiergarten
- Zoologischer Garten
- Kleine Parks im Stadtgebiet / Punktuelle Grünflächen
- neuer Grünzug entlang der Urania
- Ausbreitung der Grünstruktur Vernetzung von Grünflächen

BLUMENWIESE
Die Blumenwiese besteht aus einer Mischung aus verschiedenen einjährigen und zweijährigen Wildkräutern und mehreren Gräsern. Die Kräuter und Gräser werden in einem Anteil von jeweils 50 Prozent gesät. Durch die einjährigen Kräuter wie Centaurea, Papaver und Agrostemma entsteht bereits im ersten Jahr ein reicher Blütenflor. Im nächsten Jahr folgen die zweijährigen Kräuter. Das sind zum Beispiel Crepis, Leucanthemum, Knautia und Salvia. Der Blühzeitraum erstreckt sich von Mai bis November. Durch einen ein- bis zweischürigen Mährhythmus stehen die Pflanzen bis zur Samenreife, wodurch die erneute Aussaat und das Ernten von Saatgut ermöglicht wird.

Eine Blumenwiese hat gegenüber einer herkömmlichen Nutzwiese ökologisch und ökonomisch gesehen viele Vorteile. Sie trägt dazu bei ein positives Kleinklima in der Stadt entstehen zu lassen und erhöht die biologische Vielfalt. Vor allem für die verschiedensten Insekten bietet sie wertvollen Lebensraum. In einem ansonsten stark versiegelten Stadtraum können durch viele kleine und größere naturnahe Begrünungen (isolierte Lebensräume) wieder miteinander vernetzt werden.

Um die natürliche Aussaat zu beschleunigen werden in dem Grünzug Samen der Blumenwiese gesammelt und zu kleinen, handlichen Samenbomben verarbeitet, die dann in dem Grünzug verkauft werden können. Anwohner und Besucher können diese Samenbomben kaufen und so den Grünzug beliebig auf andere Orte wie Verkehrsbegleitgrün ausweiten.

WARUM BLUMENWIESE?
- Ökologisch wertvoller Lebensraum verschiedener Tiere
- Ästhetische Aufwertung
- Mehrwert für Besucher und Anwohner (Blumen pflücken, Samen ernten)
- Kostengünstige Erstellung
- Geringer Pflegeaufwand durch 1-2schürige Mahd

WIE FUNKTIONIERT DIE AUSSAAT?
- Ansaat verschiedener Wildblumen und Gräser
- Blumen (Samen) werden geerntet und zu „Samenbomben" verarbeitet
- Diese werden getrocknet und können in den Anwohnern und Besuchern verkauft werden
- Ausbreitung in der Stadt, Identifikation der Bewohner mit der Stadt
- Restgrünflächen in ganz Berlin werden erobert

PFLANZLISTE WIESE

Kräuter:
Achillea millefolium
Agrostemma githago
Anthemis tinctoria
Antriscus sylvestris
Campanula glomerata
Campanula rotundifolia
Carum carvi
Centaurea cyanus
Crepis biennis
Daucus carota
Dianthus carthusianorum
Dianthus superbus
Galium mollugo

Geranium pyrenaicum
Hypericum perforatum
Knautia arvensis
Leucanthemum vulgare
Lotus corniculatus
Malva moschata
Origanum vulgare
Papaver rhoeas
Pimpinella saxifraga
Plantago lanceolata
Prunella vulgaris
Salvia pratensis
Sanguisorba minor

Silene alba
Silene dioica
Silene vulgaris
Papaver rhoeas
Pimpinella saxifraga
Plantago lanceolata
Prunella vulgaris
Salvia pratensis
Sanguisorba minor
Silene dioica
Silene pratensis
Silene vulgaris
Trisetum flavescens

Gräser:
Agrostis canina
Anthoxanthum odoratum
Briza media
Bromus secalinus
Cynosurus cristatus
Festuca brevipila
Festuca nigrescens
Festuca rubra rubra
Koeleria pyramidata
Poa compressa
Poa pratensis
Poa trivialis

PFLANZLISTE WIESE - BEREICH DACH

Kräuter:
Achillea millefolium
Agrostemma githago
Anthemis tinctoria
Aster amellus
Dianthus carthusianorum
Galium verum
Leucanthemum vulgare
Linum perenne
Origanum vulgare
Prunella vulgaris

Ranunculus bulbosus
Salvia pratensis
Sanguisorba minor
Sedum acre
Sedum album
Sedum reflexum
Sedum spurium
Silene vulgaris
Thymus pulegoides
Thymus serpyllum

Gräser:
Briza media
Carex bouchannii
Festuca amethystina
Festuca ovina
Kolena ciliata
Melica ciliata
Poa alpina
Stipa capillata

COLLAGE WIESE - BEREICH DACHBEGRÜNUNG

SCHNITT 1 M1:200

◀ ▶ Peter-Joseph-Lenné-Anerkennung und Karl-Foerster-Anerkennung: Der städtebauliche Ansatz ist stark, die Nachverdichtung schlicht und zurückhaltend. So wird eine klare Struktur mit stadträumlichen Zuordnungen geschaffen. An zentralen Orten werden Rasenflächen „aufgeklappt": Pavillons für Cafés und Büros entstehen. Das zeitgeistige Element des Guerrilla Gardenings regt zur Interaktion mit dem Stadtraum an. Evelyn König und Franziska Schadzek, beide aus Hannover, wurden mit einer Peter-Joseph-Lenné-Anerkennung und einer Karl-Foerster-Anerkennung ausgezeichnet

Peter Joseph Lenné Award and Karl Foerster Award: A strong urban design gesture and carefully placed, discreet densification measures combine to create a clear urban structure with spaces that relate to their surroundings. At key locations the grass surface folds upwards to reveal pavilions for cafés or offices. An integral, contemporary guerrilla gardening element encourages people to interact with their urban surroundings. Evelyn König and Franziska Schadzek, both from Hanover, were awarded the Peter Joseph Lenné Award and Karl Foerster Award for their project

Verweilen am Wasser ein. Auch funktional wird der Freiraum weiterentwickelt. Im nördlichen Uferbereich ist ein Pflanzenfiltersystem zur Reinigung des Wassers vorgesehen. Installationen aus gerahmten Spiegeln, sogenannte Claude-Gläser, und ein über QR-Codes abrufbarer Audioguide ermöglichen neue Blickwinkel und geben Informationen zum Stadtteil.

Mehr auf die märkische Landschaft rund um Berlin als auf Lenné'sche Ideale bezieht sich der urbane *Kiefernwald* von Hagen Schmidt aus Berlin (s. S. 109). Die Jury zeichnete diese Haltung mit einer Peter-Joseph-Lenné-Anerkennung aus.

Der Entwurf schafft eine eigenständige Landschaft im Stadtgefüge und verleiht dem Raum ein überraschendes Charakteristikum. Mittels der Irritation werden die Sinne angesprochen, das Erlebnis des Aufenthalts wird dadurch intensiviert. Offene Vorzonen in den Zugangsbereichen zum Gebäude der Urania erzeugen klare Platzsituationen. Höhenunterschiede am Lützowplatz ermöglichen den direkten Zugang zum Landwehrkanal sowie die Herstellung eines stadträumlichen Bezugs zum Bauhaus-Archiv. Als eine mit Obstbäumen bestandene Wiese bietet der Lützowplatz ein Farbenspiel zur Blüte und im Herbst. Die bauliche Nachverdichtung an den Rändern erzeugt städtebauliche Potenziale wie beispielsweise eine neue Eingangssituation vor dem Hotel Berlin.

bankside area of the Landwehr Canal. Here pedestrians are able to access the water along the promenade on the south side of the canal. The open spaces are also given new functions. The north bank of the canal envisages a system of plant filters for water purification. Art installations made of framed mirrors known as Claude glasses, together with a QR-code activated audio-guide system, offer new perspectives of the area and background information on the urban quarter.

The *Kiefernwald* (Pine Forest) project by Hagen Schmidt from Berlin (cf. p. 109) draws its inspiration not from the ideals of Lenné but from the landscape of the Brandenburg Marches around Berlin, an approach that the jury commended with a Peter Joseph Lenné Award.

The design creates a landscape of its own within the grain of the city, lending the space a sense of surprise. This principle of irritation is used to stimulate the senses, heightening one's experience of being there. Open spaces in front of the entrances to the Urania building articulate a series of clearly defined urban squares. A change in height at the Lützowplatz provides direct access to the Landwehr Canal and establishes an urban connection to the Bauhaus Archives. The Lützowplatz itself is planted with fruit trees creating a play of colours in both spring and autumn. The built additions along the edges provide greater spatial definition, such as a new entrance situation in front of the Hotel Berlin.

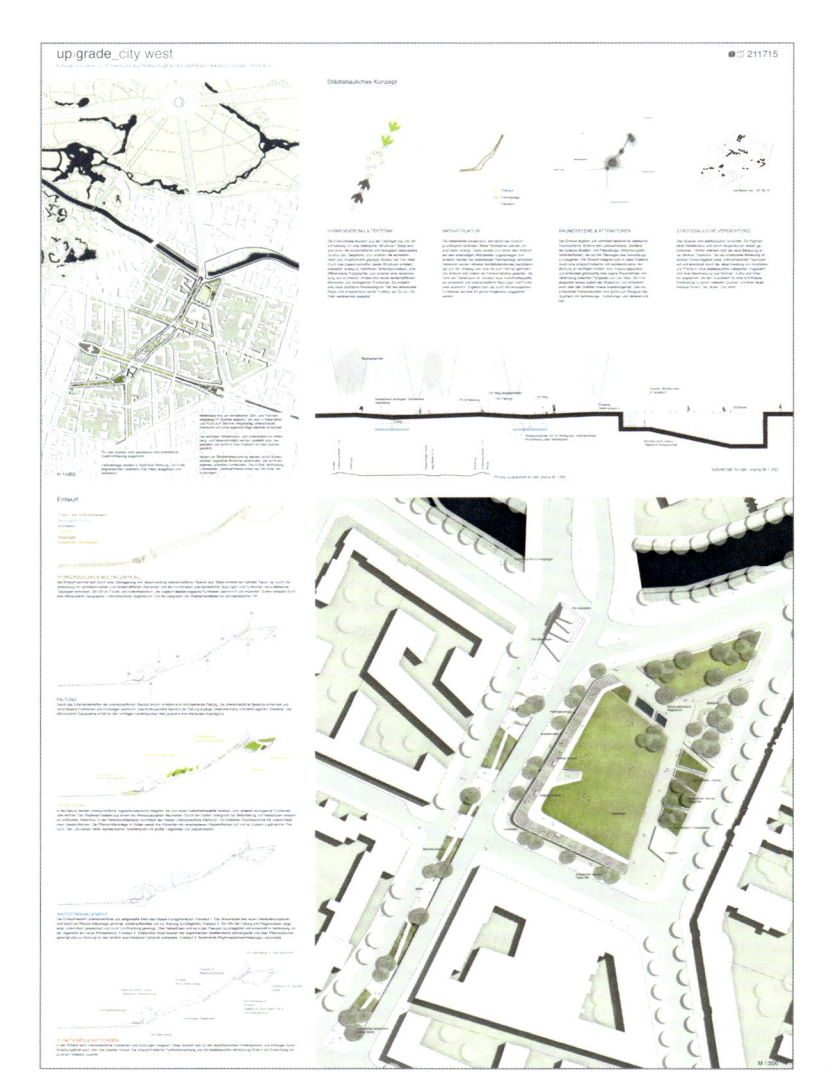

▲ Karl-Foerster-Anerkennung: Ergänzend zu Installationen zum Wassermanagement berücksichtigt die Pflanzenauswahl für diesen innerstädtischen Standort die sich verändernden klimatischen Bedingungen. Pflanz- und Farbkombinationen sowie die Höhenstaffelung der Stauden bilden das gestalterische Gerüst der Pflanzenverwendung. Mareen Leek und Fabian Karle, beide aus Berlin, wurden mit einer Karl-Foerster-Anerkennung ausgezeichnet

Karl Foerster Award: Complementing the proposed water management facilities, the project's selection of plants for this inner-city site takes account of changing climatic conditions. Combinations of plants and colours and a staggered system of shrubs at different heights serve as an underlying formal framework for the use of plants. Mareen Leek and Fabian Karle, both from Berlin, were awarded a Karl Foerster Award for their project

Die Arbeit *begreen* von Evelyn König und Franziska Schadzek, beide aus Hannover, erhielt eine weitere Peter-Joseph-Lenné-Anerkennung sowie für die Pflanzenverwendung eine Karl-Foerster-Anerkennung.

Quer durch das Entwurfsgebiet gliedert zukünftig ein grünes Band den Stadtraum. Die Nutzung dieses Freiraums durch Anwohner und Kulturtouristen schafft eine neue Verbindung eher disparater Strukturen aus der jüngeren Städtebaugeschichte. Die völlig neuartige Gestaltung des Lützowplatzes als großzügiger, gepflasterter Platzraum gibt diesem Stadtraum neues Gewicht. An zentralen Orten werden Rasenflächen „aufgeklappt": Pavillons für Cafés und Büros entstehen. Ein besonderes Element ist die am Zeitgeist orientierte Nutzung einer Blumenwiese: Anwohner und Touristen können aus der Blumenwiese gewonnene „Samenbomben" kaufen und andernorts säen. Dieses Guerrilla Gardening soll zum Dialog, zu Interaktionen im Stadtraum anregen.

Mareen Leek und Fabian Karle, beide aus Berlin, wurden mit ihrer Arbeit *upgrade city west* mit einer Karl-Foerster-Anerkennung ausgezeichnet.

Die Überlagerung der beiden stadträumlich benachbarten Strukturen Großer Tiergarten und City West mit ihrer verkehrsinfrastrukturellen Prägung erzeugt Brüche und Verwerfungen, die genutzt werden: Eine künstliche Topografie akzentuiert die Berührungs- und Kreuzungspunkte. Der verbreiterte Mittelstreifen wird zur grünen Infrastruktur. Ökologische Funktionen des Wassermanagements wie Nebler, Wasserbecken und Filter werden als Adaption an den Klimawandel integriert. Die Pflanzenauswahl ist auf einen innerstädtischen Standort ausgerichtet und berücksichtigt die sich verändernden klimatischen Bedingungen. Eine klare Farbpalette sowie die Höhenstaffelung der Stauden bilden das gestalterische Gerüst.

The *begreen* project by Evelyn König and Franziska Schadzek, both from Hanover, was commended with a further Peter Joseph Lenné Award, and also won the Karl Foerster Award for its use of plants.

The design proposes a green band that traverses the entire project site and structures the urban space. Used by residents and tourists alike, this outdoor space creates a new connection between the disparate structures of the late-20th-century surroundings. The complete redesign of the Lützowplatz as a spacious, paved urban square lends it a stronger impact in the surroundings. At key locations, the grass surface suddenly folds upwards to reveal pavilions for cafés and offices. A particular feature is the meadow of flowers, which also serves a contemporary use: residents and tourists can purchase "seed bombs" made from its flowers to sow out elsewhere. This guerrilla gardening approach is conceived as an invitation to enter into a dialogue with the urban space of the city.

Mareen Leek and Fabian Karle, both from Berlin, have also been awarded a Karl Foerster Award for their project *upgrade city west*.

The superimposition of the two urban structures of the neighbouring Große Tiergarten and traffic-dominated City West creates discontinuities and distortions in the city that can be put to use: an artificial topography accentuates the point at which the two systems touch and cross. The central reservation has been widened and becomes a form of green infrastructure. Ecological water management functions, including atomisers, pools of water and filters, have been incorporated as a means of adapting to climate change. The plants have been chosen to cope with this inner-city location and also take account of the changing climatic conditions. A clear palette of colours and staggered system of shrubs of different heights are used to create a formal framework for the plant use.

Palmen am Chiemsee
Palm trees on Lake Chiemsee

Zukunftsdialog 2013 – 2063

Futures Dialogue 2013 – 2063

SCHRÖDER Wir sind im Jahr 2063. Es geht um 150 Jahre Landschaftsarchitektur. Was ist im Jahr 2063 Landschaft? Ressource, Schönheit oder nicht mehr relevant?

THEIS Im Buch *Die Welt in 100 Jahren* von Arthur Brehmer, 1910 erschienen, heißt es: „Die reicheren Familien über ganz Afrika wohnten Tag und Nacht 1.000 bis 2.000 Meter hoch in verankerten Lufthäusern, wo sie frei waren von den Unbequemlichkeiten der tropischen und subtropischen Sonne." Das Land ist eine rein ökonomische Quelle für Landwirtschaft. Auch in heutigen Zukunftsbetrachtungen der Landschaft geht es viel mehr um Verteilungskämpfe, Zugang zu Wasser und weiteren Ressourcen als um Schönheit. Schönheit ist ein Thema, das dort eine Rolle spielt, wo es keine ökonomische Nutzung gibt oder eine gewisse Sättigung eingetreten ist und ein gewisser Reichtum herrscht.

SCHMID Die Frage sollte lauten, was ist die Gesellschaft in 50 Jahren und wie wirkt sich diese auf die Landschaft aus? Die Landschaft ist die Grundlage von allem, was hier auf diesem Planeten in der Vergangenheit passiert ist und in überschaubarer Zukunft passieren wird. Ich würde anknüpfen an Interdisziplinarität und Querschnittsorientierung.

BÖTTGER Ich denke, man sollte weiterhin den Begriff Landschaft verwenden, gerade weil er Ressource und Schönheit verknüpft. Wir werden weiter auseinanderdriften: Deutschland zerfällt in Flächen, die vor den Augen des Städters als „Landschaft" entwickelt und wahrgenommen werden, und dazwischen verbleiben sehr große Flächen, die aus den Augen des Städters nicht wahrgenommen werden und von einer globalisierten Landwirtschaft – sei es für die Nahrungs- oder die Energieerzeugung – geprägt sein werden.

GEBHARD Ich glaube nicht an die Teilung. Der Versuch des Ausgleichs wird stärker sein. Es wird Landschaften ge-

---

Karlheinz Steinmüller, Physiker, Science-Fiction-Autor, Zukunftsforscher · Physicist, Science Fiction Author, Foresight Researcher, Z_Punkt

Björn Theis, Senior Foresight Consultant, Z_Punkt

Andrea Gebhard, Landschaftsarchitektin, Präsidentin bdla · Landscape Architect, President of bdla

Arno Sighart Schmid, Landschaftsarchitekt, bdla · Landscape Architect, bdla

Johannes Böttger, Landschaftsarchitekt · Landscape Architect

Cornelia Schmidt, Landschaftsarchitektin, Hospitantin bdla · Landscape Architect, assistant of bdla

Thies Schröder, Geschäftsführer · Managing Director ts|pk

SCHRÖDER The year is 2063 and we're looking back on 150 years of landscape architecture. In the year 2063, what characterises landscape, its resources, its beauty, or is this no longer relevant?

THEIS In the book *Die Welt in 100 Jahren* (The World in 100 Years) published in 1910 by Arthur Brehmer, it says that "the richer families throughout Africa were living day and night 1000–2000 metres above the ground in airborne houses anchored to the ground, where they will be free from the discomforts of the tropical and subtropical sun." The land is used exclusively as an economic resource for agriculture. When we look to the future today, we also see that landscape is much more about competing land interests, access to water and other resources than about beauty. Beauty is an aspect that only plays a role where there is no other economic interest, where a degree of saturation has been reached, and where there is a certain level of wealth.

SCHMID The question should really be, what will society be like in 50 years and how will it influence the land-

▲ Jenseits standardisierter Spielelemente entstand auf dem Schulberg in Wiesbaden die Spielskulptur „Loop", deren Form auch städtebauliche Bezüge des weiteren Umfelds aufnimmt. Entwurf: ANNABAU Architektur und Landschaft, Berlin

Quite unlike any off-the-peg solution, the "Loop" is a sculptural playground element on the Schulberg in Wiesbaden that also makes reference to its urban surroundings. Design: ANNABAU Architektur und Landschaft, Berlin

ben, die das Zusammenspiel übernehmen, sowohl produktiv sind als auch schön und wunderbar sein werden. Eine Teilung können wir uns gar nicht leisten.
STEINMÜLLER Wenn wir über Landschaft im Jahr 2063 reden, können wir als Zukunftsforscher nicht sagen, wie die Rahmenbedingungen sein werden. Es lassen sich allenfalls große Entwicklungslinien erkennen und zu Szenarien verdichten. Es ist wesentlich, dass man nicht von vornherein alles definiert und glaubt, man habe damit alles erfasst und festgelegt. Man sollte immer den Wandel denken.
BÖTTGER Ich sehe in den Metropolräumen durchaus die Möglichkeit, dass es mehr Verknüpfungen geben wird zwischen Alltag und Landnutzen, direkte Relationen. Die sind allerdings räumlich begrenzt.

scape? The landscape is the basis for everything that has happened here on this planet in the past and in the foreseeable future. I would expect there to be more interdisciplinarity and cross-sectoral orientation.
BÖTTGER I think we should insist on the term landscape precisely because it links resources and beauty. In my view, we will drift further apart: Germany is disintegrating into areas that city-dwellers see and perceive as being "landscape" and very large areas in-between that are not on the city-dwellers' radar and serve predominantly global agricultural needs – whether for cultivating food crops or for energy production.
GEBHARD I don't think this will actually happen. The move to counteract this tendency will be stronger. There

▸ Das Motiv der wechselnden Ansichten bestimmt nicht nur die Skulptur im Innenhof des Deutschen Bundestages in Berlin, sondern auch die Pflanzenverwendung: die Gattung Hartriegel wird in farben- und blütenreichen Varianten eingesetzt. Entwurf: Hager Partner AG, Zürich mit Beat Zoderer, Wettingen

The idea of changing viewpoints was generative not just for the design of the sculpture in the interior courtyard of the German Bundestag in Berlin but also for the vegetation: dogwood has been planted in a variety of colours and blossoms. Design: Hager Partner AG, Zürich mit Beat Zoderer, Wettingen

THEIS Wenn wir in Szenarien denken, müssen wir überlegen, ob wir ausschließlich über Deutschland reden, denn wenn wir global denken, gelten andere Bedingungen.

SCHRÖDER Wir werden im globalen Maßstab einen Druck erleben, der auf guten Böden eine intensive industrielle agrarische Landnutzung erfordert. In vielen anderen Bereichen, im Bereich der postindustriellen Produktion von Gütern und Waren, im Bereich der postfossilen Energiegewinnung und im Bereich der postindustriellen Landwirtschaft, hat die Landschaftsarchitektur Vorstellungen zu entwickeln. Welche?

SCHMID Im Sinne der Zusammenführung der Wissensbereiche in einer holistischen Sichtweise ist der Landschaftsarchitekt derjenige, der ein solches Zusammenfinden verschiedener Disziplinen moderieren kann und muss.

BÖTTGER Es ist doch eher das Agrarministerium, das über die Förderkulissen Einfluss nehmen kann, als dass es Planer sind, die über räumliche Kategorien denkend Einfluss nehmen. Ich wünschte, es wäre anders.

SCHMIDT Es wird um die Strukturierung von Ressourcen gehen und auch um die Kombination mit unberührten oder wiederhergestellten Landschaften – ein Kompromiss von Ressource und Schönheit. Ich bin nicht so skeptisch. Wir haben die gesetzlichen Grundlagen. Wir haben die Methoden und Mittel, auf Entwicklungen einzuwirken. Die Frage ist: Wie verschaffen wir uns Gehör?

GEBHARD Wichtig ist die gesellschaftliche Relevanz. Eine gute Landschaftsplanung beruht ja darauf, dass ich Akteure suche und Nutzungen der Landschaft erzeuge, die gleichzeitig die anderen Fragen, wie diejenigen zum Landschaftsbild, beantworten.

STEINMÜLLER Mitte des Jahrhunderts wird es in Deutschland etwa zwei Grad wärmer sein. Wie stellen wir uns darauf ein? Brauchen wir mehr Stadtgrün? Gibt es heute schon Antworten der Landschaftsarchitektur darauf?

will be landscapes that still fulfil this combination: landscapes that are productive as well as beautiful and wonderful. I don't think we can allow these to drift apart.

STEINMÜLLER When we talk about landscape in the year 2063, we can't say as foresight researchers what the underlying parameters will be. At best, we can see general development tendencies that will gradually condense into scenarios. It is essential that we don't try and define everything in advance and think we then have everything under control. We must always keep in mind that things change.

BÖTTGER In the metropolitan areas, I think it is quite possible that there will be a greater connection and a more direct relationship between the use of rural land and everyday life, although this is probably only possible within a certain range.

THEIS If we're thinking about scenarios, then we should consider whether we are talking just about Germany, because other parameters apply if we're thinking globally.

SCHRÖDER At a global scale, there will be pressure to use fertile ground for intensive industrial-scale agriculture. In many other areas, such as the post-industrial production of goods and wares, post-fossil energy generation and post-industrial agriculture, landscape architecture will have to come up with ideas and concepts. What might they be?

SCHMID In terms of bringing together different areas of knowledge into a larger holistic way of looking at things, the landscape architect is the person who is best able to mediate between and moderate the different disciplines.

BÖTTGER The agriculture ministry can probably exert more influence through the distribution of subsidies than planner can by thinking about spatial categories, although I wish this were not so.

BÖTTGER Wir haben in Deutschland ein vergleichsweise geringes Problem mit dem Klimawandel, und im Verhältnis dazu eine breite Palette an Antworten. Hier vor Ort haben wir die Chance, „Show-Case" zu werden und als Profession exportierbare Lösungen zu entwickeln. Wir müssen uns global einbringen, das ist auch eine Frage der Verantwortung, der Schuld am Klimawandel. Aber derzeit sind bundespolitisch definierte Ziele wie die Begrenzung des Flächenverbrauchs völlig unerreicht. Diese Themen müssen wir in der Diskussion wachhalten. Es ist schwierig, aber möglich, in Einzelprojekten zugleich Systemlösungen zu erarbeiten.

STEINMÜLLER Die Bevölkerung verschiebt sich innerhalb Deutschlands, es gibt schrumpfende und wachsende Regionen. Einerseits fragmentieren sich die Städte immer mehr, weil Gewerbe- und Verkehrsflächen brachfallen und es keine Nachnutzung gibt, andererseits werden Städte verdichtet. Gibt es spezifische Antworten auf diese Prozesse?

SCHMID Für die Erarbeitung einer sinnvollen Struktur liegen riesige Chancen für diese Städte in der Verzahnung von urbanem Fabrikat und Landschaft.

SCHMIDT There will be a structuring of resources and that will also take into account unspoilt or restored natural landscapes – a compromise between resources and beauty. I'm not quite as sceptical. After all, we have statutory legislation, and we have methods and means with which to influence developments. The question is: how do we make ourselves heard?

GEBHARD An important aspect is also social relevance. Good landscape planning involves finding users and stakeholders and creating uses for the landscape that simultaneously address other aspects, such as that of the image of the landscape.

STEINMÜLLER By the middle of the century, Germany will be two degrees warmer than it is today. How do we adapt to that? Do we need more urban green? Do landscape architects have answers to this?

BÖTTGER In Germany, the problems that climate change poses are comparatively small, and our palette of possible responses is relatively large. We have the chance here to become a kind of showcase and, as a profession, to develop solutions that can be exported elsewhere. We

BÖTTGER Die Bilder dafür sind da und sogar ein gesellschaftspolitischer Konsens. Die Beispiele weisen auf eine Verzahnung von Stadt und Land. Ein Problem sind jedoch die Besitzstrukturen. Man müsste zum Beispiel eine Flurbereinigung für Einfamilienhaus-Gebiete oder Gewerbebrachen erfinden.

SCHRÖDER Was sind die strategischen Überlegungen der Landschaftsarchitektur – wer sind die Partner, die es zu gewinnen gilt, um die schon vorhandenen Prototypen der Anpassung an Demografie und Klimawandel in Angriff zu nehmen?

BÖTTGER Ich glaube, dass die große gesellschaftliche Gruppe, die über die LOHAS (nach engl. *Lifestyles Of Health And Sustainability*) definiert wird, für die Landschaftsarchitektur ein wichtiger Partner ist. Sie formuliert in der Gesellschaft Interessen, die über landschaftsarchi-

need to contribute globally too: we have a responsibility to do that not least because we have contributed to climate change. At the moment, however, we are nowhere near reaching the political objectives we have at a national level, such as limiting the consumption of land use. We must continue to raise awareness of these issues. It is difficult but achievable to develop systemic responses when working at the scale of individual projects.

STEINMÜLLER The population is shifting within Germany. Some regions are shrinking and others are growing. On the one hand, cities are becoming ever more fragmented as industrial and infrastructure sites fall into disuse but lack a follow-on concept, and on the other cities are being made denser, more built-up. Are there any specific answers to these processes?

Im abgesenkten Hof der Gorch-Fock-Schule in Hamburg entsteht ein günstiges Kleinklima, so ist er jahreszeitlich länger nutzbar. Der „Gräserwald" ist Böschungsschutz wie Spielbereich. Entwurf: DOT 2 – Groth-Rüter-Zeitznitz Landschaftsarchitekten, Hamburg

The sunken playground of the Gorch Fock School in Hamburg creates a sheltered microclimate and is usable for a longer period of the year. The grassy verges are simultaneously a play area of their own and shield the embankment. Design: DOT 2 – Groth-Rüter-Zeitznitz Landschaftsarchitekten, Hamburg

tektonische Planungen zu befriedigen wären. Hier werden privatwirtschaftlich Energien und finanzielle Mittel investiert, die für Landschaftsarchitekten interessant sind.

THEIS Wie könnte man in Zukunft diese Antworten, die ja bereits vorliegen, stärker in einen öffentlichen Diskurs bringen und die Begriffe des Nachhaltigkeitsdiskurses weiter kommunizieren?

GEBHARD Es geht um eine breite Öffentlichkeitsarbeit. Ein Problem in unserem Berufsfeld ist die relativ geringe Größe der Büros, die damit keine Ressourcen haben, sich öffentlich zu artikulieren; über Netzwerke sollen größere Einheiten, die locker organisiert sind, diesen öffentlichen Diskurs führen.

SCHMIDT Die Digitalisierung unseres Berufszweiges ist eine große Chance dafür, dass sich Netzwerke und Portale bilden, wo Wissen verknüpft wird.

SCHRÖDER Werden wir 2063 eine völlig neue Auftragsstruktur haben, die auf Ansätzen wie Crowdfunding beruht? Werden wir als Landschaftsarchitekten Lösungen vorschlagen, Partner und Finanziers suchen, statt auf den Umwegen über politische Entscheidungen und administratives Handeln mit der Lösungssuche beauftragt zu werden?

SCHMID Wir befinden uns in einer weiteren industriellen Revolution. Die Generation der Maker kann über 3D-Drucker alles selber herstellen. Das hat auch auf uns Landschaftsarchitekten gravierende Auswirkungen, weil es dann keine Auftraggeber mehr gibt, die größere Projekte an uns vergeben werden. Es ist die Frage, wie wir darauf reagieren. Sind wir dann Ideenfinder, Ideengeber und Multiplikatoren? Wie wird diese Arbeit finanziert?

STEINMÜLLER Die Landschaftsarchitekten müssen andere Aufgaben übernehmen, wie Moderation und Mediation. Wir sprechen von Open Innovation, also offenen Innovationsprozessen, aus denen sich andere Formen der Zusammenarbeit ergeben.

SCHMID For the development of sensible structures, there is great potential in these cities for bringing together urban structures and spaces, and the landscape.

BÖTTGER We do already have visions and even social and political consensus. All the examples point towards a greater interconnection of city and landscape. One problem, however, is the pattern of land ownership. We need, for example, an instrument for the reallocation of land in housing estates of single-family houses, or partially vacant commercial and industrial estates.

SCHRÖDER What strategic considerations does landscape architecture have – who are the partners it needs to team up with to start putting into effect the available prototypes for adapting to demographic and climate change?

BÖTTGER I think that a large section of society, the so-called LOHAS – Lifestyles of Health and Sustainability – will be an important partner for landscape architecture. They formulate interests in society that landscape architecture can address. These groups are investing private sector energies and financial means that are of interest for landscape architects.

THEIS How could we in future make people more aware of the answers that are already available, with a view to communicating the issues that are addressed in the discourse on sustainability?

GEBHARD Through wide-ranging public relations activities of all kinds. A problem in our profession is the relatively small size of most offices. They simply don't have the resources to undertake such publicity. But as networks, even if only informally organised, they can form larger units that are able to conduct this discourse in public.

SCHMIDT The digitisation of our professional discipline also offers an opportunity to create networks and portals that pool the available knowledge.

SCHMID Der Landschaftsarchitekt muss Fachmann sein. Im Englischen wird er als *facilitator*, „Ermöglicher", bezeichnet.
BÖTTGER Wenn man auf die Strahlkraft setzt, die Freiraum für Projekte innerhalb einer Zivilgesellschaft bedeutet, wäre ein positives Bild, dass die Landschaftsarchitekten in der Rolle von Nachhaltigkeitsmanagern eine Art Begleiter von Großprojekten werden. Der Landschaftsarchitekt wird zu einem Gewährsmann für die Gesamtnachhaltigkeit von Projekten.
THEIS In vielen Professionen sieht man neue Kooperationen. Mit welchen Berufsgruppen arbeiten die Landschaftsarchitekten im Jahr 2063 stärker zusammen?
SCHMID Mit Klimatologen; diese Zusammenarbeit wird schon sehr bald üblich werden.
BÖTTGER Es wäre interessant, Mashups bezogen auf die Landnutzer zu definieren – die großen Landverbraucher, Infrastrukturhersteller, Landwirte, Förster, die Betreiber von Gewässersystemen, die zum Teil institutionell oder staatlich sind, verstärkt aber auch privatwirtschaftlich agieren.
THEIS Welche zukünftige Technologie wird die Landschaftsarchitektur beeinflussen? Inwieweit wird Augmented Reality an Bedeutung gewinnen?

SCHRÖDER In 2063, will we have a completely new commissioning structure, perhaps based on principles similar to crowdfunding? Will we develop and propose solutions as landscape architects, then go off in search of partners and financing, instead of waiting for political decision-makers and administrative bureaucracy to commission us to start developing a solution?
SCHMID We are currently in the midst of a further industrial revolution. The generation of makers can now use 3D printers to manufacture everything themselves. That could have a great impact on us as landscape architects because there will then no longer be clients who commission larger projects. The question is: how will we respond to this? Are we going to be idea finders, idea givers and multipliers? How will this work be financed?
STEINMÜLLER Landscape architects must take on other tasks such moderation and mediation. We're talking about "Open Innovation" out of which other forms of co-operation can arise.
SCHMID Landscape architects must be experts – they must function as facilitators, as people who make things possible.
BÖTTGER If we think of the impact and reach that open spaces can have for projects in civil society, a positive

◀ Die Bewahrung des industriellen Ursprungs steht im Vordergrund der Freiraumgestaltung des Weltkulturerbes Zeche Zollverein in Essen. An strategisch wichtigen Punkten entstanden sechs Besucher-Pavillons. Entwurf: Planergruppe Oberhausen

At the world heritage site of the Zollverein Coal Mine in Essen, a primary concern of the design of the outdoor areas was to conserve industrial origins. Six visitor pavilions were created at strategically important points. Design: Planergruppe Oberhausen

▶ Das langfristig angelegte Planungskonzept „Der Zollverein – ein Park entsteht" wird schrittweise realisiert und soll die ehemals „verbotene Zone" in einen Ort zum Aneignen verwandeln

The long-term planning concept "Der Zollverein – ein Park entsteht" (Zollverein – Creation of a Park) is being realised step by step and aims to transform the former "forbidden zone" into a place that people can make their own

SCHMIDT Ich wünsche mir bessere Technik für die Arbeit unmittelbar vor Ort, um mit den Menschen direkt an Entwürfen und Planungen zu arbeiten.
STEINMÜLLER Vermutlich bekommen wir eine Art verdoppelte Landschaft: So wie Augmented Reality in den Städten Informationsschichten einblendet, wird das künftig vielleicht auch in der Landschaft erfolgen. Lernen wir Landschaften dann neu lesen?
SCHMID Ich sehe eine Chance in der Darstellung der 4. Dimension, der Zeit. Mit solchen Medien kann man natürliche Entwicklungsprozesse vorzeigen und nahebringen. So kann man Entscheidungen beeinflussen und verbessern.
GEBHARD Die Selbstvergewisserung in der realen Welt bleibt meines Erachtens sehr wichtig. Daher ist zum Beispiel das Magazin *Landlust* so erfolgreich: weil es dieses Selbstverständnis auf den Punkt bringt – „selbst pflanzen". Der Mensch braucht auch das Reale: schmecken, riechen, tasten.
STEINMÜLLER Das Neue und Typische an all diesen Technologien ist, dass es soziale Technologien sind, dass man mit ihnen mit anderen Menschen in Kontakt sein kann. Dreht man die Betrachtung in diesem Sinn um, dann ist Augmented Reality die eigentliche Realität und die Realität da draußen die physisch eingeschränkte.
BÖTTGER Ich glaube, es ist eine Selbstverständlichkeit, dass Landschaften überlagert werden und ich freue mich, dass neue Möglichkeiten auch von Erzählungen der Landschaft entstehen. Eine der wichtigsten Funktionen des öffentlichen Raums ist ja sein Erzählwert. Das ist die

image would be that of landscape architects as sustainability managers accompanying large-scale projects. The landscape architect would act as a kind of guarantor for the overall sustainability of projects.
THEIS We're seeing new forms of collaboration in many professions. Which disciplines will landscape architects be working with more intensively in the year 2063?
SCHMID With climatologists. This collaboration will soon be normal practice.
BÖTTGER It would be interesting to see what mash-ups would be possible among land users – the large land consumers, infrastructure providers, farmers, foresters, the operators of water systems, which are partially institutionalised or state-owned but are becoming increasingly commercial in their activities.
THEIS What future technologies, like augmented reality, will influence landscape architecture?
SCHMIDT I would like to see better technology for working directly on site, to work with local people directly on design and planning tasks.
STEINMÜLLER I suspect we will have a kind of dual landscape: in the same way that augmented reality presents an extra layer of information in the cities, this could perhaps also happen in the landscape. Maybe that will give us new insight into reading the landscape?
SCHMID I see an opportunity for presenting the fourth dimension: time. Using new media we can visualise and communicate natural development processes. That can inform and improve decision-making processes.

Realität, und sie wird mit Dingen wie Smartphones wesentlich komfortabler und zugänglicher. Landschaftsarchitekten sind dafür da, Räume zu gestalten und wahrnehmbar werden zu lassen. Zukünftig werden Technologien entscheidender sein, die sich mit Smart City, Smart Grids, intermodalem Verkehr beschäftigen. Da haben wir die Verantwortung präzise zu definieren: Was ist öffentlich und was ist scheinöffentlich? Was sind Spielräume? Ist ein virtuell überlagerter öffentlicher Raum privat, weil der Informationsanbieter ein privatwirtschaftliches Unternehmen ist?

STEINMÜLLER Hier gibt es zwei Felder: die Privatisierung von öffentlichen Dienstleistungen und diejenige von öffentlichen Räumen. Im Moment sehen wir ja auch Tendenzen, das Rad zurückzudrehen in Richtung Rekommunalisierung.

GEBHARD I think that people will still want to be able experience the real world first-hand. That's why magazines such as *Landlust* are so successful: they communicate this self-evident need quite directly – a kind of do-it-yourself with plants. People need something real that they can taste, smell and touch.

STEINMÜLLER What is typical of all these new technologies is that they are social technologies with which one can keep in touch with other people. Seen from this perspective, one could argue that augmented reality is the actual reality, and the reality out there is only the part that we can physically experience.

BÖTTGER I think it is become increasing normal that landscapes overlap and I look forward to the new possibilities that also arise through the narratives that the

◀ Die Installation „Florablick" ist Teil des Landschaftsparks „Das Grüne Quadrat" und bietet Ausblick auf den Goitzsche-See, eine ehemalige Tagebaugrube nahe Bitterfeld. Projektleitung: Heike Brückner, Jacques Leenhardt, Gianni Burattoni, Dessau

The "Florablick" installation is part of the "Das Grüne Quadrat" (Green Square) Landscape Park and offers a view over the lake, which was formerly an opencast mining pit near Bitterfeld. Project lead: Heike Brückner, Jacques Leenhardt, Gianni Burattoni, Dessau

▲ Der wieder geflutete Tagebau mit Relikten einer Pioniervegetation aus Sandbirke bildet inzwischen ganz unterschiedliche Gewässerzonen aus und ist als Landschafts- und Naturschutzgebiet ausgewiesen

The now flooded mine with the remains of pioneer species such as silver birch still showing. A range of different water zones have been created and the area is a landscape and nature conservation area

▲ Renaturierung und Erschließung des Schlosssees Salem gingen Hand in Hand bei der Gestaltung eines vielfältig nutzbaren Naturerlebnisparks. Entwurf: Planstatt Senner, Überlingen

The natural restoration of the Schlosssee Salem and the provision of means of access went hand in hand with the design of a multi-purpose nature discovery park. Design: Planstatt Senner, Überlingen

▶ Stege ergänzen den Rundweg um den See, der heute offen für alle ist

Walkways and footbridges complement the public footpath around the lake

Ich sehe das als Pendelbewegung. Für eine halbe oder dreiviertel Generation läuft es in die Richtung Liberalisierung, Deregulierung und Privatisierung und dann setzt eine Gegenbewegung ein, weil man gesehen hat, dass es viele Reibungsverluste, Effizienzverluste und Marktversagen gibt. Die Gegenbewegung tritt ein, bis man auch da wieder an Grenzen stößt. Insofern wäre ich für den Blick auf 2063 vorsichtig, wie weit wir in welche Richtung des Öffentlichen oder des Privaten geraten werden.

GEBHARD Die Frage, ob und wie weit Öffentlichkeit möglich ist, ist ja auch eine ethische Fragestellung. Sind diese ethischen Fragen in der Profession verankert oder ist sie davon abgekoppelt?

landscape holds. One of the most important functions of public space is this narrative capacity. That is now reality and it will become much more comfortable and accessible with the help of things like smartphones. Landscape architects are experts in designing spaces and making them legible and perceptible.

In future, technologies that cater for aspects such as Smart City, Smart Grids and intermodal mobility will play an ever more crucial role. We have to define areas of responsibility more precisely: what is public and what is pseudo-public? What are experimental spaces? Is a virtually enriched public space turned into a private space because the information provider is a private enterprise?

128

◀ Stahlwangen inszenieren die über Jahrzehnte gewachsene „Grüne Fassade" am neuen Eingang der Hamburger Parkanlage Planten un Blomen. Entwurf: A24 Landschaft, Berlin

The steel sidewalls of the new entrance to the Planten un Blomen park in Hamburg contrast with the "green façade", which has grown over many decades. Design: A24 Landschaft, Berlin

◀ Eine gefaltete Rampe führt ins Innere der Parkanlage. In den wertvollen Gehölzbestand wurde nur minimal eingegriffen

A folded metal ramp leads into the interior of the park, minimising the impact on the valuable trees and vegetation

SCHMID Wir haben nicht die Macht, die Eigentumskategorien zu verändern. Aber wir sind mit dem, was wir tun, egal ob privat oder öffentlich, der Gesellschaft gegenüber verpflichtet.

BÖTTGER Es wird meiner Meinung nach eine Bastardisierung von Privatem und Öffentlichem geben. Die Landschaftsarchitekten werden dabei als Gestalter, als Identitätsbildner eine wichtige Rolle spielen. Eine Krise sehe ich aber dennoch. Denn wer hat den Überblick? Die Städte haben ja jetzt schon Schwierigkeiten mit der Steuerung.

SCHRÖDER Liegen in der Steuerung komplexer Prozesse erweiterte Aufgaben der Landschaftsarchitektur?

BÖTTGER Städte müssen wieder in die Rolle kommen, zu führen anstatt zu reagieren. In Zukunft wird es vermehrt vorkommen, dass man sich mit Projekten um Gelder bewirbt, die nicht unbedingt nur aus kommunalen Kassen kommen. Gartenschauen sind beispielsweise Großprojekte, bei denen viel bewegt wird, zum Beispiel in Bezug auf Stadtentwicklung, und in denen Landschaftsarchitekten eine große Verantwortung haben. Ich kann mir vorstellen, dass es künftig mehr konzeptionelle Planungen geben wird, mit denen Kommunen oder Regionen nach draußen gehen, um nach einer Projektierung Finanzen zu akquirieren.

STEINMÜLLER Werden Landschaften zukünftig auf Zeit geplant? So dass die nächste Generation alles wieder neu plant?

SCHMID Nein, ich setze eher auf Nachhaltigkeit und Kontinuität.

STEINMÜLLER Ich habe an die Architekten gedacht, die früher bis zum nächsten großen Stadtbrand geplant

STEINMÜLLER There are two aspects at play here: the privatisation of public services and that of public spaces. At the moment we can also observe tendencies that turn back the wheel towards re-nationalisation. I think that is a pattern that swings back and forth: for half or three-quarters of a generation, it swings in the direction of liberalisation, deregulation and privatisation before the backswing sets in because we have seen that too much is lost through friction, lack of efficiency and market failure. This countermovement continues until it reaches its limits. As such, I'd be cautious about making any predictions for 2063 concerning how far we will be in one or the other direction, whether more public or more private.

GEBHARD The question of whether and to what degree things are open and public is also an ethical issue. Are such ethical questions anchored in the profession or separate from it?

SCHMID We don't have the power to change ownership categories. But in everything that we do, regardless of whether public or private, we have a responsibility to society.

BÖTTGER In my opinion, we will have a bastardisation of private and public. And landscape architects, as designers, as givers of identity, stand to play an important role. Even so, I do foresee a crisis. After all, who knows the current state of things and is knowledgable enough to compare? The cities already have difficulties with steering the direction of development processes.

SCHRÖDER Is there potential for landscape architects to assume a role in the steering of processes?

▲ Mit der städtebaulich-(landschafts-)architektonischen Definition von Raumkanten und Bodenbelägen wird die Ortsmitte Eugendorf als neues Ensemble gefasst. Entwurf: Harry Dobrzanski und Hannes Krauss, Penzberg

The urban definition of the new ensemble at the town centre of Eugendorf is accentuated with the help of architectonic and landscape elements such as paving and elements that frame the space. Design: Harry Dobrzanski and Hannes Krauss, Penzberg

▲ Arbeit mit dem klassischen Repertoire der Landschaftsarchitektur: Eine texturierte Betonwand mit Pergola bildet eine Abschirmung zwischen multifunktionalem Platz und Parkplatz

The classical repertoire of landscape architecture: a textured concrete wall with pergola marks the division between a car park and a multi-purpose square

haben. In der Gründerzeit sollten die Häuser ca. 80 Jahre stehen. Heute geht man davon aus, dass nach 30 Jahren eine Umnutzung stattfindet. Auch werden Häuser heute gleich so gebaut, dass sie möglichst umweltfreundlich rückgebaut und recycelt werden können. Ich habe entsprechend an recycelbare Landschaften gedacht.

BÖTTGER Innerstädtische Grünflächen haben eine unermessliche Resilienz. Schon im Titel von *Die Besitzergreifung des Rasens* wies Günther Grzimek darauf hin, dass sich die Art der Nutzung eines Freiraums ständig wandelt. Aber der Wert einer unversiegelten Fläche mit einem Baumbestand in der Innenstadt ist völlig unstrittig ein dauerhafter.

GEBHARD Es wird meiner Meinung nach künftig fast nur noch städtische Lebensweisen geben. Landleben wird von den Ansprüchen her zum Stadtleben.

SCHMID In 20 Jahren wird man sich der Wechselbeziehungen zwischen Stadt und Land ganz selbstverständlich annehmen.

THEIS Was ist Ihr persönliches Wunschbild für die Landschaftsarchitektur im Jahr 2063?

BÖTTGER The cities need to get back into the role of leading instead of reacting. In future they will increasingly find themselves seeking financing for projects that will not necessarily come from the state or federal purse. Regional garden shows are, for example, large-scale projects that can achieve a great deal, especially in the area of urban development, and in which landscape architects have great responsibility. I can imagine that in future there will be more conceptual planning projects which the municipalities or regions then use to go out and seek funding for their realisation.

STEINMÜLLER Will new landscapes in future be planned for a limited time frame? So that the next generation can plan everything anew?

SCHMID No, sustainability and continuity will prevail.

STEINMÜLLER I was thinking of the architects in the past who conceived of their houses lasting only until the next great fire. In the late 18th, early 19th century, houses were built to last 80 years. Today it seems that buildings are converted every 30 years or so. Houses are now being built so that they can be disassembled and recycled

▲ Die Parkerweiterung Killesberg in Stuttgart verknüpft den bestehenden Höhenpark Killesberg mit neu entstehenden Stadtquartieren auf dem ehemaligen Messegelände. Entwurf: Rainer Schmidt Landschaftsarchitekten und Stadtplaner, Rainer Schmidt, München

The extension to Killesberg Park in Stuttgart links the existing high-level Killesberg Park with the new urban quarters being built on the site of the former trade fair grounds. Design: Rainer Schmidt Landschaftsarchitekten und Stadtplaner, Rainer Schmidt, Munich

BÖTTGER Landschaftsarchitektur wird sich mehr über künstlerische Positionen bestimmen. Die Profession muss stark genug sein, einzelnen Personen so etwas auch zu „erlauben".

GEBHARD Schließlich galt schon im Barock der Landschaftsarchitekt als einer der angesehensten Künstler. Die Ansätze dafür, die in der Profession da sind, besonders die Querschnittsorientierung, werden 2063 stärker gewürdigt sein als heute.

SCHMIDT Man wird Kompromisse finden zwischen dem Ökonomischen, dem Gestalterischen und dem eigenen Lebensstil.

SCHRÖDER Der über Jahrzehnte erkämpfte Professionalisierungsgrad der Landschaftsarchitekten beinhaltet Kompetenzen, die verallgemeinerungsfähig sind. Wenn Landschaftsarchitektur es schafft, diesen Expertenstatus nicht zu verlassen, sondern mehr als bisher in bürgerschaftlich getragenen Prozessen zusammenzuarbeiten, dann werden Kompetenz und Bedeutung zu- und nicht abnehmen. Künftig werden Landschaftsarchitekten noch stärker prozessual steuernd eingreifen.

again in an environmentally friendly way. As such, I was thinking about whether this could apply to landscapes – can they be made recyclable in the same way?

BÖTTGER Inner-city green spaces are amazingly resilient. In Günther Grzimek's book *Die Besitzergreifung des Rasens* (Taking Possession of the Lawn), he notes that the way we use spaces changes continually, but that the value of an unsealed surface in the city with a stock of trees is without question of lasting permanence.

GEBHARD The urban way of life will be the predominant way of life in future. People living in the countryside will have the same demands as those living in cities.

SCHMID In 20 years' time, we will have grown accustomed to the interplay between city life and rural life.

THEIS What is your personal wish for landscape architecture in the year 2063?

BÖTTGER That landscape architecture defines itself more strongly through its artistic positions. The profession must be resilient enough for individual persons to "take this liberty".

▲ Die tiefer liegenden Wege lassen eine Vielzahl von unterschiedlichen Perspektiven entstehen und spielen mit der Wahrnehmung von Raum und Maßstab

The lower lying paths provide opportunities for all kinds of new perspectives to arise and play with our perception of space and scale

▶ Der Entwurf verwebt die Historie eines Steinbruchs mit der umgebenden, naturnahen Landschaft in einer künstlichen Topografie aus Rasenkissen, die von weißen Betonelementen gefasst sind

The design weaves the history of a quarry with the surrounding naturalistic landscape by fashioning an artificial topography of lawn cushions, edged with white concrete elements

SCHMID „Palmen am Chiemsee" wäre ein schönes Szenario: Sandstrände, Palmen, Hängematten, die Alpen im Blick.

GEBHARD Yes, in the Baroque, the landscape gardener was one of the most highly respected of all artists. My wish is that the indications already afoot in the profession, especially with regard to cross-sectoral orientation, will be accorded greater respect in 2063.

SCHMIDT That we will find compromises between economic and artistic demands and our own ways of life.

SCHRÖDER That landscape architects manage to use and apply more widely the competences that they have acquired over the past decades. If landscape architecture is able to retain the expert status it has earned, and to collaborate more often than at present in processes driven by society and its citizens, its competencies and its standing will increase and not decrease. In future, landscape architects will play a more active role in steering processes.

SCHMID "Palm trees on Lake Chiemsee" would be an attractive scenario: sandy beaches, palm trees and hammocks with the Alps visible on the horizon.

Palmen am Chiemsee | Palm trees on Lake Chiemsee | 133

Von Entitäten zu Identitäten

From entities to identities

Verortungen der Landschaftsarchitektur im 100. Jahr des bdla

Situating landscape architecture in the hundredth year of the Federation of German Landscape Architects

von · by Nicole Uhrig

Identität. Die erste Annäherung an diesen Begriff zeigt: Identität ist ein vielfältig zu fassendes Phänomen. Von der Charakterisierung von Personen über die Psychologie und Soziologie bis hin zur Mathematik findet dieser wenig eindeutige Begriff Verwendung. Spricht man als Planer und Gestalter von Identität, grenzt sich das Feld merklich ein. So nimmt die Landschaftsarchitektur meist Bezug auf einen Ort oder ein Objekt, charakterisiert dessen Eigentümlichkeiten und begibt sich auf die Suche nach dem Genius Loci. Neben der zu entdeckenden und in der Gestaltung zu betonenden Eigentümlichkeit, dem Geist des Ortes, werden entsprechend der Planungsaufgabe noch eine Reihe weiterer Identitäten in den kreativen Prozess einbezogen: einerseits personenbezogene Identitäten künftiger Nutzer in Form von Ziel- oder Lebensstilgruppen, kulturelle Identitäten, Bauherrenidentitäten wie die eines Gartenbesitzers oder die Corporate Identity eines Unternehmens[1], andererseits ortsbezogene Stadt- oder Regionalidentitäten mit Marketingrelevanz.

Neben den funktionalen, räumlichen, ästhetischen, ökologischen oder wirtschaftlichen Aspekten der Landschaftsarchitektur sind ihre ideellen Dimensionen von wesentlicher Bedeutung. Wie wirkt ein Platz oder ein Park als Kommunikationssystem? Welche Bedeutungsebenen schwingen zwischen den Zeilen mit? Vermittelt er Atmosphäre, ist er Quelle oder Resonanzraum für Stimmungen? Können sich Benutzer und Betrachter damit identifizieren? Stiftet er Identität? Was ist sein Mehrwert, sein Beitrag zur Entität?

Als Entität bezeichnen wir einer gemeinsamen Betrachtung unterliegende Objekte, die eine Einheit bilden und als kohärentes System erscheinen. Bleibt eine Landschaftsarchitektur bloße Entität, begreift man sie lediglich als systemische Einheit.

Identity. Even a cursory examination is enough to discover that identity is a phenomenon that can be understood in many different ways. This somewhat vague term is used to characterise people as well as in the fields of psychology and sociology and in mathematics. But when planners and designers speak of identity, the field of possible meanings narrows considerably. Landscape architecture usually relates to a place or an object, characterises its singular particularities and does its best to tap into its *genius loci*. In addition to the specific qualities and spirit of the place that need to be identified and then transported through the design, a whole series of other identities can also play a role in the creative process of designing that depend on the task at hand: these include the personal identities of the future users in the form of target groups or lifestyle groups, cultural identities, the identities of the client, such as the owner of the garden or the corporate identity of a company,[1] not to mention the identity of the locality or region and its respective marketing potential.

Alongside the functional, spatial, aesthetic, ecological or economic aspects of landscape architecture, its idealistic dimensions are of key importance. How does a square or a park function as a system of communication? What layers of meaning can be revealed by reading between the lines? Does it communicate an atmosphere, does it serve as a source or space of resonance for moods? Do its users and viewers identify with it? Does it engender a sense of identity? What is its added value, how does it contribute to its entity?

An entity describes a constellation of subordinate objects that together form a unit and that we perceive as a coherent system. If landscape architecture remains

▲ Die Varianz der Parkbank: Temporäre Gestaltung des Berliner Spittelmarkts. Entwurf: BERNARD und SATTLER Landschaftsarchitekten, Berlin

The variance of the park bench: temporary design of the Spittelmarkt in Berlin. Design: BERNARD und SATTLER Landschaftsarchitekten, Berlin

Landschaftsarchitekten sind bemüht, nicht nur Entitäten, also funktionale, ökologische oder ästhetische systemische Einheiten, zu entwerfen, sondern sie wollen darüber hinaus ideelle Ebenen einflechten und jene abstrakten Einheiten mit charakteristischen Eigenschaften und mit einem Eigennamen versehen – damit schaffen sie Identitäten.

Was ist Identität? Vereinfacht betrachtet ist Identität nichts anderes als die individuelle Eigentümlichkeit eines Wesens oder Objektes, die es von anderen deutlich unterscheidbar macht. Und Identität ist nicht statisch, sie ist ein Konstrukt der Interaktion und immer im Fluss. Identität tritt tagtäglich mit ihrer Außenwelt in Kontakt, entwickelt und verändert sich und ist letztlich das Ergebnis eines kontinuierlichen Kommunikationsprozesses. Dies

merely an entity, we see it only as a systemic unit. Landscape architects strive not only to create entities, i.e. functional, ecological or aesthetic systemic units, but also to invest them with layers of conceptual meaning and to infuse these abstract entities with characteristic qualities and a name of their own – all of which are means of creating identities.

So, what is identity? Put simply, identity is nothing other than the specific individual characteristic of a being or object that distinguishes it clearly from others. Identity is also not a static notion: it is a construct formed out of interaction and is always in flux. It is in constant contact with the outside world, developing and changing continually as the product of an ongoing process of communication. This is especially true of personal identities

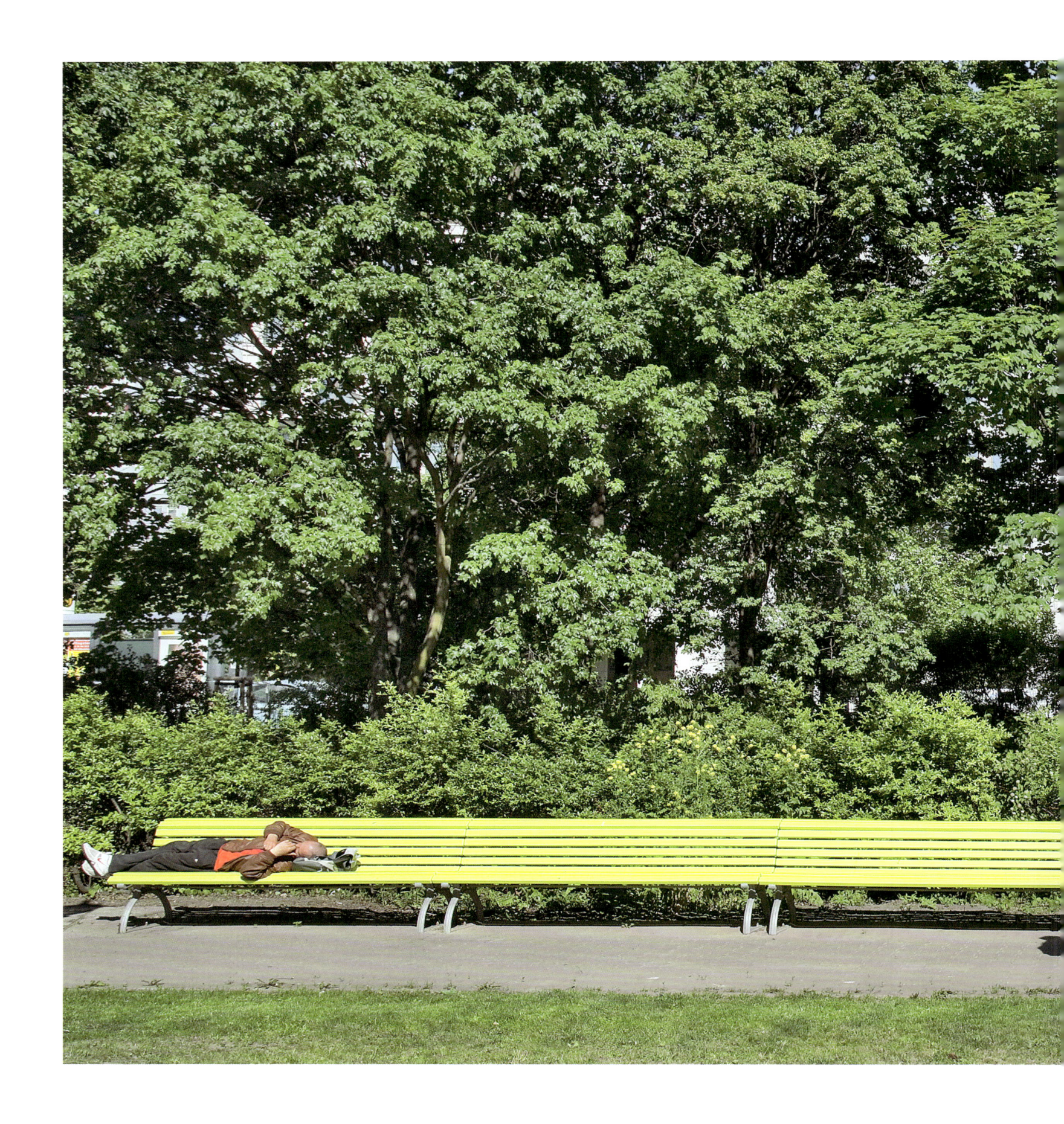

▲ Mit wenigen Mitteln erhielt einer der ehemals wichtigsten
Stadtplätze Berlins eine neue Aufenthaltsqualität

Simple means improve the urban quality of what was once
one of the most important urban squares in Berlin

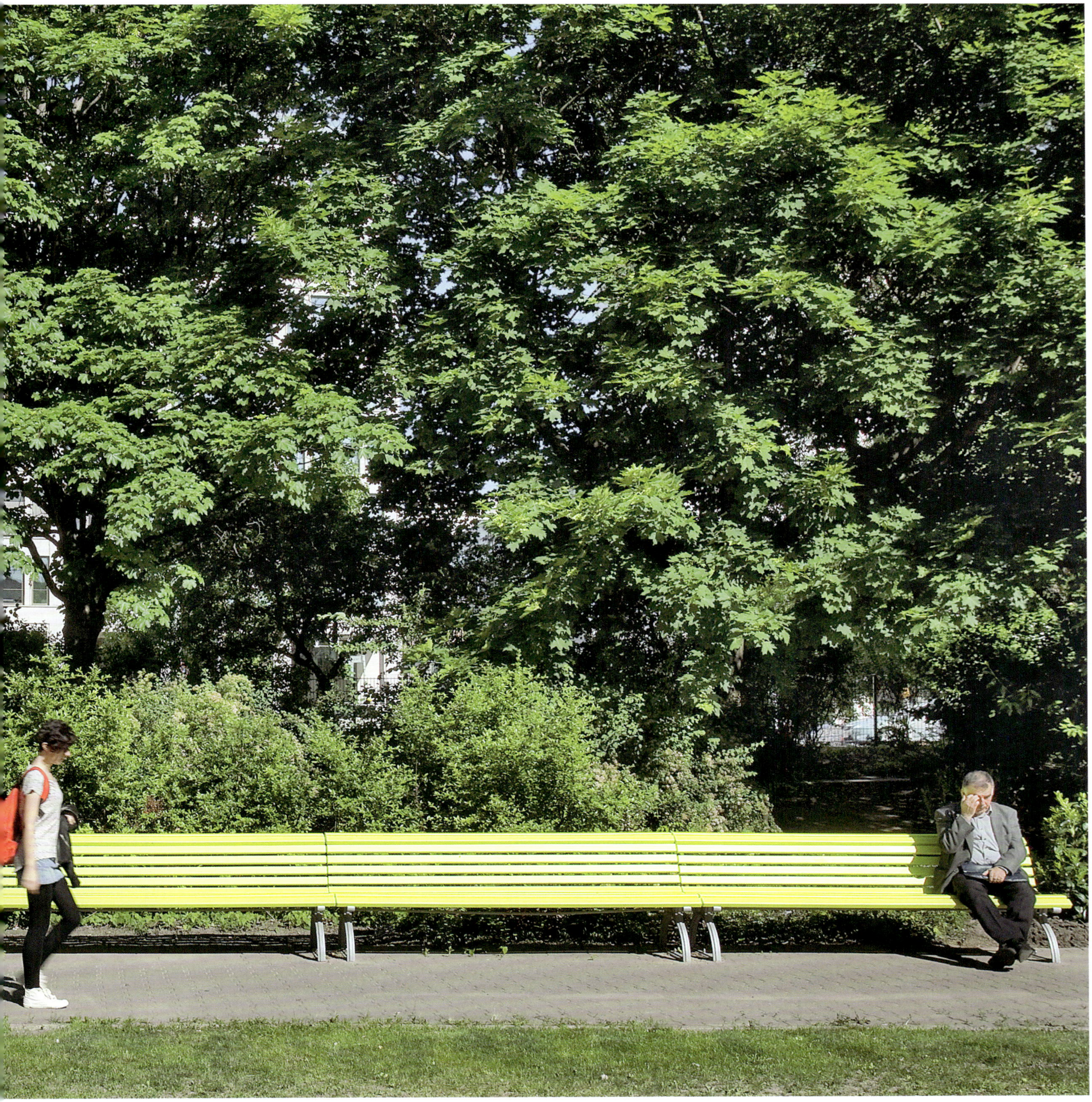

gilt insbesondere für die personenbezogene, aber auch für die ortsbezogene Identität; zudem beeinflussen sich beide wechselseitig, was die Konstellation ungleich komplexer macht.

Eben diese beiden Kategorien, die personenbezogene Identität des Landschaftsarchitekten[2] und die Identität des Ortes, erscheinen für die Landschaftsarchitektur besonders relevant. Im Rahmen dieser Publikation, die den Titel *Zeiträume* trägt, liegt es nahe, den Blick sowohl auf die Wandelbarkeit des professionellen Selbstverständnisses der Landschaftsarchitekten als auch auf die veränderlichen Identitäten von Orten und Landschaftsarchitekturen zu richten.

but also of place-related identities and, to complicate things still further, the two also influence one another.

It is these two categories – the personal identity of the landscape architect[2] and the identity of the place – that are of particular relevance for landscape architecture. This book, entitled *Time Scales*, provides us with an excellent opportunity to take a closer look both at the changing nature of the professional self-image of landscape architects as well as the changing identities of places and landscape architectures.

◀ Ein Durchgangsraum wird zum Ort: Murbrücke zwischen Bad Radkersburg in Österreich und Gornja Radgona in Slowenien. Die beweglichen Kunststoffscheiben am Brückengeländer bieten visuelle wie akustische Bereicherung. Entwurf: bauchplan).(, München und michellerundschalk, München

A transit space is turned into a place: the Mur bridge at the border between Bad Radkersburg in Austria and Gornja Radgona in Slovenia. Movable plastic discs attached to the bridge railings are a visual and acoustic attraction. Design: bauchplan).(, Munich and michellerundschalk, Munich

IDENTITÄT SUCHEN: WER SIND WIR?

„*Wo* sind wir?" fragen die Protagonisten im Film *Les Mystères du Château de Dé* von Man Ray. Eingebettet in die surrealistisch anmutende Geschichte zweier Reisender, die ihre Reisepläne zwei Spielwürfeln überlassen, zeigt das filmische Portrait aus dem Jahr 1929 die Villa Noailles in Hyères an der französischen Riviera, eine Ikone moderner Architektur und Gartenkunst.

Uns zeigt dieses historische Dokument der Moderne noch etwas anderes. Zwischen den Zeilen geht es um eine handfeste Identitätskrise in Zeiten des Umbruchs. „*Wer* sind wir?" ist die eigentliche Frage, die den Plot beherrscht und die durch die strumpfverhüllten Gesichter der Figuren zum Ausdruck gebracht wird. Ausgelöst durch die in der Moderne herrschende Aufbruchsstimmung, den Erneuerungswillen und die harsche Infragestellung des Status quo in allen gestalterischen Belangen, befand sich die moderne Gesellschaft in einem Zustand der Irritation und Neuorientierung.

Auch die gestaltenden Professionen standen trotz aller Euphorie und Experimentierfreude vor der Aufgabe, die neu aufgekommenen Werte, darunter den modernen Technologie- und Fortschrittsglauben, zu reflektieren und in einen neuen Formenkanon umzusetzen. Damit formierten sie ihr neues Selbstverständnis als Profession, ihre neue Identität.

Die Landschaftsarchitektur hat in ihrer Geschichte eine Reihe von Identitätskrisen und Brüchen erlebt. Im Übergang zur Aufklärung von der Stilepoche des Barock, in der die Gartenkunst als hochangesehene Kunstgattung sich dem Zenit ihrer Wertschätzung näherte, machte das Selbstverständnis der Gartenkünstler seine bisher wohl größte Krise durch. Vor dem Hintergrund einer großen ästhetischen Revolution, welche die Vorherrschaft des formal-geometrischen Gartens zu Gunsten der natürlich

IN SEARCH OF IDENTITY: WHO ARE WE?

In Man Ray's cinematic portrait *Les Mystères du Château de Dé* (The Mysteries of the Chateau of Dice) from 1929, the protagonists ask, "*Where* are we?" This surrealistic tale of two travellers who allow their journey to be decided by rolling two dice, is set partly in the Villa Noailles in Hyères on the French Riviera, an icon of modern architecture and garden design.

Aside from its value as a historical document of the age of modernism, the film also tells us something else: reading between the lines, we see the story of a crisis of identity in a time of upheaval. The question that the plot really concerns is "*Who* are we?", which we see expressed by the stocking-masked faces of the protagonists. The age of modernism was accompanied by a spirit of optimism, a desire for innovation but also harsh criticism of the status quo in all spheres of art and design, and this in turn gave rise to a sense of uncertainty and reorientation in society.

The design professions too, despite the euphoria and experimental enthusiasm, were faced with the task of getting to grips with new emerging values, such as the unwavering belief in modern technology and progress, and of transforming these into a new formal canon. In effect they were forming a new self-image of their profession, a new identity for themselves.

In the history of landscape architecture, the profession has experienced a series of crises of identity and reorientation phases. Probably the most serious crisis to befall the profession of the garden designer occurred during the period of transition to the Age of Enlightenment from the epoch of the Baroque style, a period in which garden design as a much-respected art form was probably more highly regarded than at any other time. The aesthetic revolution that accompanied this period

erscheinenden Form stürzte, wechselte der Gestalter die Fronten und strebte nach einem neuen Naturbild. Vom ehemals unverkennbaren Bezwinger der Natur wurde er zu ihrem Fürsprecher, Schutzherrn und scheinbaren Gefolgsmann.

Der nächste Kurswechsel in Richtung Moderne zu Beginn des 20. Jahrhunderts rehabilitierte nicht nur das Verhältnis zur orthogonalen architektonischen Form im Freiraum, sondern er verschob insbesondere den gartenkünstlerischen Fokus von ästhetischen Wertmaßstäben in Richtung einer sozial motivierten und funktionalistischen Planung und machte somit den vormaligen Gartenkünstler zum Gartenarchitekten.

Im Jahr 1972 benannte sich der 1913 gegründete Bund Deutscher *Garten*architekten um in Bund Deutscher *Landschafts*architekten und kommunizierte damit wiederum eine neue Werthaltung und Identität nach außen. Die Profession hatte sich weiterentwickelt und zeichnete sich inzwischen durch ein stärker großmaßstäbliches Denken und durch eine umfassende Sicht auf die Landschaft in all ihren Dimensionen aus. Die ökologische Komponente gewann zunehmend an Gewicht und machte viele Landschaftsarchitekten fortan zu ökosystemischen Denkern und Biotop-Planern. Die Aufspaltung in den Zweig der

toppled the prevailing dominance of formal, geometric garden arrangements in favour of naturalistic forms, forcing the artists and designers to switch sides and adopt a new idealised view of nature. Where once they had demonstratively bent nature to their will, they now cast themselves as advocates of nature, as its protectors and apparent followers.

The next change of direction came with the advent of modernism in the early 20th century, which not only rehabilitated the relationship to orthogonal architectural forms in outdoor spaces but also shifted the focus of garden design away from aesthetic criteria towards socially motivated and functionalist planning objectives. Consequently, the garden artists became garden architects.

In 1972, the Federation of German *Garden* Architects, which was founded in 1913, renamed itself the Federation of German *Landscape* Architects, reflecting the general shift in values and the new identity in its name. The profession had continued to develop and its work was meanwhile characterised by thinking at a larger scale and a more comprehensive view of the landscape in all its dimensions. Ecological aspects had gained greater importance and many landscape architects saw themselves

◀ Mit Korrespondenz und Verfremdung der regionalen Industriearchitektur spielen die überdimensionierten Wohnzimmer-Möbel aus Backstein im Mündungspark am Alten Hafen in Köln-Worringen. Entwurf: Dirk Melzer, Köln

In the spirit of the regional industrial architecture but also strangely out of place, these over-sized pieces of living room furniture made of brick stand in the Debouchment Park at the Old Harbow in Cologne-Worringen. Design: Dirk Melzer, Cologne

▲ Der Mündungspark ist in die Fahrradroute Kölner Randkanal integriert, diese wiederum Bestandteil eines neuen regionalen Grünkorridors mit Anknüpfung an den „dritten", äußeren Kölner Grüngürtel

The Debouchment Park is connected to the cycle path along Cologne's Randkanal, which is in turn part of a new regional green corridor linked to the "third" Outer Green Belt around Cologne

ökologisch orientierten, regionalmaßstäblich arbeitenden Landschaftsplaner und in die mehr objektplanerisch entwerfenden Landschaftsarchitekten, die sich Ende der 1980er Jahre wieder vermehrt der kreativ-gestalterischen Seite und den architektonischen Aspekten ihrer Profession zuwandten, war notwendig und zeigt die Erneuerungskraft jener Krisen.

Heute beherrscht ein gesunder Stilpluralismus die Landschaftsarchitektur, und die Profile der Landschaftsarchitekten sind mittlerweile breit aufgestellt. Diese multiplen Identitäten generieren eine große Anpassungsfähigkeit, welche der Profession genug Stabilität verleiht, um neuartigen Anforderungen vorerst ohne tiefgreifende

increasingly as ecosystem thinkers and biotope planners. The ensuing split in the profession into two branches – ecologically-oriented landscape planners who worked at a regional scale on the one hand, and the more design-oriented landscape architects who worked on projects on an object scale on the other and who from the late 1980s onwards focused increasingly on creative design and architectonic aspects – proved to be necessary and shows the process of renewal that the crisis set in motion.

Today, there is a healthy degree of pluralism in the field of landscape architecture, and the profiles of landscape architects are now quite diverse. This multiplicity of identities also provides greater adaptability, giving the

Identitätskrisen begegnen zu können. Angesichts massiver Veränderungen unserer Lebensumwelt im Zuge der Energiewende, gleichzeitig ablaufender Prozesse von Schrumpfung und Wachstum unserer Siedlungsstrukturen, inklusive der hochspezialisierten Nutzungsanforderungen an zeitgemäße Räume und der Komplexität heutiger Planungsaufgaben zeichnet sich der nächste Umbruch und ein neuer Zyklus im Selbstverständnis der Landschaftsarchitekten jedoch schon ab.

Um all diese Herausforderungen einer postindustriellen Gesellschaft bewältigen zu können, ist heute ein weiter Blick gefragt. Landschaftsarchitekten betrachten ihre profession sufficient stability to respond to new challenges without, at present, precipitating a fundamental identity crisis. Nevertheless, new challenges to the profession are already appearing on the horizon: the dramatic changes to our living environment as a result of the shift in energy policies, the simultaneous shrinkage and expansion processes affecting our urban settlements, the highly specialised functional requirements of contemporary spaces and the complexity of current planning tasks are just some aspects that may well necessitate a renewed cycle of self-critical analysis within the profession.

◀ Der Freiraum der Siedlung Wohnen am Buchheimer Weg in Köln-Ostheim folgt dem „fließenden Raum" der geknickten Baukörper. Private Mietergärten sind ebenso integriert wie Stellplätze, Kita-Garten oder öffentliche Spiel- und Gartenflächen. Entwurf: urbane gestalt johannes böttger landschaftsarchitekten, Köln

The outdoor areas of the Buchheimer Weg housing estate in Cologne-Ostheim follow the "flowing space" of the angular buildings and incorporate private gardens for tenants, car parking, a children's nursery as well as communal playgrounds and gardens. Design: urbane gestalt johannes böttger landschaftsarchitekten, Cologne

Arbeit in holistischer Manier als Teil eines übergeordneten Gesamtwerks. Es werden Allianzen mit anderen Professionen geknüpft, die Landschaftsarchitektur erobert sich den städtebaulichen Maßstab zurück[3], ästhetisch-künstlerische und naturwissenschaftlich-technische Herangehensweisen verschmelzen wieder miteinander und Landschaftsplaner und Landschaftsarchitekten sitzen vermehrt im gleichen Boot oder vereinen sich in einer Person zum weitblickenden Landschaftsstrategen.

IDENTITÄT VORFINDEN: GENIUS LOCI

Neben dem Aspekt der personenbezogenen Identität der Landschaftsarchitekten nimmt die am Ort vorgefundene Identität großen Einfluss auf die Entwicklung der Landschaftsarchitektur. Spätestens seit dem Einzug des Englischen Landschaftsgartens ist die vorgefundene Ortsidentität, der Genius Loci, eine wichtige Referenzgröße für die landschaftsarchitektonische Entwurfsarbeit. Eine umfassende, sensible, bisweilen auch erfinderische Analyse[4] des Ortes, das Aufspüren, gekonnte Verstärken, Integrieren, Inszenieren oder Uminterpretieren vorhandener, teils historischer Spuren gehören heute zum Repertoire zeitgenössischer Landschaftsarchitektur, wie es viele erfolgreich beplante Konversionsflächen und industrielle Landschaften beispielhaft belegen. Jene Art des „wesensspezifischen Entwerfens" basiert auf einer messerscharfen Dechiffrierung des Genius Loci. Sie kreist um die Identität des Ortes und versucht sie freizulegen.

Der vorgefundenen Identität eines Ortes wird ein großes Gewicht für anstehende Planungen zugesprochen. In so manchem Partizipationsverfahren wird deshalb um den Erhalt vorhandener Identifikationsobjekte gekämpft, und es besteht Scheu vor einer gezielt geplanten Neuinterpretation des Ortes. Gleichwohl sind Identitäten auch ohne Zutun der Planer einer stetigen Veränderung unterworfen;

In order to manage the challenges presented by today's post-industrial society, we need to be far-sighted. Landscape architects see their work in a holistic manner as part of a large overall system. Alliances are being established with other professions, landscape architecture is once again working at an urban scale,[3] aesthetic and artistic approaches are increasingly going hand in hand with natural-scientific and technical approaches, and landscape planners and landscape architects are once again sitting in the same boat, or merging into one to become far-sighted landscape strategists.

DISCOVERING IDENTITY: GENIUS LOCI

In addition to the aspect of the personal identity of landscape architects, the identity of place has a strong influence on the development of landscape architecture. Ever since the emergence of the English landscape garden, the inherent identity of a place, its *genius loci*, has been an important aspect of the design of landscape architecture. The comprehensive, sensitive, sometimes even inventive analysis[4] of a place, the discovery, skilful emphasis, incorporation, portrayal or reinterpretation of existing, often historical traces are part of the repertoire of contemporary landscape architecture, as many successful wasteland conversion projects and industrial landscapes can testify to. This kind of "character-specific design" necessitates razor-sharp skills in the decoding of the *genius loci*. It revolves around the identity of the place and attempts to reveal it.

The existing identity of a place is accorded great importance for the later design project. In some public participation procedures, there is therefore strong support for retaining existing objects of identification and a reluctance to embrace even sensitive proposals for a planned reinterpretation of the place. But even without

◀ In einer „bildhauerischen" Strategie werden durch Rodungen und Ergänzungen im Baumbestand die verschwundenen Raumstrukturen des Konzentrationslagers Bergen-Belsen in der Gedenkstätte in der Lüneburger Heide nachgezeichnet. Entwurf: sinai Gesellschaft von Landschaftsarchitekten, Berlin

Using a "sculptural" strategy, clearings and additional insertions in the existing vegetation are used to reveal the earlier spatial structure of the Bergen-Belsen concentration camp as part of the memorial site in the Lüneburg Heath. Design: sinai Gesellschaft von Landschaftsarchitekten, Berlin

sie sind per se als dynamisches Konstrukt zu betrachten, wie dies Christian Norberg-Schulz aus der Sicht der Postmoderne formuliert: "Den Genius Loci zu beschützen und zu bewahren heißt deshalb gerade, sein Wesen in immer neuen historischen Kontexten zu korrigieren."[5] Doch besitzt das noch unsichtbare und deshalb schwer zu vermittelnde Neue häufig weniger Überzeugungskraft, während man auf das Vorhandene immer verweisen kann.

IDENTITÄT STIFTEN: STIMMIG KOMMUNIZIEREN

Soll mit Hilfe von Landschaftsarchitektur eine bestimmte Ortsidentität konstruiert bzw. eine bestehende negativ besetzte Identität am Ort umgeprägt werden, bieten sich unterschiedliche Ansatzpunkte an, die aus einer Entität heraus Identität erzeugen können. Beispielsweise fußt ortsbezogene Identität stark auf dem soziologisch hergeleiteten Phänomen der Aneignung und kann sich durch Beziehungen ausbilden, die zwischen Menschen und ihrer räumlichen Umgebung entstehen. Daher widmet die Landschaftsarchitektur den Nutzungsmöglichkeiten eines Raums viel Aufmerksamkeit, können diese Nutzungen doch eine physisch und mental erfahrbare Verbindung zum Ort herstellen. Aus einer solchen positiven Interaktion zwischen Mensch und Ort entstehen emotionale Beziehungen wie Zugehörigkeitsgefühl, Vertrautheit oder das Gefühl von Heimat, worauf auch die Partizipation in Planungsverfahren abzielt. Vorhandene Spuren individueller und kollektiver Handlungen können diesen Prozess unterstützen[6]. Menschen stellen Beziehungen zwischen ihrer persönlichen Identität und Objekten her, indem sie sich mit dem betreffenden Objekt identifizieren. Dieses Objekt kann auch ein signifikanter Ort sein[7]. Unter ästhetisch-emotionalen Aspekten erscheinen die Ausstrahlung und

the input of the planner, identities are constantly shifting; they can be regarded as inherently dynamic constructs as Christian Norberg-Schulz formulates in the context of postmodernism: "To protect and conserve the 'genius loci' in fact means to concretize its essence in ever new historical contexts."[5] But still, that which is new is invisible and therefore harder to communicate and often less compelling, while one can always point to that which exists.

ENGENDERING IDENTITY: COHERENT COMMUNICATION

If landscape architecture is to help construct the identity of a particular place, or to reconfigure the negative identity of a place, there are a variety of approaches to generating identity out of an entity. For example, location-based identity is strongly rooted in the sociological phenomenon of appropriation and can manifest itself as a relationship between people and their spatial environment. Landscape architecture therefore devotes considerable attention to the ways a space can be used so that these functions can help people develop a physical and mental connection to the place. This kind of positive interaction between people and place is responsible for engendering emotional relationships such as a sense of belonging, of familiarity or of being on "home ground", which is what public participation procedures aim to achieve. Existing traces of individual or collective activities can reinforce this process.[6] People establish relationships between their own personal identity and objects by identifying with the respective object. This object can equally be a significant place.[7] From an aesthetic-emotional aspect, the atmosphere and poetics of a place

▶ Der „Steinerne Weg" führt als „entleerter Raum" vom Dokumentationszentrum in die Weite des Lagergeländes der Gedenkstätte Bergen-Belsen

The "Stony Path" is a "voided space" that leads from the documentation centre into the depths of the site of the concentration camp memorial

▼ Mit den „Nachzeichnungen" im Maßstab 1:1 wird die Dimension des ehemaligen Konzentrationslagers erlebbar

1:1 scale clearings in the woodland serve as "markings" that make the dimensions of the former concentration camp legible

die Poetik eines Ortes als wichtigstes Kriterium für ortsbezogene Identität[8].

Neben jenen schwer fassbaren, immateriellen Kriterien, welche die Landschaftsarchitektur mit Hilfe von Atmosphären, Sinnesqualitäten, Assoziationsfeldern, Emotionalität oder Ausstrahlung in der Ausbildung von Identität unterstützen können, sind auch handfestere Komponenten zu nennen. Zum Handwerkszeug des Identitätsstifters gehören unter anderem die Prägnanz im Entwurf, die Steigerung der Aufmerksamkeit, das Herstellen von Wiedererkennbarkeit und das Alleinstellungsmerkmal – was beispielsweise mit Hilfe der Integration von Kunst an exponierten Stellen erreicht werden soll. Wo eine spezifische Raumqualität nicht reproduzierbar ist, kann Identität

would seem to be the most important criteria for place-related identity.[8]

Aside from those hard-to-grasp, immaterial criteria that influence how landscape architecture acquires identity, such as through atmospheres, sensory qualities, association fields, emotions or personality, there are also more tangible components. The designer's toolbox includes a range of identity-imparting design strategies such as clarity and succinctness of the design idea, ways of attracting attention, of heightening recognisability as well as creating distinct and unique situations – which can, for example, be achieved by incorporating art at prominent positions. Identity can develop where the quality of a space is not reproducible, and particularly

Heller Muschelkalk, gegliedert durch dunkle Basaltbänder, nimmt das Fassadenraster eines anliegenden Warenhauses auf und bestimmt die Neugestaltung des Fuldaer Borgiasplatzes. Entwurf: Planergruppe Oberhausen, Reith und Wehner Architekten, Fulda

Light-coloured shell limestone paving interspersed with dark basalt strips replicate the grid of the façade of a nearby department store for the design of the Borgiasplatz in Fulda. Design: Planergruppe Oberhausen, Reith und Wehner Architekten, Fulda

entstehen – im Fall einer besonders starken Identität kann eine Landschaft oder Landschaftsarchitektur sogar zur Marke werden. Soll ein Projekt maßgeblich der Stiftung von Identität und deren erfolgreicher Kommunikation dienen, bedarf es allerdings der Abwägung zwischen aufmerksamkeitssteigernden Gestaltungsmitteln und den subtileren kommunikativen Zeichen des Ortes. Solche „leisen" Zeichen sind als wertvolles Vor-Ort-Potenzial zu werten, das die Qualität einer Landschaftsarchitektur maßgeblich beeinflusst und das es unbedingt zu nutzen gilt.

Die Ziele, die mit der Identitätsstiftung einhergehen, richten sich sowohl nach außen als auch nach innen. So unterstützen beispielsweise besonders prägnante Leuchtturmprojekte wie seinerzeit der Landschaftspark Duisburg-Nord regionale und metropolitane Identitäten und sind durch ihre starke Außenwirkung von großer Bedeutung für Stadtmarketing und Wirtschaftsförderung. Zielt die Identitätsbildung auf eine Innenwirkung ab, geht es darum, dass sich Nutzer, Anwohner oder ansässige Gewerbetreibende mit einem Ort identifizieren, ihn annehmen und ihm Wertschätzung entgegenbringen. Im Rahmen der IBA Hamburg sollen unter anderem mit Hilfe von ortsbezogener Identität kulturelle und soziale Barrieren überwunden werden. Die starke Identität von Orten wird hier als verbindendes Element genutzt, um ein Zusammengehörigkeitsgefühl zu schaffen, das sich mehr über den Ort definiert – „wir wohnen *hier*"– als über soziale oder kulturelle Zugehörigkeiten.

Letztlich beruht Identität auf einer Reihe von Kommunikationsprozessen auf unterschiedlichsten Ebenen. Um diese Prozesse in Gang zu bringen, braucht es möglichst viele Anknüpfungspunkte und kommunikative Schnittstellen. Gleichzeitig sind es die Stimmigkeit jener Ebenen und ein ganzheitliches Erscheinungsbild, die der konstruierten Identität Kraft und Glaubwürdigkeit verleihen.

distinctive landscapes or landscape architecture can even achieve a trademark quality. Where the aim of a project is expressly to bring out and communicate the identity of a place, the designer must weigh up the value of attention-generating design means versus working with the more subtle communicative signs of the place. These softer signs represent a valuable potential of the site that can lend the landscape architecture a particularly distinctive quality and should be used wherever possible.

The aims associated with creating a sense of identity can be directed both inward and outward. For example, particularly distinctive flagship projects, such as the Duisburg Nord Landscape Park, are an effective means of generating regional and metropolitan identity, and through their strong visibility are important instruments for local marketing and economic development. More inwardly oriented aims include improving a sense of local identity so that a space is used, appropriated and valued by its users, local residents and businesses. As part of the Hamburg International Building Exhibition, the creation of a sense of local identity aims to help overcome cultural and social barriers. Where places have a strong sense of identity, they can serve as a uniting element in which the sense of community, of belonging, is defined more by place – "*here* is where we live" – than by social or cultural milieu.

Ultimately, identity is based on a series of communication processes that take place at quite different levels. To set these processes in motion, we need to establish as many possible points of contact and communicative interaction as possible. At the same time, it is the coherence and consistency of these levels and the overall image of the place that lend this constructed sense of identity strength and credibility.

IDENTITÄT NUTZEN: VERORTUNG VERSUS ESKAPISMUS

„Ich bin der Welt abhanden gekommen"

(FRIEDRICH RÜCKERT)[9]

Der Eskapismus, das Phänomen der Realitätsflucht in eine vermeintlich bessere Wirklichkeit, ist uns wichtig. Die gedankliche Flucht aus den Schwierigkeiten und Anstrengungen der realen Welt ist ein Ausgleich, der uns zur Ruhe kommen lässt und mitunter auch neue Perspektiven auf Bekanntes eröffnet und uns kreativ macht. Jeder Garten kommt eskapistischen Tendenzen entgegen. Der Garten ist noch heute der Metapher des verlorenen Paradieses verhaftet und steht für die Sehnsucht nach einer besseren

USING IDENTITY: ROOTEDNESS VERSUS ESCAPISM

"I am lost to the world"

(Friedrich Rückert)[9]

Escapism, the phenomenon of fleeing reality into a supposedly better reality, is for us a valuable outlet. The ability to mentally remove ourselves from the difficulties and rigours of the real world is a form of emancipation that allows us to calm down, to see familiar problems in a new light, and can stimulate creativity. Every garden is in some way or another conducive to escapist tendencies. Gardens were and still are a metaphor for paradise lost, and embody within them a yearning for a better world.

◀ Die bewegte Mittelgebirgslandschaft Nordrhein-Westfalens inspirierte die temporäre, begehbare Holzskulptur des NRW-Pavillons für die Weltgartenausstellung Floriade 2012 in Venlo, Niederlande. Entwurf: RMP Stephan Lenzen, Bonn

The rolling upland landscape of North Rhine-Westphalia inspired the design of the temporary walk-on wooden sculpture of the pavilion for the Floriade 2012 international garden show in Venlo, The Netherlands. Design: RMP Stephan Lenzen, Bonn

▲ In der Symbolisierung von Hügeln und Tälern wird das Landschaftsbild zu einer Landschafts-Architektur

Through the symbolisation of hills and valleys, the image of the landscape becomes landscape architecture

Welt. In unserer Gesellschaft macht sich Eskapismus häufig fest an Konsum und Unterhaltung, seien es digitale Phantasiewelten oder reale Disney-World-Landschaften. Jene Art eskapistischen Fluchtverhaltens impliziert aber auch, dass der Blick von gesellschaftlichen Anforderungen und Zielen und letztlich auch von gesellschaftlicher Verantwortung abgewandt wird. Um die reale Welt als erlebenswert empfinden zu können, braucht es ein Gefühl des Verhaftetseins mit ihr. Erst dann gibt es auch Möglichkeiten, Einfluss auf die Qualität der eigenen realen Lebensumwelt zu nehmen.

Räumliche Identität hat das Potenzial, den Betrachter in der Realität zu verorten. Identität wirkt somit als Gegenspieler zum Eskapismus. Insbesondere uns Landschafts-

In contemporary society, the most common avenues of escapism are consumerism and entertainment, whether virtual fantasy worlds or real Disneyland landscapes. An implicit aspect of such kinds of escapist behaviour, however, is that of taking a step back from social demands and aims, and with it of turning one's back on social responsibility. In order to view the world around us as worthwhile and valuable, one needs to feel a sense of attachment to it. Only then can one actively influence the quality of one's own living environment.

Spatial identity has the potential to root the viewer in reality. Identity therefore serves as a counterpoint to escapism. As landscape architects, we are particularly responsible for transforming entities into identities.

▲ Als „Gesamtkunstwerk aus Stein" schreiben die Außenanlagen die Fassaden des Hambacher Schlosses in Neustadt an der Weinstraße fort. Entwurf: LOMA architecture.landscape.urbanism, Kassel

Conceived as a "Gesamtkunstwerk made of stone", the outdoor areas pick up the form and materiality of the façades of Hambach Castle in Neustadt. Design: LOMA architecture.landscape.urbanism, Kassel

▶ Die Neuordnungen verstehen sich als „chirurgische Eingriffe" in den historischen Bestand, mit denen auch an den Hambacher Festzug des Jahres 1832, die „Geburtsstunde der deutschen Demokratie", erinnert wird

The reconfiguration takes the form of "surgical interventions" in the historical substance of the original, and commemorates the Hambach Festival procession in 1832, which is regarded as the birth of German democracy

architekten kommt die Aufgabe zu, aus Entitäten Identitäten zu machen. Um neu geschaffene und neu interpretierte Orte benennbar und wiedererkennbar zu machen, geben wir ihnen ein unverwechselbares Gesicht. Solche Orte zeigen klare Bilder und setzen Anker, die uns durch eine komplexe, manchmal auch eigenschaftsarme Umwelt navigieren. Identität schafft Verortung und verhindert letztlich, dass wir der Welt abhanden kommen.

Whether a newly created place or a newly interpreted place, we give it a name and make it recognisable by lending it a unique and distinctive face. Such places communicate clear images and create anchors that help us navigate through a complex and sometimes featureless environment. Identity creates a sense of rootedness and ultimately prevents us from becoming lost to the world.

1 Die Corporate Identity eines Unternehmens ist allerdings keine echte personenbezogene Identität, sondern sie ist vielmehr als theoretisches Konstrukt einer „Ich-Identität" im Rahmen des strategischen Managements zu betrachten.

2 In der Psychologie steht der personalen (Ich-)Identität der Aspekt der sozialen (Wir-)Identität gegenüber. In diesem Sinn nimmt auch das Zugehörigkeitsgefühl zur sozialen bzw. beruflichen Gruppe der Landschaftsarchitekten Einfluss auf die individuelle Identität jedes Landschaftsarchitekten.

3 Im Jahr 2012 erhielt Häfner/Jiménez Büro für Landschaftsarchitektur aus Berlin den Deutschen Städtebaupreis für das Projekt „Neugestaltung der historischen Mitte in Staßfurt".

4 „Erfinderische Analyse" ist ein Kernbegriff in der Arbeit des französischen Landschaftsarchitekten Bernard Lassus. Vgl. Bernard Lassus, *The Landscape Approach*, University of Pennsylvania Press, Philadephia, 1998.

5 Christian Norberg-Schulz, *Genius Loci – Landschaft, Lebensraum, Baukunst*, Klett-Cotta, Stuttgart, 1982, S. 18.

6 Vgl. Annemarie Bucher, „Landschaft, Landschaftsbewusstsein und landschaftliche Identität als Potenziale für die regionale Entwicklung", in: GAIA 19/3, 2010, S. 213 – 222; Susanne Hauser, „Lokale Identität, Ästhetik und die urbanisierte Landschaft", in: *Jahrestagung Forum Landschaft*, „Den Wandel gestalten – Periurbane Landschaften", Basel, 15. April 2008 (www.forumlandschaft.ch/archiv/…/08/links/Hauptreferat_Hauser.pdf, aufgesucht am 01.12.2012); Amos Rapoport, *The Meaning of the Built Environment*, Sage Publications, Beverly Hills, 1982.

7 Vgl. Peter Weichhart, *Raumbezogene Identität*, Steiner, Stuttgart, 1990.

8 Vgl. u. a. Detlev Ipsen, *Ort und Landschaft*, VS Verlag für Sozialwissenschaften, Wiesbaden, 2006.

9 „Ich bin der Welt abhanden gekommen", Gedicht von Friedrich Rückert aus dem Jahr 1821.

1 The corporate identity of a company is not a true personal identity but rather a theoretical construct equivalent to a personal identity, and is shaped by the company's strategic management policy.

2 In the field of psychology, personal (self-)identity is discussed in relation to social (collective) identity. In this respect, the sense of belonging to a social or professional group of landscape architects influences the individual self-identity of each landscape architect.

3 In 2012, Häfner/Jiménez Büro für Landschaftsarchitektur in Berlin was awarded the German Urban Design Prize for their project for the "Redesign of the historic centre of Staßfurt".

4 "Inventive Analysis" is a key concept in the work of the French landscape architect Bernard Lassus. Cf. Bernard Lassus, *The Landscape Approach*, Philadelphia, University of Pennsylvania Press, 1998.

5 Christian Norberg-Schulz, *Genius loci: Towards a Phenomenology of Architecture*, New York, Rizzoli, 1980, p. 18.

6 Cf. Annemarie Bucher, "Landschaft, Landschaftsbewusstsein und landschaftliche Identität als Potenziale für die regionale Entwicklung", in: GAIA 19/3, 2010, pp. 213 – 222; Susanne Hauser, "Lokale Identität, Ästhetik und die urbanisierte Landschaft", in: *Jahrestagung Forum Landschaft*, "Den Wandel gestalten – Periurbane Landschaften", Basel, 15 April 2008 (http://www.forumlandschaft.ch/archiv/jahrestagungen/08/links/Hauptreferat_Hauser.pdf, accessed 01/12/2012); Amos Rapoport, *The Meaning of the Built Environment*, Beverly Hills, Sage Publications, 1982.

7 Cf. Peter Weichhart, *Raumbezogene Identität*, Stuttgart, Steiner, 1990.

8 See also Detlev Ipsen, *Ort und Landschaft*, Wiesbaden, VS Verlag für Sozialwissenschaften, 2006.

9 *Ich bin der Welt abhanden gekommen*, poem by Friedrich Rückert from 1821.

ANHANG | APPENDIX

Über die Preisträger Deutscher Landschaftsarchitektur-Preis 2013

About the prize winners of the German Landscape Architecture Prize 2013

DEUTSCHER LANDSCHAFTSARCHITEKTUR-PREIS 2013

hutterreimann Landschaftsarchitektur GmbH, Berlin mit thoma architekten, Berlin/Zeulenroda – Park am Löbauer Wasser, Löbau
Das Büro hutterreimann Landschaftsarchitektur wurde 2001 von Barbara Hutter und Stefan Reimann gegründet. Sie entwickeln spezifische Freiräume, die vom Ort und seiner Geschichte inspiriert sind. Im kreativen Umgang mit dem Vorgefundenen erzeugen sie spannungsreiche, charakteristische Landschaften mit neuer Identität. Der nachhaltige Umgang mit den zur Verfügung stehenden Ressourcen, den ökologischen wie sozialen Konditionen und die Angemessenheit der Mittel sind die bestimmenden Grundsätze dieser Gestaltung. In der Reduktion auf das Wesentliche liegt die Kraft ihrer Arbeiten. Dazu gehört auch der Mut zur „großen Geste", die, wenn sie angemessen erscheint, als klare Setzung polarisieren kann. www.hr-c.net

**relais Landschaftsarchitekten, Berlin –
Der Christliche Garten (Gärten der Welt), Berlin**
relais Landschaftsarchitekten wurde 2001 von Gero Heck und Marianne Mommsen gegründet. Das Büro setzt sich mit der Planung von Freiräumen im urbanen und landschaftlichen Kontext, vom städtebaulichen Maßstab bis zum konkreten Objekt auseinander. Grundlage dieser Entwurfstätigkeit ist die Auseinandersetzung mit der gewachsenen Situation des Ortes, mit dessen Atmosphäre und sozialer Bedeutung. Den Freiraum sieht das Büro als Topos, der nicht nur semantisch, sondern auch essenziell im Widerspruch zu optischer und funktionaler Reglementierung steht. Ziel der Entwurfsarbeit ist daher die Schaffung vielschichtig erlebbarer und prägnanter Räume, deren klare Struktur und offene Konzeption sich im Rahmen der Nutzung als entwicklungsfähig erweisen. www.relaisLA.de

WGF Landschaft, Nürnberg – Grüngürtel: Impuls 2012, Köln
WGF Landschaft wurde 1974 von Gerd Aufmkolk gegründet und wird heute von ihm und den Geschäftsführern Hubert Hintermeier, Michael Voit und Sigrid Ziesel als GmbH getragen. Schwerpunkte sind die Grün- und Landschaftsplanung im Bereich der Bauleitplanung, Verkehrs- und

GERMAN LANDSCAPE ARCHITECTURE PRIZE 2013

hutterreimann Landschaftsarchitektur GmbH, Berlin with thoma architekten, Berlin/Zeulenroda – Löbauer River Park, Löbau
The office hutterreimann Landschaftsarchitektur was founded in 2001 by Barbara Hutter and Stefan Reimann and develops specific outdoor spaces that are inspired by their place and its history. Taking a creative approach to the existing situation, they produce stimulating and characteristic landscapes, lending them a new sense of identity. The sustainable use of available resources, respect for the ecological and social conditions and the use of appropriate means are the guiding principles of their design approach. The strength of their work lies in revealing what is essential. This also means having the courage to make an appropriate "strong gesture" that, through the clarity of its expression, can be potentially polarising. www.hr-c.net

**relais Landschaftsarchitekten, Berlin –
The Christian Garden (Gardens of the World), Berlin**
relais Landschaftsarchitekten was founded by Gero Heck and Marianne Mommsen in 2001. The office concentrates on the planning of open spaces in urban and rural contexts, with projects ranging from an urban design scale to the scale of a specific object. Their designs are based on an exploration of the respective situation and its evolution, its atmosphere and social meaning. The office sees open space as a topos that contrasts, not only semantically but also in its very essence, with visual and functional regimentation. In their design work they aim to create characteristic and yet multi-layered experiences and spaces, with a clear structure and open conceptual approach that enables them to develop in the course of continued use. www.relaisLA.de

WGF Landschaft, Nuremberg – Green Belt: Impuls 2012, Cologne
WGF Landschaft was founded in 1974 by Gerd Aufmkolk and is now run by himself and his partners Hubert Hintermeier, Michael Voit and Sigrid Ziesel as a limited company. The focus of their work lies in the design of green spaces and landscapes, especially in conjunction

Gewässerplanung. Die Erfahrungen betreffen sowohl förmliche Planungsinstrumente als auch informelle Planungen, die sich mit den Möglichkeiten der Freiraumentwicklung in ländlichen und verdichteten Stadtregionen auseinandersetzen. Dabei stehen die Qualifizierung und die Gestaltung der Landschaft als Schlüssel für alle weiteren sich anlagernden Ziele im Vordergrund. www.wgf-nuernberg.de

club L94 Landschaftsarchitekten GmbH, Köln – Elsbethenareal und Schrannenplatz, Memmingen

Das Büro club L94 Landschaftsarchitekten GmbH schafft starke Bilder, die ein hohes Maß an Identität im Freiraum stiften. Im Vordergrund steht die Befriedigung differenzierter Nutzungsansprüche an die Gestaltung. Die inhaltliche Reduktion auf wenige Elemente, die sich in die Systematik einer Gesamtkonzeption integrieren, verleiht den Entwürfen Ruhe und Klarheit. Formal stehen die Entwürfe der jungen Moderne nah. Die Planer streben im Wissen um die landschaftsarchitektonischen Traditionen nach spannungsreicher Interpretation und Transformation. In der Realisierung der Entwürfe legen sie großen Wert auf bautechnische Professionalität und Detailgenauigkeit in der Ausführung. www.clubl94.de

lohrer.hochrein landschaftsarchitekten bdla, München/Magdeburg/Perach a. Inn – Park Phoenix West, Dortmund

Das Büro von Ursula Hochrein und Axel Lohrer besteht seit 1993. Als Team von Landschaftsarchitekten und Stadtplanern beschäftigen sie sich mit den vielfältigen Facetten von Freiraum zwischen urbaner Dichte und landschaftlicher Weite. Im offenen Dialog, in interdisziplinären Teams, in Wettbewerben oder als Preisrichter suchen sie nach dem Wesentlichen und Unverwechselbaren eines Ortes als Basis für ihre gestalterische Arbeit. Von der ersten Idee über die städtebauliche Konzeption bis hin zur landschaftsarchitektonischen Objektplanung sind sie bestrebt, die jeweils eingenommene Haltung bis ins Detail zu realisieren. www.lohrer-hochrein.de

Lützow 7 Cornelia Müller, Jan Wehberg, Landschaftsarchitekten, Berlin – Elisengarten, Aachen

Das Büro Lützow 7 Cornelia Müller, Jan Wehberg, Landschaftsarchitekten ist seit 1997 selbstständig tätig. Schwerpunkte liegen in der Landschaftsarchitektur und Gartenkunst, der Objektplanung im privaten und öffentlichen Raum, in städtebaulich-landschaftsplanerischen Aufgaben sowie Gutachten und Parkpflegewerken. Lützow 7 legt beson-

with land-use planning, traffic infrastructure and watercourse planning. Their experience covers both formal and informal planning concepts that explore the possibilities of landscape development in rural as well as densely built-up urban regions. Their emphasis lies on the qualitative improvement and design of the landscape as the key to resolving all associated aims. www.wgf-nuernberg.de

club L94 Landschaftsarchitekten GmbH, Cologne – Elsbethenareal and Schrannenplatz, Memmingen

club L94 Landschaftsarchitekten GmbH creates strong images that help people to identify readily with outdoor spaces. A central focus is the fulfilling of different functional requirements, while the reduction of their designs to a few key elements, integrated within the framework of an overall concept, lends their work a sense of calm clarity. The office is influenced by the formal language of the emergent Modernism and draws on its knowledge of the history and tradition of landscape architecture to achive stimulating interpretations and transformations. The office also places great value on the best possible workmanship and attention to detail in the realisation of their designs. www.clubl94.de

lohrer.hochrein landschaftsarchitekten bdla, Munich/Magdeburg/Perach a. Inn – Park Phoenix West, Dortmund

Founded in 1993, the office of Ursula Hochrein and Axel Lohrer consists of landscape architects and urban designers and is experienced in the design of open spaces in both dense urban and expansive rural contexts. In their work in interdisciplinary teams, on competitions or as jury members, they seek through open dialogue to identify the essential and distinctive quality of a place as the generator for its design. From the first idea to the urban design concept and the landscaping and design of the particular project, the office strives to articulate the respective conceptual position at all levels of detail in the realisation of the project. www.lohrer-hochrein.de

Lützow 7 Corneila Müller, Jan Wehberg, Landschaftsarchitekten, Berlin – Elisengarten, Aachen

Lützow 7 Cornelia Müller, Jan Wehberg, Landschaftsarchitekten is a freelance office founded in Berlin in 1997. The main focus of their work lies in landscape architecture and garden design, projects in private and public space, large-scale urban and landscape planning projects as well as expert reports and park maintenance concepts.

deren Wert auf die Magie des Ortes, das Harmonisieren vermeintlicher Gegensätze zwischen Ästhetik und Gebrauch, zwischen der Faszination der Natur und dem behutsamen gestaltenden Eingriff sowie eine ästhetische Konzeption, bei der die Vielfalt des Einzelnen zur Einfachheit des Ganzen als nachhaltige Planungsprämisse wird. Neben zahlreichen national und international prämierten und realisierten Wettbewerben, wie das neue Regierungsviertel in Berlin, erhielt das Büro für seine Arbeiten mehrere Anerkennungen. www.luetzow7.com

Stefan Fromm Landschaftarchitekten, Dettenhausen –
Drei neue Parks für Nagold
Stefan Fromm ist seit 1988 als freischaffender Landschaftsarchitekt tätig. 1990 gründete er sein eigenes Büro in Böblingen, 1994 erfolgte der Umzug nach Dettenhausen bei Tübingen. Tätigkeitsschwerpunkt des etwa zehnköpfigen Teams ist die Planung öffentlicher und privater Freiräume aller Größenordnungen sowie städtebaulicher Projekte in enger Zusammenarbeit mit Architekten und Stadtplanern. Aus Wettbewerbserfolgen entstanden zahlreiche Planungsaufträge, unter anderem für vier Landesgartenschauen (zuletzt Nagold 2012). Kennzeichnend für die Arbeit von Stefan Fromm sind die intensive Auseinandersetzung mit den Gegebenheiten des Ortes, die Berücksichtigung räumlicher und funktionaler Bezüge, sowie eine sorgfältige planerische Ausarbeitung bis ins Detail. www.fromm-landschaftsarchitekten.de

Topotek 1 Gesellschaft von Landschaftsarchitekten mbH, Berlin –
Superkilen, Kopenhagen/Dänemark
Das Büro Topotek 1, 1996 gegründet, geleitet von Martin Rein-Cano und Lorenz Dexler, ist im Feld der Gestaltung städtischer Freiräume verwurzelt. Ausgehend von einem kritischen Verständnis vorhandener Realitäten finden ihre konzeptionellen Lösungsansätze ihren Niederschlag in klaren Statements im urbanen Kontext. In der Umsetzung orientiert sich Topotek 1 an den Bedürfnissen nach Variabilität, Kommunikation und Sinnlichkeit. Zugleich unternimmt das Büro Ausflüge in die Konzeption und Realisierung von Ausstellungen und Kunstinstallationen. Dieser Ansatz wurde mit zahlreichen Preisen ausgezeichnet, darunter dem Nationalen Preis für integrierte Stadtentwicklung und Baukultur für das Projekt Campus der Martin-Luther-Universität in Halle/Saale 2009, dem Institute Honor Award by the National AIA Award 2013, dem Civic Trust Award 2013 sowie dem reddot design award: best of the best 2013. www.topotek1.de

Lützow 7 places special emphasis on uncovering the specific spirit of a place, on resolving the apparent contradictions between aesthetics and use and between the fascination of nature and sensitive design interventions. Individual diversity leads to holistic simplicity as a sustainable premise for planning. In addition to winning and realising numerous national and international competitions, such as the new government quarter in Berlin, the work of the office has also received several prizes and awards. www.luetzow7.com

Stefan Fromm Landschaftarchitekten, Dettenhausen –
Three new parks for Nagold
Stefan Fromm has worked as a freelance landscape architect since 1988. In 1990, he founded his own office in Böblingen, relocating in 1994 to Dettenhausen near Tübingen. The main focus of the work of the ten-person-strong team is the planning of public and private outdoor spaces at all scales, as well as urban design projects in close cooperation with architects and urban planners. Numerous planning commissions have resulted from successful competition entries, among them four state garden shows (most recently Nagold in 2012). They feature an intensive examination of the existing situation of the site, the consideration of all spatial and functional interdependencies and meticulous attention to detail in planning and execution. www.fromm-landschaftsarchitekten.de

Topotek 1 Gesellschaft von Landschaftsarchitekten mbH, Berlin –
Superkilen, Copenhagen/Denmark
The work of the office of Topotek 1, founded in 1996 by Martin Rein-Cano and Lorenz Dexler, is rooted in the design of urban open spaces. Starting from a critical comprehension of the existing realities of the site, they develop conceptual approaches that are ultimately manifested as clear statements in an urban context. In the articulation of their designs, Topotek 1 respond to the need for variability, communication and sensory experience. In addition to investigating urban issues, the office undertakes excursions into the conception and realisation of exhibitions and art installations. The work of the office has been awarded numerous prizes including the National Prize for Integrated Urban Development and Building Culture for the design of outer spaces on the Campus of Martin Luther University in Halle/Saale 2009, the AIA Institute Honor Award 2013, the Civic Trust Award 2013 and the reddot design award: best of the best 2013. www.topotek1.de

Straub Thurmayr Landschaftsarchitekten und Stadtplaner, München und Winnipeg/Kanada – Folly Forest, Strathcona School, Winnipeg/Kanada

Dietmar Straub und Anna Thurmayr sind die leitenden Partner von Straub Thurmayr Landschaftsarchitekten. Sie lehren Landschaftsarchitektur an der University of Manitoba in Kanada. Seit mehr als 20 Jahren arbeiten und leben sie zusammen. Dietmar Straubs breites Wissen über gegenwärtige und historische Landschaftsarchitektur sowie seine Begeisterung für Materialität, Technologie und auch für Ingenieurwesen und Kunst liegen seiner Entwurfstätigkeit zugrunde. Anna Thurmayr begann ihre Karriere mit dem Entwurf von begrünten Dächern und hat in der Projektleitung und -durchführung von zahlreichen exponierten Projekten gearbeitet. Ihre Forschungsinteressen gehen aus der vielfältigen Projektarbeit hervor und umfassen die visuelle Sprache der Landschaftsarchitektur, Baumaterialien in nördlichen Klimazonen sowie Dachgärten. Dietmar Straub und Anna Thurmayr konnten während ihrer beruflichen Laufbahn als Lehrende, Landschaftsarchitekten und Städtebauer für eine Vielzahl von Aufträgen an sehr unterschiedlichen Orten, Bauplätzen und in vielen Ländern arbeiten.

RMP Stephan Lenzen Landschaftsarchitekten, Bonn – Masterplan emscher:zukunft

RMP Stephan Lenzen Landschaftsarchitekten, gegründet 1951, wird seit 2004 von Stephan Lenzen als alleinigem Inhaber geführt. Die Arbeit des Büros deckt die gesamte Bandbreite der Objekt- und der Landschaftsplanung ab. Neben der Auseinandersetzung mit der Gestaltung urbaner Lebensräume bestehen besondere Kompetenzen in Machbarkeitsstudien, Planung und Realisierung von Projekten zu den Themen Stadt am Fluss sowie Gartenschauen in Stadt und Land. Dabei versteht das Büro Landschaftsarchitektur nicht als Kunst, sondern als kongeniale Zusammenführung von kreativer Ingenieurleistung und gärtnerischem Handwerk. Was zählt, ist das Wohlfühlen der Menschen und die Erfüllung der funktionalen Anforderungen an den Ort. www.rmp-landschaftsarchitekten.de

ASTOC Architects and Planners, Köln – Masterplan emscher:zukunft

ASTOC Architects and Planners ist seit rund 20 Jahren in Köln zu Hause und bearbeitet städtebauliche und architektonische Projekte in Deutschland und im benachbarten Ausland. ASTOC Architects and Planners hat in den eigenständigen Disziplinen Architektur und Städtebau zahlreiche Projekte realisiert, viele davon für langjährige Auftraggeber aus der privaten Wirtschaft und von öffentlichen Institutionen.

Straub Thurmayr Landschaftsarchitekten und Stadtplaner, Munich and Winnipeg/Canada – Folly Forest, Strathcona School, Winnipeg/Canada

Dietmar Straub and Anna Thurmayr are the principal partners of Straub Thurmayr Landschaftsarchitekten and teach landscape architecture at the University of Manitoba, Canada. They have been working and living together for more than 20 years. Dietmar Straub's broad knowledge of contemporary and historical landscape architecture, his passion for materiality, technology, and also for engineering and art are the foundation of his design work. Anna Thurmayr began her professional career in green roof design and has since acted as a lead designer and project manager on several high-profile projects. Her research interests, derived from the wide range of projects she has undertaken, are the visual language of landscape architecture, materials in northern climates and roof gardens. Both have had the opportunity to deal with a wide range of assignments in their careers, and to work in very different places, sites and countries – both as teachers and as landscape architects and urban designers.

RMP Stephan Lenzen Landschaftsarchitekten, Bonn – Emscher Future master plan

RMP Stephan Lenzen Landschaftsarchitekten, founded in Bonn in 1951, has been run since 2004 by Stephan Lenzen as the sole director. The work of the office covers the entire spectrum of project and landscape planning. In addition to designing urban living environments, the office has particular competencies in drawing up feasibility studies, the planning and realisation of projects concerned with riverside cities as well as regional and national garden shows. The office sees landscape architecture not as an art but as a perfectly matched synthesis of creative engineering skills and the craft of gardening. Ultimately what matters is that people feel at home in landscape architecture and that it meets the functional demands placed on a particular object or the place. www.rmp-landschaftsarchitekten.de

ASTOC Architects and Planners, Cologne – Emscher Future master plan

ASTOC Architects and Planners has been based in Cologne for about 20 years and creates urban design and architectural projects in Germany and neighbouring countries. ASTOC Architects and Planners have realised numerous projects in the separate disciplines of architecture and urban design, many of them in long-term partnerships with commercial clients and public institutions. The office's urban

Dabei profitieren die städtebaulichen Projekte von den Erfahrungen in der Konzeption und Realisierung von Gebäuden, und die Hochbauprojekte erhalten durch die Kenntnisse um die städtebaulichen Zusammenhänge einen präzise verorteten architektonischen Ausdruck. Zahlreiche Preise und Auszeichnungen bestätigen die Qualität der Projekte. www.astoc.de

Landschaft planen + bauen GmbH, Berlin und Dortmund – Masterplan emscher:zukunft

Das Büro Landschaft planen + bauen GmbH arbeitet seit seiner Gründung vor 31 Jahren in den Segmenten Landschaftsarchitektur, Landschaftsplanung, Gewässerentwicklung, Regenwassermanagement, Erschließungsplanung und Projektmanagement. Die themen- und segmentübergreifend zusammengestellten Teams verfolgen gestalterisch hochwertige und ökologisch nachhaltige Projektziele, insbesondere auch in komplexen und technisch aufwändigen Fragestellungen. Besonderes Augenmerk der nutzerbezogenen Lösungs- und Planungsansätze liegt auf dem Lebenselement Wasser. Das umfassende Leistungsspektrum des Büros umfasst die verschiedenen Projektphasen von der übergeordneten Rahmenkonzeption bis zur detaillierten ausführungsreifen Einzellösung. www.lpb-berlin.de

Norbert Post · Hartmut Welters Architekten und Stadtplaner GmbH, Dortmund und Köln – Masterplan emscher:zukunft

Das Büro Post · Welters, gegründet 1990 von den Architekten und Stadtplanern Norbert Post und Hartmut Welters, ist mit ca. 25 Mitarbeitern unterschiedlicher Fachrichtungen in den Bereichen Architektur, Städtebau und Wettbewerbsmanagement tätig. Ziele im Tätigkeitsfeld Städtebau sind Erhalt und Schaffung lebenswerter Stadtquartiere, lebendiger Innenstädte und zukunftsfähiger Stadtstrukturen, die zur Bewältigung der globalen, energetischen und kulturellen Herausforderungen der Zukunft beitragen. In diesem Sinne entwickelt und plant das Team unter anderem gemeinschaftliche und innovative Wohnprojekte. Eine wichtige Rolle spielen dabei Energieeffizienz, das Wohnen für alle Lebensphasen und unterschiedliche Zielgruppen und die qualitätsvolle Gestaltung des Übergangs zwischen öffentlichem und privatem Raum. www.post-welters.de

design projects benefit from their experience in the conceptualisation and realisation of buildings, while ASTOC's knowledge of urban design issues in turn lends their building projects a strong architectural personality that is born of its place. Numerous awards and commendations confirm the high quality of their work. www.astoc.de

Landschaft planen + bauen GmbH, Berlin and Dortmund – Emscher Future master plan

The office of Landschaft planen + bauen GmbH has worked in the fields of landscape architecture, landscape planning, watercourse development, rainwater management, access planning and project management since its founding 31 years ago. Project teams consist of members from different disciplines and backgrounds with a view to achieving design solutions that are ecologically sustainable and of a high quality, especially where project tasks are complex and technically demanding. A special focus of the office's user-oriented design and planning approach is the vital element of water. The comprehensive spectrum of services offered by Landschaft planen+bauen covers the entire planning process from the overall conceptual framework to detailed construction planning. www.lpb-berlin.de

Norbert Post · Hartmut Welters Architekten und Stadtplaner GmbH, Dortmund and Cologne – Emscher Future master plan

Founded in 1990 by the architects and urban planners Norbert Post and Hartmut Welters, the office Post · Welters now numbers 25 members of staff and works in the fields of architecture, urban design and competition management. Its aims in the field of urban design are to maintain and to create liveable urban neighbourhoods, vibrant city centres and sustainable urban structures that contribute to overcoming the global, energy-related and cultural challenges of the future. To this end, the team also develops and plans innovative and communal housing schemes. Important aspects in this context are energy efficiency, the provision of living environments for all phases of life, a mix of different residents and the careful design of the transition between public and private space. www.post-welters.de

Wartner & Zeitzler Landschaftsarchitekten bdla und Stadtplaner, Landshut/Plattling – Gänsdorf Solar Field: a model for future renewable energy generation

The work of Wartner & Zeitzler encompasses most aspects of landscape and project planning. Their designs are characterised by a clear formal language with high-quality work in detail and adhere to the

Wartner & Zeitzler Landschaftsarchitekten bdla und Stadtplaner, Landshut/Plattling – Solarfeld Gänsdorf: ein wahres Märchen zur Energiewende

Das Büro Wartner & Zeitzler bearbeitet die meisten Bereiche der Landschafts- und Objektplanung. Die Planungen zeichnet eine klare Formensprache mit hoher Detailqualität aus, ganz im Sinne von „weniger ist oft mehr". Ziel ist dabei auch immer der sparsame Umgang mit den Schutzgütern Boden und Wasser und mit Rohstoffen. In allen Planungen versucht das Büro durch frühzeitige Kommunikation und Öffentlichkeitsarbeit Konflikte verschiedener Interessengruppen zu vermeiden. Bei der Umsetzung stärken die Planungsansätze die örtlichen Potenziale. www.wartner-zeitzler.de

Planergruppe Oberhausen, Oberhausen – Parkautobahn A42, Emscher Landschaftspark

Landschaft zu gestalten heißt für die 1973 gegründete Planergruppe Oberhausen, Raum erlebbar zu machen. Um die Wahrnehmung des Betrachters für die spezifischen Eigenschaften eines Ortes zu schärfen, werden architektonische Elemente und Materialien zurückhaltend, aber bewusst verwendet. Der Standort des Büros inmitten von Industrie- und Siedlungsraum ermöglicht eine detaillierte Sicht auf die Potenziale und Probleme der Ruhr-Emscher-Region. Sie schärft das Problembewusstsein auch für Projekte in anderen Regionen, ist die Basis für pragmatische Lösungsansätze und einen pfleglichen Umgang mit der Vegetation als Baumaterial. Die Planergruppe macht Räume durch Interpretation erfahrbar und nutzbar.
www.planergruppe-oberhausen.de

foundation 5+ landschaftsarchitekten, Kassel – Parkautobahn A42, Emscher Landschaftspark

foundation 5+ landschaftsarchitekten arbeiten seit 2002 in allen Bereichen und Maßstäben der Freiraumplanung, von der Objektplanung und dem Freiflächenmanagement über Rahmenplanungen bis zur regionalen und strategischen Freiraumplanung. Schwerpunkte liegen im öffentlichen Stadtraum, bei sozialen Trägern, im Wohnungsbau sowie in regionalen Freiraumsystemen. Durch prägnante, ordnende Eingriffe und Setzungen wird versucht, den jeweiligen Freiraum auf vielfältige Weise lesbar zu machen und Identifikationsmöglichkeiten anzubieten. Statt auf starre, konservierende Bilder setzt unsere Planung auf Entwicklung und Pflege als anpassungsfähige gestalterische Strategie.
www.foundation-kassel.de

principle of "less is often more". The aim is always to make responsible use of valuable resources such as soil, water and raw materials. The office takes a proactive, up-front approach to communications and publicity to avoid conflicts between different interest groups. The office's planning approach is always directed towards strengthening the respective potential of the site. www.wartner-zeitzler.de

Planergruppe Oberhausen, Oberhausen – A42 Park Motorway, Emscher Landscape Park

For the landscape architecture office Planergruppe Oberhausen, founded in 1973, designing landscapes is about enabling people to experience spaces. To raise awareness among users and visitors of the specific qualities of a place, the office makes careful but deliberate use of architectural elements and materials. The office's location in the heart of an industrial conurbation enhances the team's knowledge of the potential and problems of the Ruhr-Emscher region. This heightens the office's consciousness for challenges in other regions, serves as a basis for developing pragmatic approaches and for dealing sensitively with vegetation as a building material. Through a process of interpretation, the Planergruppe turns spaces into usable places and tangible experiences.
www.planergruppe-oberhausen.de

foundation 5+ landschaftsarchitekten, Kassel – A42 Park Motorway, Emscher Landscape Park

Since 2002, foundation 5+ landschaftsarchitekten has worked in all areas and at all scales of the planning of outdoor spaces, from individual projects and the management of outdoor facilities to land-use planning and regional and strategic development. Their work focuses on designs for the public urban realm, for social agencies and housing, and for outdoor spaces at a regional scale. Through the use of well-placed interventions and insertions that order space, the site is made legible at different levels to create opportunities for identification. Rather than preserving a fixed image of the landscape, the office aims, with the help of ongoing gardening measures, to formulate adaptable design strategies that develop over time.
www.foundation-kassel.de

planungsgruppe grün gmbh, Bremen – A281 – Zwischen Hightech, Laubenpieper und Natura 2000, Bremen

Die planungsgruppe grün wurde 1972 gegründet und ist in der Freiraumplanung und Umweltplanung tätig. Das Büro bearbeitet Projekte in allen Leistungsphasen und auf allen Maßstabsebenen. In der Freiraumplanung umfasst das Aufgabenspektrum die Gestaltung von nachhaltigen Freiräumen, ästhetisch, funktional, ökologisch und sozial konsistenten Freiraumstrukturen im urbanen und landschaftlichen/suburbanen Umfeld. Dies ist damit auch ein wichtiger Teil der Stadtplanung. In der Umweltplanung werden Vorhabenträger bei der Entwicklung und Umsetzung ihrer Projekte unterstützt; dazu gehören floristische und faunistische Erfassungen, die Erstellung umweltplanerischer Fachbeiträge (UVS, LBP, FFH-VP, Artenschutz) für Genehmigungsverfahren sowie die Verfahrensbegleitung. www.pgg.de

herrburg Landschaftsarchitekten, Berlin – BIGyard Gartenhof, Berlin

Seit 2003 realisieren herrburg Landschaftsarchitekten Freiräume an den Schnittstellen zwischen öffentlichem Raum, halböffentlichen Räumen und privaten Refugien. Ein sensibles Gespür für den Ort und die Bedürfnisse der Nutzer beeinflusst die Gestaltung von Schulen, Kitas, Spielplätzen und Einrichtungen für Menschen mit Behinderung. Dialoge mit Bauherren, Bürgerbeteiligung oder Workshopverfahren sind Grundlage für individuelle Lösungen. In die Bewältigung komplexer räumlicher oder logistischer Konstellationen fließt die langjährige Erfahrung der Büroteilhaber Mareike Schönherr, Susanne Friedburg und Markus Schönherr ein. Mit Leidenschaft für den gestalteten Raum werden die Projekte vom Konzept bis zum Bau umgesetzt. www.herrburg.de

Arbeitsgemeinschaft Almuth Krause, Landschaftsarchitektin, Leipzig und Susanne Schnorbusch, Architektin, Berlin – kiezPARK FORTUNA, Berlin

Almuth Krause gründete 1999 das Büro Spiel.Raum.Planung. Die Tätigkeit des Büros umfasst neben den klassischen Feldern wie Wohnumfeld, Spielräumen für Kinder und Parkanlagen auch gartendenkmalpflegerische Projekte. Seit 2003 besteht eine projektbezogene Zusammenarbeit mit der Architektin und Urban Designerin Su Schnorbusch, die seit 1995 selbstständig tätig ist. Schwerpunkt der Arbeitsgemeinschaft ist die gestalterische Aufwertung und gesellschaftliche Aktivierung von Rückbauflächen durch partizipative Planungsprozesse. Der kreative und transparente Austausch von Anwohnern und Eigentümern wird methodisch vorbereitet, fachlich kompetent begleitet, die finanzielle Umsetzbarkeit und maßstabsgerechte Entwicklung des

planungsgruppe grün gmbh, Bremen – A281 – Between high-tech, allotment gardens and Natura 2000, Bremen

Founded in 1972, the planungsgruppe grün works in the field of open space planning and environmental planning. The office conducts projects and provides services for all planning phases and at all scales of the landscape. The emphasis is on designing sustainable, aesthetic, functional, ecological and socially consistent outdoor spaces in urban and rural or suburban contexts, which are considered as an integral part of urban design. The office supports project developers in the development and realisation of their projects. This includes cataloguing the existing flora and fauna, documentation for planning permission applications (environmental impact assessments, landscape management plans, flora and fauna habitat assessments, protection of species) and assistance in the application procedure. www.pgg.de

herrburg Landschaftsarchitekten, Berlin – BIGyard garden courtyard, Berlin

Since 2003, the Berlin-based landscape architects herrburg Landschaftsarchitekten have been creating open spaces at the intersection of public space, semi-public space and private refuges. With a keen sense for the character of a place and the needs of users, the office designs outdoor spaces for schools, children's nurseries, playgrounds and facilities for the disabled. Dialogue with the client, public participation procedures or workshops serve as a basis for developing individual solutions. Through their combined years of experience, the office partners Mareike Schönherr, Susanne Friedburg and Markus Schönherr are proficient in handling complex spatial configurations or difficult logistical situations. They conduct all their projects from conception to completion. www.herrburg.de

Almuth Krause, landscape architect, Leipzig and Susanne Schnorbusch, architect, Berlin – kiezPARK FORTUNA, Berlin

Almuth Krause founded the office Spiel.Raum.Planung in 1999. The work of the office covers not only the classical disciplines of outdoor spaces for residential areas, playground areas for children and parks but also projects for historical garden conservation. Since 2003, Krause has worked on individual projects together with the freelance architect and urban designer Su Schnorbusch. The main focus of their collaborative work is the upgrading and social activation of disused sites, using participative planning processes. The creative and open exchange with residents and property owners is methodically prepared, professionally managed and ensures the financially viable realisation

Ortes gesichert. Ziel ist es, Beiräte zur eigenständigen Weiterentwicklung der häufig mit Fördermitteln finanzierten Freiräume zu bilden. www.su-schnorbusch.de, www.hobusch-kuppardt.de/frames/spielraum.html

Helleckes Landschaftsarchitektur, Karlsruhe – Grünzug Centro Verde, Mannheim

Das Büro Helleckes Landschaftsarchitektur wurde 1999 von Stefan Helleckes gegründet. Arbeitsschwerpunkte liegen in den Bereichen der Objektplanung Landschaftsarchitektur sowie städtebaulich-landschaftsarchitektonischer Wettbewerbe und Studien. Ziel ist es, Orte zu schaffen, die strukturell lesbar und identitätsstiftend sind. Stefan Helleckes ist als Preisrichter tätig und lehrt seit 1997 an mehreren Hochschulen in den Studiengängen Landschaftsarchitektur und Architektur. www.helleckes-landschaftsarchitektur.de

Glück Landschaftsarchitektur, Stuttgart – Privatgarten B, Stuttgart

Glück Landschaftsarchitektur wurde 2001 von Michael Glück gegründet. Die Projekte des Büros bewegen sich größtenteils im städtebaulichen und architektonischen Kontext. Neben Aufgaben im öffentlichen Raum gestaltet das Büro auch zahlreiche Privatgärten. Wesentliches Ziel im Entwurfsprozess ist es, die oftmals fragmentierte Umgebung neu zu ordnen, um damit Orientierung zu schaffen. Die Bearbeitung vielfältiger Wettbewerbsaufgaben ist ständige Inspiration für die Entwicklung des Büros. Die meist interdisziplinär geführten Arbeitsprozesse fördern Flexibilität und Kreativität. Das Büro wurde durch zahlreiche Wettbewerbserfolge ausgezeichnet. www.buero-glueck.de

Outside! Landschaftsarchitekten, Hamburg – Wohnumfeldverbesserung Wohnquartier Essener Straße, Hamburg

Outside! Landschaftsarchitekten wurde 1999 von Gerd Grunau und Gottfried Neder gegründet. Arbeitsschwerpunkte liegen in der Objektplanung, insbesondere im sozialen Wohnungsbau, öffentlichen Frei- und Spielräumen, Freizeitflächen und Kindertageseinrichtungen – wenn gewünscht mit intensiven Beteiligungsverfahren. Ziel ist es, die Potenziale eines Ortes zu erkennen und eine harmonische Einheit zwischen diesem und den Nutzern zu erreichen. Aus individuellen Ansätzen können Erlebnisräume entstehen, bei deren Entwicklung bereits die Herstellungs- und Folgekosten im Auge behalten werden. www.buero-outside.de

---

of a project at a scale that is appropriate for the development of the site. The aim is to establish committees that can continue to develop the spaces as public funding becomes available. www.su-schnorbusch.de, www.hobusch-kuppardt.de/frames/spielraum.html

Helleckes Landschaftsarchitektur, Karlsruhe – Centro Verde green corridor, Mannheim

Stefan Helleckes founded Helleckes Landschaftsarchitektur in 1999 in Karlsruhe. The office's main areas of work include project-based landscape architecture as well as urban design and landscape architecture competitions and studies. The office strives to design places that are structurally legible and create a sense of identity. Stefan Helleckes acts as a member of competition juries and since 1997 has taught at various universities on the subjects of landscape architecture and architecture. www.helleckes-landschaftsarchitektur.de

Glück Landschaftsarchitektur, Stuttgart – Private garden B, Stuttgart

Glück Landschaftsarchitektur was founded in 2001 by Michael Glück. While projects are mostly in a public urban design or architectural context, the office also designs numerous private gardens. The primary aim of the design process is to lend new order to the frequently fragmented surroundings so as to provide orientation. The office regularly takes part in a variety of competitions as a means of generating fresh inspiration for developing the office. Such projects often entail interdisciplinary working processes and foster flexibility and creativity, as evidenced by the numerous competition prizes the office has won. www.buero-glueck.de

Outside! Landschaftsarchitekten, Hamburg – Residential area improvements, Essener Strasse, Hamburg

Outside! Landschaftsarchitekten was founded in 1999 by Gerd Grunau and Gottfried Neder. The office focuses on social housing, the design of public open spaces and playgrounds, recreation areas and children's day-care centres – including comprehensive participation procedures as required. Their work aims to identify the potential of a place and to establish a harmonious balance between the place and its users. Individually developed approaches can result in the creation of spaces that facilitate a range of experiences, and in which the cost of implementation and later maintenance is considered during the development process. www.buero-outside.de

Über den bdla

Im Bund Deutscher Landschaftsarchitekten bdla haben sich Garten- und Landschaftsarchitekten zusammengeschlossen, um ihre beruflichen Interessen zu vertreten. Zu den Zielen des bdla gehört die Förderung der sozial und ökologisch orientierten Siedlungs- und Landschaftsentwicklung sowie der Freiraumplanung auf der Basis fundierter planerischer und gestalterischer Kenntnisse. Mit dem seit 1993 verliehenen Deutschen Landschaftsarchitektur-Preis würdigt der bdla, ohne Beschränkung auf seine Mitglieder, herausragende Planungsleistungen, die sowohl ästhetisch anspruchsvolle Lösungen als auch ökologische Zielsetzungen aufweisen. Der bdla ist Mitglied der International Federation of Landscape Architects IFLA und der IFLA Europe. Der Bundesverband hat seinen Sitz in Berlin.

DIE JURY 2013

August Forster, Bundesverband Garten-, Landschafts- und Sportplatzbau BGL, Bad Honnef

Dr. Bernd Hunger, GdW Bundesverband deutscher Wohnungs- und Immobilienunternehmen e.V., Berlin

Prof. Dr. Falk Jaeger, freier Architekturkritiker, Berlin

Prof. Dr.-Ing. Josef Kunz, Bundesministerium für Verkehr, Bau und Stadtentwicklung, Bonn

Norbert Portz, Deutscher Städte- und Gemeindebund, Bonn

Till Rehwaldt, Rehwaldt Landschaftsarchitekten, Dresden

Prof. Cornelius Scherzer, Fakultät Landbau/Landespflege, Hochschule für Technik und Wirtschaft, Dresden

Lukas Schweingruber, Schweingruber Zulauf Landschaftsarchitekten BSLA, Zürich/Schweiz

Prof. Antje Stokman, Institut für Landschaftsplanung und Ökologie ILPÖ, Universität Stuttgart

About the bdla

The Federation of German Landscape Architects (Bund Deutscher Landschaftsarchitekten or bdla) is the professional association for garden and landscape architects in Germany. Its goals include socially and ecologically oriented environmental development, as well as open-space planning based on competent planning and design skills. The German Landscape Architecture Prize, awarded since 1993 and also open to non-members, is the Federation's way of acknowledging outstanding achievements that combine sophisticated aesthetic solutions and ecological objectives. The bdla is a member of the International Federation of Landscape Architects (IFLA) and of IFLA Europe. The Federation's national headquarters are situated in Berlin.

THE JURY 2013

August Forster, Federal Association for Garden, Landscape and Sports Ground Construction (BGL), Bad Honnef

Dr. Bernd Hunger, German Association of Housing and Real Estate Companies (GdW e.V.), Berlin

Prof. Dr. Falk Jaeger, freelance architecture critic, Berlin

Prof. Dr.-Ing. Josef Kunz, Federal Ministry of Transport, Building and Urban Development, Bonn

Norbert Portz, German Federation of Cities and Municipalities, Bonn

Till Rehwaldt, Rehwaldt Landschaftsarchitekten, Dresden

Prof. Cornelius Scherzer, Faculty of Agriculture/Landscape Management, University of Applied Sciences (HTW), Dresden

Lukas Schweingruber, Schweingruber Zulauf Landschaftsarchitekten BSLA, Zurich/Switzerland

Prof. Antje Stokman, Institute for Landscape Planning and Ecology (ILPÖ), University of Stuttgart

Über die Autoren

JOHANNES BÖTTGER, geb. 1976, ist Landschaftsarchitekt und leitet das Büro urbane gestalt in Köln. Nach Studium an der TU München und der Universidade de Évora, Portugal, Diplom 2002 bei Prof. Peter Latz mit Auszeichnung des bdla, Gründung von jbbug 2006, heute: urbane gestalt johannes böttger landschaftsarchitekten. Zu den Projekten, die aus gewonnenen Wettbewerben hervorgingen, gehören der Klagesmarkt (Hannover City 2020+), die Siedlung Buchheimer Weg in Köln und der Friedhof Ingelheim. Auszeichnung im Deutschen Städtebaupreis, Deutscher Bauherrenpreis mit bdla-Preis für Freiraumgestaltung und urban quality award der Eurohypo AG in Silber. Johannes Böttger ist außerdem als Preisrichter und Gutachter tätig. Er war 2005–2011 Mitarbeiter der Leibniz Universität Hannover, lange bei Prof. Dr. Udo Weilacher. Lehrtätigkeit seit 2009 an der Texas A&M University, der Pennsylvania State University und als Gast in Seminaren und Workshops im In- und Ausland.

ANDREA GEBHARD ist Landschaftsarchitektin und Präsidentin des bdla. Sie studierte Geographie, Soziologie und Landespflege unter anderem an der Technischen Universität Berlin und der Universität Hannover. Ihre berufliche Laufbahn begann sie 1984 in zwei Architekturbüros, ehe sie in das Planungsreferat der Stadt München wechselte. 1993 wurde sie dort zur Leiterin der Abteilung Grünplanung berufen. Im Jahr 2000 übernahm sie die Geschäftsführung der BUGA München 2005 GmbH. 2006 gründete sie das Büro gebhard konzepte; seit 2009 führt sie das Büro mahl-gebhard-konzepte. 1990 trat sie in den bdla ein, 1992–1997 war sie 2. Vorsitzende des bdla Bayern, 2006–2007 bdla-Vizepräsidentin und seit 2007 steht Andrea Gebhard an der Spitze des Verbandes. Sie ist Mitglied des Beirates der Bundesstiftung Baukultur, Mitglied des Wissenschaftlichen Beirats des Bundesinstituts für Bau-, Stadt- und Raumforschung, Mitglied im Deutschen Werkbund, in der Deutschen Akademie für Städtebau und Landesplanung und im IBA-Expertenrat. 2011 berief Bundesbauminister Dr. Ramsauer sie in das Kuratorium zur Nationalen Stadtentwicklungspolitik.

ULRICH GROBER, geb. 1949, studierte Germanistik und Anglistik an der Goethe-Universität Frankfurt am Main und der Ruhr-Universität Bochum. Anschließend Tätigkeit in der Erwachsenenbildung und beim Aufbau eines soziokulturellen Zentrums im Ruhrgebiet. Seit 1992 ist er

About the authors

JOHANNES BÖTTGER, born in 1976, is a landscape architect and runs the office urbane gestalt in Cologne. After studying at the Technische Universität München and Universidade de Évora, Portugal, completing his diploma in 2002 (a bdla prize winner) under Prof. Peter Latz, he founded jbbug in 2006, which is now urbane gestalt johannes böttger landschaftsarchitekten. The office's projects are often the product of competition successes, among them the Klagesmarkt (Hanover City 2020+), the Buchheimer Weg estate in Cologne and Ingelheim Cemetery. He has earned numerous prizes including the German Urban Design Prize, the German Building Owners' Prize with a bdla Prize for Landscape Design and a Silver Urban Quality Award from the Eurohypo AG. Johannes Böttger also serves on competition juries and is an expert assessor. From 2005 until 2011, he worked at the Leibniz Universität Hannover under Prof. Dr. Udo Weilacher and since 2009 he has taught at Texas A&M University and at Pennsylvania State University. He is also a guest tutor for seminars and workshops in Germany and abroad.

ANDREA GEBHARD is a landscape architect and president of the bdla. She studied geography, sociology, landscape management and other fields at the Technische Universität Berlin and University of Hanover. She started work in two architecture offices in 1984 before joining the City of Munich Planning Authority. In 1993 she was appointed director of the Parks and Landscape Department, and in 2000 she became managing director of the BUGA München 2005 GmbH. In 2006 she founded the office gebhard konzepte, which became mahl-gebhard-konzepte in 2009. She first joined the bdla in 1990, serving from 1992–1997 as vice-chair of the Bavarian section. From 2006–2007 she was vice-president of the bdla before becoming president of the association in 2007. She is a member of the Council of the Federal Foundation of Baukultur, a member of the Scientific Committee of the Federal Institute for Research on Building, Urban Affairs and Spatial Development, a member of the Deutsche Werkbund, of the German Academy for Urban Design and Regional Planning and of the expert commission of the International Building Exhibition. In 2011, the Federal Minister of Building, Dr. Ramsauer, appointed her to the National Urban Development Policy Commission.

freier Autor, Journalist und Publizist. Zahlreiche Beiträge für Radio und Printmedien in den Themenfeldern Kulturgeschichte, Ökologie, Nachhaltigkeit und nachhaltige Lebensstile. Sein erstes Buch *Ausstieg in die Zukunft* über Projekte einer alternativen Ökonomie erschien 1998. Es folgte ein Buch über das Wandern als Übung zur Naturwahrnehmung und Entschleunigung (*Vom Wandern – neue Wege zu einer alten Kunst*, 2006). In der „Begriffsarchäologie" *Die Entdeckung der Nachhaltigkeit – Kulturgeschichte eines Begriffs* (2010, englische Ausgabe *Sustainability – a cultural history*, 2012) geht er den historischen Aufladungen des modernen Nachhaltigkeitsbegriffs nach. Seitdem zahlreiche Vorträge und Seminare zum Thema.

MICHAEL MÜLLER, geb. 1964, ist als Senator für Stadtentwicklung und Umwelt seit 2011 für wichtige Zukunftsfragen Berlins verantwortlich – von Stadtplanung und Baukultur, über Wohnen und Verkehr bis zum Klimaschutz und zur Entwicklung des Stadtgrüns. Als SPD-Mitglied seit 1981 hat er sich in seinem Heimatbezirk Berlin-Tempelhof engagiert und wechselte 1996 ins Berliner Abgeordnetenhaus, wo er ab 2001 Fraktionsvorsitzender der SPD war. Von 2004 bis 2012 war er Landesvorsitzender der Berliner SPD. Seit der Abgeordnetenhauswahl 2011 ist er Bürgermeister von Berlin und leitet die größte Berliner Verwaltung.

TILL REHWALDT, geb. 1965, studierte von 1985 bis 1990 an der Technischen Universität Dresden und war am dortigen Institut für Landschaftsarchitektur bis 1996 als wissenschaftlicher Mitarbeiter tätig. Nach dem Gewinn eines Wettbewerbs war der Landschaftspark Zittau-Olbersdorf 1999 sein erstes bedeutendes Werk. Inzwischen sind eine Reihe von Projekten hinzugekommen, die sich vor allem mit Fragestellungen im öffentlichen Raum befassen. Die Planung des ULAP-Platzes in Berlin-Mitte erhielt 2009 den Deutschen Landschaftsarchitektur-Preis. Von 2006 bis 2008 war Till Rehwaldt Gastprofessor am Fachgebiet Objektplanung und Entwerfen der Technischen Universität Berlin. Regelmäßig ist er als Preisrichter in Wettbewerbsverfahren sowie als Gutachter und Autor tätig.

CHRISTOPH ROSENKRANZ, geb. 1981, studierte Stadt- und Regionalplanung an der Brandenburgischen Technischen Universität Cottbus. DAAD-Stipendium an der Technischen Universität Graz. Seit 2008 ist er bei ts|pk thies schröder planungskommunikation in Berlin in den Bereichen innovative Beteiligungsverfahren, Publikationen zur Landschaftsarchitektur sowie Erarbeitung von Stadt- und Regionalentwicklungskonzepten tätig. Im Mittelpunkt der Projektbetreuung stehen die

ULRICH GROBER, born in 1949, studied German and English literature at the Goethe University Frankfurt am Main and the Ruhr-Universität Bochum. After working in adult education and establishing a sociocultural centre in the Ruhr conurbation, he became a freelance author, journalist and publicist in 1992. He has written numerous contributions for radio and print media on the topics of cultural history, ecology, sustainability and sustainable lifestyles. His first book, *Ausstieg in die Zukunft*, on projects for an alternative economic model was published in 1998. In 2006, a second book followed on kiking as an exercise in appreciating nature and slowing down (*Vom Wandern – neue Wege zu einer alten Kunst*, 2006). In his etymological-archaeological investigation *Sustainability – a cultural history*, first published in German in 2010 and translated into English in 2012, he traces the historical origins of the modern notion of sustainability. Since then he has given numerous lectures and seminars on the subject.

MICHAEL MÜLLER, born in 1964, has been Berlin Senator for Urban Development and the Environment since 2011 and is responsible for important issues concerning the development of Berlin including urban design and architecture, housing and transport, climate control and the development of Berlin's urban green. As a member of the Social-Democratic Party (SPD), he has been actively involved in his home district, Berlin-Tempelhof since 1981, joining the Berlin House of Representatives in 1996 where he became Chairman of the SPD parliamentary group in 2001. From 2004 to 2012, he was Chairman of the SPD in the federal state of Berlin, and after the elections in the House of Representatives in 2011, he became Mayor of Berlin, a position below the Governing Mayor, heading the largest of the city's senate departments.

TILL REHWALDT, born in 1965, studied from 1985 to 1990 at the Technische Universität Dresden, where he stayed on as a member of staff at the Institute for Landscape Architecture until 1996. His first important work, the Landscape Park in Zittau-Olbersdorf, was realised in 1999 after winning the competition. Since then a series of projects have followed, all of which deal primarily with aspects of public space. His design for the ULAP Square in Berlin-Mitte was awarded the German Landscape Architecture Prize in 2009. From 2006 to 2008, Till Rehwaldt was visiting professor at the Department of Landscape Architecture and Environmental Planning at the Technische Universität Berlin. He regularly serves as a competition juror and also works as an expert assessor and author.

Erarbeitung gemeinsamer Lösungen mit unterschiedlichen Interessengruppen sowie die Steuerung der Kommunikation von Konzeption und Vorbereitung bis zur Durchführung und Dokumentation.

PROFESSOR ARNO SIGHART SCHMID, geb. 1937. Nach Gärtnerlehre Studium der Garten- und Landschaftsgestaltung an der Staatlichen Lehr- und Forschungsanstalt für Gartenbau Weihenstephan/Ingenieurschule für Gartenbau (später FH). 1961–1973 als Resident Landscape Architect in der Karibik tätig. 1974 Partner im Büro Eppinger-Schmid, Freie Landschaftsarchitekten in Leonberg, ab 1993 als Partnerschaft Prof. Schmid | Treiber | Partner, ab 2002 zusätzliches Büro Prof. Arno S. Schmid + Manfred Rauh Landschaftsarchitekten in Neu-Ulm. Mitglied im bdla seit 1961, Fellow der American Society of Landscape Architects, Korrespondierendes Ehrenmitglied des britischen Landscape Institute, Mitglied der Deutschen Akademie für Städtebau und Landesplanung (DASL). Diverse Ehrenämter im bdla und in der European Foundation for Landscape Architecture (EFLA)/IFLA Europe. 1983–1989 Präsident des bdla, 1996–2000 Präsident der International Federation of Landscape Architects (IFLA), 2004–2010 Präsident der Bundesarchitektenkammer.

CORNELIA SCHMIDT, geb. 1986, studierte Landschaftsarchitektur an der Technischen Universität Dresden und der Haute École Charlemagne ISI in Gembloux. Sie ist Preisträgerin des Studentenwettbewerbes Mitteldeutschland des bdla 2009 und 2010. Ihre Diplomarbeit über das Thema Licht im Freiraum von 2011 wurde mit der Sonja-Bernadotte-Medaille für Gartenkultur und dem Kurt-Beyer-Preis 2011 prämiert. Arbeit als Diplom-Ingenieurin für Landschaftsarchitektur bei BGHplan in Trier im Bereich Objektplanung/Landschaftsplanung; Hospitantin des bdla; ehrenamtliche Tätigkeit im Vorstand des Landesverbandes der DGGL Saar-Mosel.

THIES SCHRÖDER, geb. 1965, leitet ts|pk thies schröder planungskommunikation und den L&H Verlag in Berlin. Er studierte Landschaftsplanung an der Technischen Universität Berlin. Er ist Fachjournalist, Redakteur und Autor im Bereich Landschaftsarchitektur, Städtebau und Regionalentwicklung und entwickelt und betreut Kommunikationsprodukte und -konzepte in Zusammenarbeit mit privaten und öffentlichen Auftraggebern. Zu seinen Buchpublikationen zählen unter anderem *Inszenierte Naturen. Zeitgenössische Landschaftsarchitektur in Europa*, *Gartenkunst 2001* sowie *Mögliche Räume. Stadt schafft Landschaft*. Thies Schröder ist zudem Geschäftsführer der Ferropolis GmbH und betreibt in diesem Projekt eine Standortentwicklung per Kulturevents.

CHRISTOPH ROSENKRANZ, born in 1981, studied town and regional planning at Brandenburg University of Technology in Cottbus and at Graz University of Technology on a DAAD scholarship. In 2008 he joined ts|pk thies schröder planungskommunikation in Berlin and has worked on innovative public participation procedures, landscape architecture publications and the development of town and regional development concepts. A central aspect of his project consultancy work is the elaboration of joint solutions together with different interest groups as well as the guiding of communications from the concept and preparation phase through to implementation and documentation.

PROFESSOR ARNO SIGHART SCHMID, born in 1937, studied garden and landscape design at the State School and Research Institute for Horticulture in Weihenstephan/Engineering School for Horticulture (now the University of Applied Sciences) after a prior apprenticeship as a gardener. From 1961–1973 he was a resident landscape architect in the Caribbean. In 1974 he co-founded the landscape architecture partnership Eppinger-Schmid in Leonberg, renamed Prof. Schmid | Treiber | Partner in 1993, and in 2002 additionally established Prof. Arno S. Schmid + Manfred Rauh Landscape Architects in Neu-Ulm. He is an honorary corresponding member of the British Landscape Institute, a member of the German Academy for Urban and Regional Spatial Planning (DASL) and undertakes voluntary work for the bdla and the EFLA/IFLA Europe. From 1983–1989 he was president of the bdla, from 1996–2000 president of the International Federation of Landscape Architects (IFLA) and from 2004–2010 president of the Federal Chamber of German Architects.

CORNELIA SCHMIDT, born in 1986, studied landscape architecture at the TU Dresden and the Haute École Charlemagne ISI in Gembloux. In 2009 and 2010, she was a recipient of the student award for the Central Germany section of the bdla and her diploma project on the subject of light in open spaces, completed in 2011, was awarded the Sonja Bernadotte Medal for Garden Culture and the Kurt Beyer Prize in 2011. She has since worked as qualified landscape architect for BGHplan in Trier and as an intern with the bdla. She is a honorary member of the board of the Saar-Mosel division of the German Society for Garden Architecture and Landscape Culture (DGGL).

THIES SCHRÖDER, born in 1965, is director of ts|pk thies schröder planungskommunikation and the L&H Verlag publishing company in Berlin. He studied landscape planning at the Technische Universität

DR. KARLHEINZ STEINMÜLLER, geb. 1950, war nach dem Physik- und Philosophiestudium in Chemnitz und Berlin zuerst an der Ostberliner Akademie der Wissenschaften mit der Modellierung von Ökosystemen befasst. In den 1980er Jahren hat er gemeinsam mit seiner Frau Angela Steinmüller mehrere Science-Fiction-Bücher geschrieben. 1991 ging er an das Sekretariat für Zukunftsforschung in Gelsenkirchen, das vorwiegend Zukunftsstudien für die Landesregierung NRW durchführte. 1997 gründete er mit Klaus Burmeister die Z_punkt GmbH The Foresight Company, deren Wissenschaftlicher Direktor er jetzt ist. Z_punkt ist ein international tätiges Beratungsunternehmen für strategische Zukunftsfragen, das sich mit der Übersetzung von Trend- und Zukunftsforschung in die Praxis des strategischen Managements befasst. Der private Think Tank mit Sitz in Köln arbeitet zumeist für namhafte deutsche und internationale Unternehmen, aber auch für öffentliche Auftraggeber. Zu den Publikationen von Angela und Karlheinz Steinmüller gehören die Sachbücher *Wild Cards* (2004) und *Die Zukunft der Technologien* (2006) sowie das Science-Fiction-Buch *Computerdämmerung* (2010).

BJÖRN THEIS, geb. 1976, ist Senior Foresight Consultant bei Z_punkt mit einem Arbeitsschwerpunkt Szenario-Entwicklung in den Bereichen Gesellschaft, Politik, Sicherheit und Consumer Goods. Ein weiterer Schwerpunkt ist die Identifizierung und Analyse von Emerging Issues und Weak Signals. Daneben befasst er sich mit digitaler Kultur sowie der Übertragung von ethnologischen Forschungsmethoden in die Zukunftsforschung. Neben seiner Tätigkeit bei Z_punkt unterrichtet Björn Theis Zukunftsforschung an der Freien Universität Berlin.

PROFESSOR DR. KLAUS TÖPFER ist Exekutivdirektor des Institute for Advanced Sustainability Studies (IASS) Potsdam sowie ehemaliger Exekutivdirektor des Umweltprogramms der Vereinten Nationen (UNEP). Er absolvierte ein Studium der Volkswirtschaftslehre und promovierte in Münster. Er war Bundesminister für Umwelt, Naturschutz und Reaktorsicherheit und Bundesminister für Raumordnung, Bauwesen und Städtebau sowie Mitglied des Deutschen Bundestages. Zu Professor Töpfers zahlreichen Auszeichnungen und Ehrungen zählen das Große Bundesverdienstkreuz, der Deutsche Umweltpreis der Deutschen Bundesstiftung Umwelt (DBU) und der Deutsche Nachhaltigkeitspreis für sein Lebenswerk. 2012 wurde er in die Earth Hall of Fame Kyoto aufgenommen.

Berlin. He is a journalist, editor and author in the fields of landscape architecture, urban and regional development and develops and oversees communication products and concepts in cooperation with private and public clients. His published works include *Changes in Scenery – Contemporary Landscape Architecture in Europe*, *Garden Art 2001*, and *Mögliche Räume. Stadt schafft Landschaft*. Thies Schröder is also director of Ferropolis GmbH and promotes the location through the means of cultural events.

DR. KARLHEINZ STEINMÜLLER, born in 1950, studied physics and philosophy in Chemnitz and Berlin before joining the East German Academy of Sciences where he was involved in modelling ecosystems. In the 1980s, together with his wife Angela Steinmüller, he wrote several science fiction books. In 1991 he joined the Secretariat for Futures Studies at Gelsenkirchen undertaking futures studies for the government of North Rhine-Westphalia in particular. In 1997, together with Klaus Burmeister, he founded Z_punkt GmbH The Foresight Company, of which he is scientific director. Z_punkt is an internationally operating strategy and foresight consultancy that translates findings derived from trend and futures research into practical advice for strategic management. The private think tank based in Cologne works predominantly for prominent German and international businesses but also for public institutions. Publications by Angela and Karlheinz Steinmüller include *Wild Cards* (2004), *Die Zukunft der Technologien* (2006) and the science fiction book *Computerdämmerung* (2010).

BJÖRN THEIS, born in 1976, is a senior foresight consultant at Z_punkt, working predominantly on developing scenarios in the fields of society, politics, security and consumer goods. A further focal area of work is the identification and analysis of "emerging issues" and "weak signals". In addition, he investigates digital culture and the transfer of ethnological research methods into futures research. Alongside his work for Z_punkt, he teaches Futures Research at the Freie Universität Berlin.

PROFESSOR DR. KLAUS TÖPFER is the executive director of the Institute for Advanced Sustainability Studies (IASS) in Potsdam and former executive director of the United Nations Environment Programme (UNEP). He studied economics, earning his doctorate from the University of Münster. He was German Federal Minister for

DR.-ING. NICOLE UHRIG, geb. 1970, ist freiberufliche Landschaftsarchitektin und Fachautorin. Sie schloss ihr Studium der Landschaftsplanung an der Technischen Universität Berlin 1997 ab und studierte ein Jahr Landschaftsarchitektur und Städtebau an der Escola Tècnica Superior d'Arquitectura in Barcelona. Sie war bis 2004 in den Planungsbüros Gabriele Kiefer und ST raum a. in Berlin tätig und 2004–2008 wissenschaftliche Mitarbeiterin am Lehrstuhl Landschaftsarchitektur und Entwerfen von Prof. Dr. Udo Weilacher an der Leibniz Universität Hannover. Sie promovierte 2011 zum Thema „Landschaftsarchitektur als Baustein unternehmerischer Corporate Identity-Konzepte" an der Technischen Universität München. Nicole Uhrig ist an verschiedenen Universitäten und Hochschulen in Lehre und Forschung tätig und seit 2013 Gastprofessorin an der Hochschule Anhalt.

PROFESSOR GÜNTHER VOGT, geb. 1957, ist Landschaftsarchitekt, Inhaber und Geschäftsführer von Vogt Landschaftsarchitekten Zürich, London und Berlin. Er lehrt seit 2005 als Professor für Landschaftsarchitektur an der ETH Zürich. 2012 hatte er eine Gastprofessur an der Graduate School of Design der Harvard University. Günther Vogt war von 2007 bis 2011 Vorsitzender des Netzwerk Stadt und Landschaft (NSL) der ETH Zürich. 2010 gründete er das Case Studio VOGT als Büro und Hochschule verbindende Plattform. 2012 wurde er vom Schweizer Bundesamt für Kultur mit dem Prix Meret Oppenheim für seine herausragenden Leistungen als Landschaftsarchitekt, seine städtebaulichen Projekte und Untersuchungen sowie seine intensive und wechselseitig befruchtende Zusammenarbeit mit Architektur- und Kunstschaffenden ausgezeichnet.

the Environment, Nature Conservation and Nuclear Safety and subsequently Federal Minister for Regional Planning, Housing and Urban Development and a member of the German Bundestag. Professor Töpfer has received numerous awards and honours, including the Federal Cross of Merit, the German Environmental Award of the Deutsche Bundesstiftung Umwelt and the German Sustainability Award for his lifetime achievements in the field of sustainability. In 2012 he was inducted in the Kyoto Earth Hall of Fame.

DR.-ING. NICOLE UHRIG, born in 1970, is a freelance landscape architect and author. She completed her studies in landscape planning at the Technische Universität Berlin in 1997 and spent a year studying landscape architecture and urban design at the Escola Tècnica Superior d'Arquitectura in Barcelona. She worked for the offices of Gabriele Kiefer and ST raum a. in Berlin before joining the Chair for Landscape Architecture and Design at the Leibniz Universität Hannover under Prof. Dr. Udo Weilacher from 2004–2008. In 2011 she completed her doctorate with a dissertation on landscape architecture as an integral part in corporate identity concepts at the Technische Universität München. Nicole Uhrig has taught and researched at various universities and universities of applied sciences and in 2013 became visiting professor at Anhalt University of Applied Sciences.

PROFESSOR GÜNTHER VOGT, born in 1957, is a landscape architect, founder and managing director of Vogt Landschaftsarchitekten with offices in Zurich, London and Berlin. Since 2005, he has been Professor of Landscape Architecture at the ETH Zurich. In 2012 he took up a guest professorship at the Graduate School of Design at Harvard University. From 2007 to 2011, he was director of the Network City and Landscape (NSL) at the ETH Zurich and in 2010 he founded Case Studio VOGT as a platform for connecting office and university. In 2012 he was awarded the Prix Meret Oppenheim of the Swiss Bundesamt für Kultur for his outstanding services as a landscape architect, for his urban design projects and studies as well as his intensive and mutually beneficial collaborations with architects and artists.

Über die Förderer der Publikation

ALLIANZ UMWELTSTIFTUNG Anlässlich ihres 100-jährigen Firmenjubiläums gründete die Allianz SE im Jahr 1990 die Allianz Umweltstiftung. Ziel der Stiftungstätigkeit ist, zu neuen Entwicklungen für Mensch und Umwelt anzuregen, zu außergewöhnlichen Leistungen anzuspornen und zur Kreativität zu ermuntern. Seit 1990 bewilligte die Allianz Umweltstiftung mehr als 60 Mio. Euro als Fördermittel für mehr als 90 Groß- und ca. 4.200 Kleinprojekte. Bundesweit führt die Stiftung die Aktion „Blauer Adler" durch; die jährliche Verleihung des Deutschen Klimapreises an Schulen/Schüler sowie die Benediktbeurer Gespräche runden die Aktivitäten ab. https://umweltstiftung.allianz.de/

BRUNS-PFLANZEN-EXPORT GMBH & CO. KG Bruns-Pflanzen-Export wurde 1876 durch den ersten Gärtner der Familie, Diedrich-Gerhard Bruns, gegründet und ist eine der größten Baumschulen Europas. Die mehr als 500 Hektar umfassenden Anbauflächen liegen im Ammerland rund um das Zwischenahner Meer. 80 Prozent der Pflanzen werden über den Garten- und Landschaftsbau für die Objekt- und Landschaftsbegrünung für private und auch öffentliche Investoren geliefert. 20 Prozent des Umsatzes liegen im Gartencenter-Bereich. Produktionsschwerpunkte sind Solitärgehölze und bis zu 40-jährige Solitärbäume sowie die Produktion von Formgehölzen. Die Pflanzen werden deutschland-, aber auch europaweit verkauft. www.bruns.de

BUNDESVERBAND GARTEN-, LANDSCHAFTS- UND SPORTPLATZBAU E.V. (BGL) Der Bundesverband Garten-, Landschafts- und Sportplatzbau e.V. (BGL) ist ein Wirtschafts- und Arbeitgeberverband. Er vertritt die Interessen des deutschen Garten-, Landschafts- und Sportplatzbaus auf Bundesebene und in Europa. In seinen zwölf Landesverbänden sind über 3.500 vorwiegend kleinere und mittelständische Mitgliedsunternehmen organisiert. Als Dienstleister geben sie sich am geschützten Signum mit dem Zusatz „Ihre Experten für Garten & Landschaft" zu erkennen und bieten maßgeschneiderte, individuelle Lösungen rund ums Bauen mit Grün. Damit erzielen sie zurzeit über 60 Prozent des gesamten Marktumsatzes von über 6 Mrd. Euro im GaLa-Bau in Deutschland. Präsident ist August Forster. www.galabau.de

COMPUTERWORKS GMBH Die ComputerWorks GmbH, 1989 in Lörrach gegründet, entwickelt und vertreibt Softwarelösungen für Apple Macintosh® und Microsoft Windows®. In Lörrach und Basel betreuen mehr

About the sponsors of the publication

ALLIANZ UMWELTSTIFTUNG The Allianz SE founded the Allianz Umweltstiftung on the occasion of its centenary in 1990. The activities of the foundation are directed towards promoting new developments for people and the environment, motivating outstanding initiatives and stimulating creativity. Since 1990, the Allianz Umweltstiftung has provided more than 60 million Euros of funding for more than 90 large and approximately 4,200 smaller projects. The foundation runs the nationwide "Blauer Adler" campaign, awards the annual Deutscher Klimapreis to schools and its pupils, and organises the Benediktbeurer Gespräche series of dialogues. https://umweltstiftung.allianz.de

BRUNS-PFLANZEN-EXPORT GMBH & CO. KG Bruns-Pflanzen-Export was founded in 1876 by Diedrich-Gerhard Bruns, the first gardener in the family. Over the course of 130 years, Bruns has become one of the largest tree nurseries in Europe. Its plants are cultivated on over 500 hectares of land in the Ammerland region around the Lake Zwischenahner Meer. Eighty percent of the plants it produces are sold to private or public clients via gardening and landscaping contractors, while 20 percent of the turnover is generated in garden centre sales. Bruns specialises in solitaire woody plants and up to 40-year-old solitary trees as well as the production of form-clipped woody plants. Bruns' plants are sold throughout Germany and Europe. www.bruns.de

BUNDESVERBAND GARTEN-, LANDSCHAFTS- UND SPORTPLATZBAU E. V. (BGL) The Federal Association for Garden, Landscape and Sports Ground Construction is an umbrella organisation for the industry and employers. It represents the interests of gardeners, landscaping companies and sports venue constructors at a national and European level. Its twelve federal associations represent the interests of over 3,500 predominantly small and medium-sized businesses. As a service provider, the association presents itself as "Your Expert for Gardens and Landscaping", offering made-to-measure, individual solutions for all aspects of landscaping and garden construction. Its members account for over 60 percent of the 6 billion Euros total market turnover in gardening and landscaping in Germany. The president of the association is August Forster. www.galabau.de

COMPUTERWORKS GMBH ComputerWorks GmbH, founded in 1989 in Lörrach, develops and sells software for Apple Macintosh® and

als 50 Mitarbeiter den deutschsprachigen Markt. ComputerWorks ist spezialisiert auf Software für Bauwesen und Design. Der Schwerpunkt liegt bei der CAD-Software Vectorworks. Mit mehr als 450.000 Anwendern weltweit ist Vectorworks das meistgenutzte CAD-Programm auf dem Apple Macintosh und eines der führenden für Windows. Zu den Anwendern zählen z. B. Landschaftsarchitekten, Architekten, Innenarchitekten, Städtebauer, Garten- und Landschaftsbauer, technische Zeichner, Designer, Eventveranstalter und Kommunen. www.computerworks.de

DEUTSCHER MIETERBUND E. V. Der Deutsche Mieterbund (DMB) ist der Dachverband von 320 örtlichen Mietervereinen mit mehr als 500 Beratungsstellen in ganz Deutschland. Die Mietervereine sind Interessenvertreter und Rechtsberater vor Ort. Der Dachverband vertritt die politischen Interessen aller Mieter. Zu den Themen gehören sowohl „klassische" Mieterthemen als auch Fragen der energetischen Modernisierung und des verstärkten Einsatzes erneuerbarer Energien, des Städtebaus, der Städtebauförderung und der Gestaltung des Wohnumfeldes. Die Arbeit wird aus Mitgliedsbeiträgen finanziert. Eine öffentliche Förderung gibt es nicht. www.mieterbund.de

GDW BUNDESVERBAND DEUTSCHER WOHNUNGS- UND IMMOBILIENUNTERNEHMEN Der GdW Bundesverband deutscher Wohnungs- und Immobilienunternehmen vertritt als größter deutscher Branchendachverband bundesweit und auf europäischer Ebene rund 3.000 kommunale, genossenschaftliche, kirchliche, privatwirtschaftliche, landes- und bundeseigene Wohnungsunternehmen. Sie bewirtschaften rund sechs Millionen Wohnungen, in denen über 13 Mio. Menschen wohnen. Der GdW repräsentiert damit Wohnungsunternehmen, die fast 30 Prozent aller Mietwohnungen in Deutschland bewirtschaften. www.gdw.de

RINN BETON- UND NATURSTEIN GMBH & CO. KG Rinn Beton- und Naturstein ist ein modernes Familienunternehmen in der vierten Generation. Es produziert das komplette Sortiment an Betonsteinprodukten für Garten- und Landschaftsbau sowie Stadtgestaltung. Spezialitäten sind großformatige Magnumplatten für öffentliche Flächen, Maßanfertigungen und Sonderfarben. Als einziger Hersteller hat Rinn Betonsteine mit Teflon®-Schutz entwickelt, die besonders reinigungsfreundlich, farbstabil und strapazierfähig sind. Nachhaltiges Denken bestimmt das Handeln von Rinn, mit dem Ziel einer Balance zwischen ökologischen, sozialen und ökonomischen Ansprüchen. www.rinn.net

Microsoft Windows®. In Lörrach and Basel, over 50 staff cater for the German language market. ComputerWorks specialises in software for the construction and design industries, most notably the CAD software Vectorworks. With more than 450,000 installations worldwide, Vectorworks is the most widely used CAD software on the Apple Macintosh and a leading program on Windows, used by landscape architects, architects, interior designers, urban designers, garden and landscaping firms, draughtsmen, industrial designers, event designers and public authorities, among others. www.computerworks.de

DEUTSCHER MIETERBUND E.V. The German Tenants' Association (DMB) is an umbrella organisation for 320 local tenants' associations that represent tenants locally, with more than 500 legal advice centres throughout Germany. The DMB represents the interests of all tenants on a political level. The associations deal with both traditional tenants' issues as well as aspects such as energy-efficient modernisation, the increased use of renewable energy resources, issues of urban planning and grant funding and the design of living environments. The work of the association is financed by membership fees; the organisation receives no public funding. www.mieterbund.de

GDW BUNDESVERBAND DEUTSCHER WOHNUNGS- UND IMMOBILIENUNTERNEHMEN The GdW, the German Association of Housing and Real Estate Companies, as the largest sectoral German umbrella organisation, represents nationwide and at a European level some 3,000 municipal, cooperative, church-run, commercial, state and national housing associations. Together, they manage some six million apartments housing 13 million people. The GdW therefore represents housing associations that together manage almost 30 percent of all rented accommodation in Germany. www.gdw.de

RINN BETON- UND NATURSTEIN GMBH & CO. KG Rinn is a modern fourth-generation family business and produces a complete range of pre-cast concrete and stone products for use in garden and landscape architecture and urban environments. Specialist products include large-format Magnum paving slabs for public areas as well as made-to-measure items and special colours for individual solutions. Rinn is the only manufacturer to have developed pre-cast concrete products with Teflon® protection that makes them easy to clean, colourfast and hard-wearing. Rinn is committed to sustainability and strives to achieve a balance between ecological, social and economic aims in all its activities. www.rinn.net

Personen- und Projektregister

A24 Landschaft	
Planten un Blomen, Eingang Neue Messe, Hamburg	129
Andritzky, Michael	6
ANNABAU Architektur und Landschaft	
Spielplatz auf dem Schulberg, Wiesbaden	117
ASTOC Architects and Planners	157
Masterplan emscher:zukunft	76, 78–81
Atelier Dreiseitl	
Bishan Ang-Mo Kio Park, Singapur	20
Zollhallenplatz, Freiburg/Breisgau	17
Aufmkolk, Gerd	63
bauchplan).(	
grenze als ort. brücke als gelenk. Murbrücke zwischen Bad Radkersburg/Österreich und Gornja Radgona/Slowenien	139
Bauer, Friederike	37
bbz landschaftsarchitekten	
:terra nova, Rhein-Erft-Kreis	18
BERNARD und SATTLER Landschaftsarchitekten	
Temporäre Freiflächengestaltung am Spittelmarkt, Berlin	135
BIG – Bjarke Ingels Group	
Superkilen, Kopenhagen	72–73
Bloch, Ernst	30
Böttger, Johannes	116–133, 143, 163
Brehmer, Arthur	116
Brock, Bazon	42
Brückner, Heike	
Das Grüne Quadrat – ein Park für Bitterfeld, Bitterfeld-Wolfen	28, 125
Bucher, Annemarie	151
Burattoni, Gianni	
Das Grüne Quadrat – ein Park für Bitterfeld, Bitterfeld-Wolfen	28, 125
Burckhardt, Lucius	38, 47
Campe, Joachim Heinrich	10
Carlowitz, Hans Carl von	13, 14, 15, 17, 22, 27
Case Studio VOGT	42
Charles, Prinz von Wales	11
club L94 Landschaftsarchitekten GmbH	155
Elsbethenareal und Schrannenplatz, Memmingen	48, 64–65
Crutzen, Paul	27
De Andrade Adauto Costa, Isabella	107, 108
Debord, Guy-Ernest	42
Dexler, Lorenz	73
Dobrzanski, Harry	
Ortsmitte Eugendorf	130
DOT 2 Groth-Rüter-Zeitnitz Landschaftsarchitekten	
Gorch-Fock-Schule, Hamburg	121
el:ch landschaftsarchitekten	
Wohnanlage Gern 64, München	35
Evelyn, John	12, 13, 23
Felber, Stephan	102
Flor, Frank	65
Forster, August	162
foundation 5+ landschaftsarchitekten	159
Parkautobahn A42, Emscher Landschaftspark	76, 84–85
Freiherr von Wendt, Maximilian	
Golf Resort Castelfalfi, Montaione	9
Friedburg, Susanne	89
Fromm, Stefan	14, 48, 71, 156
Fugger-Babenhausen, Annina Gräfin	102
Gebhard, Andrea	6–7, 116–132, 163
Geitz, Peter	10

Index of persons and projects

A24 Landschaft	
Planten un Blomen, Neue Messe entrance, Hamburg	129
Andritzky, Michael	6
ANNABAU Architektur und Landschaft	
Playground on the Schulberg, Wiesbaden	117
ASTOC Architects and Planners	157
Emscher Future master plan	77, 78–81
Atelier Dreiseitl	
Bishan Ang-Mo Kio Park, Singapore	20
Zollhallenplatz, Freiburg/Breisgau	17
Aufmkolk, Gerd	63
bauchplan).(	
grenze als ort. brücke als gelenk. Mur bridge at the border between Bad Radkersburg/Austria and Gornja Radgona/Slovenia	139
Bauer, Friederike	37
bbz landschaftsarchitekten	
:terra nova, Rhine-Erft district	18
BERNARD und SATTLER Landschaftsarchitekten	
Temporary design of the Spittelmarkt, Berlin	135
BIG – Bjarke Ingels Group	
Superkilen, Copenhagen	72–73
Bloch, Ernst	30
Böttger, Johannes	116–133, 143, 163
Brehmer, Arthur	116
Brock, Bazon	42
Brückner, Heike	
Green Square landscape park, Bitterfeld-Wolfen	28, 125
Bucher, Annemarie	151
Burattoni, Gianni	
Green Square landscape park, Bitterfeld-Wolfen	28, 125
Burckhardt, Lucius	38, 47
Campe, Joachim Heinrich	10
Carlowitz, Hans Carl von	13, 14, 16, 20, 27
Case Studio VOGT	42
Charles, Prince of Wales	11
club L94 Landschaftsarchitekten GmbH	155
Elsbethenareal and Schrannenplatz, Memmingen	49, 64–65
Confucius	9
Crutzen, Paul	27
De Andrade Adauto Costa, Isabella	107, 108
Debord, Guy-Ernest	42
Dexler, Lorenz	73
Dobrzanski, Harry	
Eugendorf town centre	130
DOT 2 Groth-Rüter-Zeitnitz Landschaftsarchitekten	
Gorch Fock School, Hamburg	121
el:ch landschaftsarchitekten	
Gern 64, residential estate, Munich	35
Evelyn, John	11, 12, 13, 22
Felber, Stephan	102
Flor, Frank	65
Forster, August	162
foundation 5+ landschaftsarchitekten	159
A42 Park Motorway, Emscher Landscape Park	77, 84–85
Freiherr von Wendt, Maximilian	
Castelfalfi Golf Resort, Montaione	9
Friedburg, Susanne	89
Fromm, Stefan	14, 49, 71, 156
Fugger-Babenhausen, Annina Gräfin	102
Gebhard, Andrea	6–7, 116–133, 163

Glück Landschaftsarchitektur	161
Privatgarten B, Stuttgart	76, 96 – 97
Glück, Michael	96, 161
Gracián, Balthasar	30
Grober, Ulrich	7, 8 – 25, 163
Grunau, Gerd	99
Gysin, Pascal	13
Haeckel, Ernst	16
Häfner/Jiménez Büro für Landschaftsarchitektur	151
Energieberg Georgswerder, Hamburg-Wilhemsburg	24
Hager Partner AG	
Innenhof Bundestag, Berlin	118
Hauser, Susanne	151
Heidegger, Martin	23
Helleckes Landschaftsarchitektur	161
Grünzug Centro Verde, Mannheim	76, 94 – 95
Helleckes, Stefan	95, 61
herrburg Landschaftsarchitekten	160
BIGyard Gartenhof, Berlin	76, 88 – 91
Homann, Jörg	65
Hunger, Dr. Bernd	162
hutterreimann Landschaftsarchitektur GmbH	154
Park am Löbauer Wasser, Löbau	48, 50 – 59
Ipsen, Detlev	151
Jaeger, Prof. Dr. Falk	162
Karle, Fabian	114, 115
Kiefer, Prof. Gabriele	102
Klose, Götz	65
Konfuzius	10
König, Evelyn	112, 113, 115
Krause, Almuth	160
kiezPARK FORTUNA, Berlin	76, 92 – 93
Krauss, Hannes	
Ortsmitte Eugendorf	130
Kunz, Prof. Dr.-Ing. Josef	162
Landschaftsarchitekturbüro Geitz & Partner GbR	
Pilotprojekt Umgehungsgerinne und Neckarseitenarm, Ludwigsburg	10
Landschaft planen + bauen	158
Masterplan emscher:zukunft	76, 78 – 81
Lassus, Bernard	151
Leek, Maren	114, 115
Leenhardt, Jacques	
Das Grüne Quadrat – ein Park für Bitterfeld, Bitterfeld-Wolfen	28, 125
Linné, Carl Nilsson	15, 16, 20
Lohrer, Axel	67, 155
lohrer.hochrein landschaftsarchitekten bdla	155
Park Phoenix West, Dortmund	48, 66 – 67
LOMA architecture.landscape.urbanism	
Hambacher Schloss, Neustadt an der Weinstraße	150
Lützow 7 Cornelia Müller, Jan Wehberg, Landschaftsarchitekten	155
Elisengarten, Aachen	48, 68 – 69
Maier-Harth, Isabel	104, 105, 106
Malzahn, Lasse	110, 111, 113
Melzer, Dirk	
Mündungspark am Alten Hafen und Fahrradroute Kölner Randkanal, Köln	141
michellerundschalk	
grenze als ort. brücke als gelenk. Murbrücke zwischen Bad Radkersburg/Österreich und Gornja Radgona/Slowenien	139
Müller, Michael	100 – 101, 164

Geitz, Peter	10
Glück Landschaftsarchitektur	161
Private Garden B, Stuttgart	77, 96 – 97
Glück, Michael	96, 161
Gracián, Balthasar	30
Grober, Ulrich	7, 8 – 25, 164
Grunau, Gerd	99
Gysin, Pascal	13
Haeckel, Ernst	15
Häfner/Jiménez Büro für Landschaftsarchitektur	151
Georgswerder Energy Hill, Hamburg-Wilhemsburg	24
Hager Partner AG	
Interior courtyard of the Bundestag, Berlin	118
Hauser, Susanne	151
Heidegger, Martin	23
Helleckes Landschaftsarchitektur	161
Centro Verde green corridor, Mannheim	77, 94 – 95
Helleckes, Stefan	95, 161
herrburg Landschaftsarchitekten	160
BIGyard garden courtyard, Berlin	77, 88 – 91
Homann, Jörg	65
Hunger, Dr. Bernd	162
hutterreimann Landschaftsarchitektur GmbH	154
Löbau River Park, Löbau	49, 50 – 59
Ipsen, Detlev	151
Jaeger, Prof. Dr. Falk	162
Karle, Fabian	114, 115
Kiefer, Prof. Gabriele	102
Klose, Götz	65
König, Evelyn	112, 115
Krause, Almuth	160
kiezPARK FORTUNA, Berlin	77, 92 – 93
Krauss, Hannes	
Eugendorf town centre	130
Kunz, Prof. Dr.-Ing. Josef	160
Landschaftsarchitekturbüro Geitz & Partner GbR	
Bypass channel along the Neckar, Ludwigsburg	10
Landschaft planen + bauen	158
Emscher Future master plan	77, 78 – 81
Lassus, Bernard	151
Leek, Maren	114, 115
Leenhardt, Jacques	
Green Square landscape park, Bitterfeld-Wolfen	28, 125
Linnaeus, Carl Nilsson	14, 20
Lohrer, Axel	67, 155
lohrer.hochrein landschaftsarchitekten bdla	155
Park Phoenix West, Dortmund	49, 66 – 67
LOMA architecture.landscape.urbanism	
Hambach Castle, Neustadt an der Weinstraße	150
Lützow 7 Cornelia Müller, Jan Wehberg, Landschaftsarchitekten	155
Elisengarten, Aachen	49, 68 – 69
Maier-Harth, Isabel	104, 105, 106
Malzahn, Lasse	110, 111, 113
Melzer, Dirk	
Debouchment Park at the Old Harbor and cycle path along Cologne's Randkanal, Cologne	141
michellerundschalk	
grenze als ort. brücke als gelenk. Mur bridge at the border between Bad Radkersburg/Austria and Gornja Radgona/Slovenia	139
Müller, Michael	100 – 101, 164
Neder, Gottfried	99
Norberg-Schulz, Christian	144, 151

Neder, Gottfried	99
Norberg-Schulz, Christian	144, 151
Norbert Post · Hartmut Welters Architekten und Stadtplaner GmbH	158
Masterplan emscher:zukunft	76, 78–81
Outside! Landschaftsarchitekten	161
Wohnumfeldverbesserung Wohnquartier Essener Straße, Hamburg-Langenhorn	76, 98–99
Petrarca, Francesco	42
pg landschaften	
Merian-Gärten, Basel	13
Planergruppe Oberhausen	159
Neugestaltung Universitätsplatz und Borgiasplatz, Fulda	147
Parkautobahn A42, Emscher Landschaftspark	76, 84–85
Der Zollverein – ein Park entsteht, Essen	123
Planstatt Senner, Überlingen	
Naturerlebnispark Schlosssee Salem	126
planungsgruppe grün gmbh	160
A 281, Bremen	76, 86–87
Popper, Karl	30
Portz, Norbert	162
Preißmann, Rainer	
Golf Resort Castelfalfi, Montaione	9
Pytlik, Dennis	104, 105, 106
Rainer Schmidt Landschaftsarchitekten und Stadtplaner	
Parkerweiterung Killesberg, Stuttgart	131
rajek barosch landschaftsarchitektur	
Der Weingarten – Neue Siedlerbewegung – Pichlgasse, Wien	17
Rapoport, Amos	151
Rauch, Lucas	110, 111, 113
Ray, Man	139
Rehwaldt, Till	50–59, 162, 164
Rein-Cano, Martin	73
Reith und Wehner Architekten	
Neugestaltung Universitätsplatz und Borgiasplatz, Fulda	147
relais Landschaftsarchitekten	154
Der Christliche Garten (Gärten der Welt), Berlin-Marzahn	48, 60–61
RMP Stephan Lenzen Landschaftsarchitekten	157
Masterplan emscher:zukunft	76, 78–81
NRW-Pavillon, Floriade 2012, Venlo	149
Rosenkranz, Christoph	102–115, 164
Roy, Arundhati	24
Rückert, Friedrich	148, 151
Schadzek, Franziska	112, 113, 115
Scherzer, Prof. Cornelius	162
Schmid, Prof. Arno Sighart	116–132, 165
Schmidt, Cornelia	116–132, 165
Schmidt, Hagen	108, 109, 113
Schmidt, Rainer	131
Schnorbusch, Susanne	160
kiezPARK FORTUNA, Berlin	76, 92–93
Schönherr, Mareike	89
Schönherr, Markus	89
Schröder, Thies	26–37, 116–132, 165
Schweingruber, Lukas	162
sinai Gesellschaft von Landschaftsarchitekten mbH	
Außengelände der Gedenkstätte Bergen-Belsen, Lohheide	144
Speer, Albert	62
Spitzer, Klaus	6
Stefan Fromm Landschaftsarchitekten	156
Drei neue Parks für Nagold	48, 70–71
Tübinger Mühlenviertel, Tübingen	14
Steinmüller, Dr. Karlheinz	116–132, 166

Norbert Post · Hartmut Welters Architekten und Stadtplaner GmbH	158
Emscher Future master plan	77, 78–81
Outside! Landschaftsarchitekten	161
Residential area improvements Essener Straße, Hamburg-Langenhorn	77, 98–99
Petrarca, Francesco	42
pg landschaften	
Merian Gardens, Basel	13
Planergruppe Oberhausen	159
Design of Universitätsplatz and Borgiasplatz, Fulda	147
A42 Park Motorway, Emscher Landscape Park	77, 84–85
Zollverein Coal Mine, Essen	123
Planstatt Senner, Überlingen	
Nature Discovery Park Schlosssee Salem	126
planungsgruppe grün gmbh	160
A 281 – Between high-tech, allotment gardens and Natura 2000, Bremen	77, 86–87
Popper, Karl	30
Portz, Norbert	162
Preißmann, Rainer	
Castelfalfi Golf Resort, Montaione	9
Pytlik, Dennis	104, 106, 107
Rainer Schmidt Landschaftsarchitekten und Stadtplaner	
Extension to Killesberg Park, Stuttgart	131
rajek barosch landschaftsarchitektur	
Vineyard, Pichlgasse housing complex, Vienna	17
Rapoport, Amos	151
Rauch, Lucas	110, 111, 113
Ray, Man	139
Rehwaldt, Till	50–59, 162, 164
Rein-Cano, Martin	73
Reith und Wehner Architekten	
Universitätsplatz and Borgiasplatz, Fulda	147
relais Landschaftsarchitekten	154
The Christian Garden (Gardens of the World), Berlin-Marzahn	49, 60–61
RMP Stephan Lenzen Landschaftsarchitekten	157
Emscher Future master plan	77, 78–81
North Rhine-Westphalia Pavilion, Floriade 2012, Venlo	149
Rosenkranz, Christoph	102–115, 165
Roy, Arundhati	23
Rückert, Friedrich	148, 151
Schadzek, Franziska	112, 115
Scherzer, Prof. Cornelius	162
Schmid, Prof. Arno Sighart	116–132, 165
Schmidt, Cornelia	116–132, 165
Schmidt, Hagen	108, 109, 113
Schmidt, Rainer	131
Schnorbusch, Susanne	160
kiezPARK FORTUNA, Berlin	77, 92–93
Schönherr, Mareike	89
Schönherr, Markus	89
Schröder, Thies	26–37, 116–132, 165
Schweingruber, Lukas	162
sinai Gesellschaft von Landschaftsarchitekten mbH	
Grounds of the Bergen-Belsen Memorial	144
Speer, Albert	62
Spitzer, Klaus	6
Stefan Fromm Landschaftsarchitekten	156
Three new parks for Nagold	49, 70–71
Mühlenviertel residential quarter, Tübingen	14
Steinmüller, Dr. Karlheinz	116–132, 166
Stokman, Prof. Antje	162

Stokman, Prof. Antje	162
Straub Thurmayr Landschaftsarchitekten und Stadtplaner	157
FollyForest, Strathcona School, Winnipeg	48, 74 – 75
Straub, Prof. Dipl.-Ing. Dietmar	75
SUPERFLEX	
Superkilen, Kopenhagen	48, 72 – 73
Tauscher, Christoph	63
Theis, Björn	116 – 132, 166
Thiel, Elisabeth	106, 107
Thurmayr, Prof. Dipl.-Ing. Anna	75
thoma architekten	48, 50 – 59
Töpfer, Prof. Dr. Klaus	7, 26 – 37, 166
Topotek 1 Gesellschaft von Landschaftsarchitekten mbH	156
Superkilen, Kopenhagen	48, 72 – 73
Uhrig, Dr. Ing. Nicole	7, 134 – 151, 167
urbane gestalt johannes böttger landschaftsarchitekten	
Freianlagen der Siedlung Wohnen am Buchheimer Weg, Köln-Ostheim	143
Vogt, Prof. Günther	7, 38 – 47, 102, 167
Vogt Landschaftsarchitekten	38
Wartner & Zeitzler Landschaftsarchitekten bdla und Stadtplaner	159
Solarfeld Gänsdorf	76, 82 – 83
Wartner, Helmut	83, 159
Weeramantry, Christopher G.	9
Wegener, Burkhard	65
Weichhart, Peter	151
WGF Landschaft	154
Grüngürtel: Impuls 2012, Köln	48, 62 – 63
Yang, Jun	107, 108
Zeitzler, Rupert	83, 159
Zoderer, Beat	
Innenhof Bundestag, Berlin	118
Straub Thurmayr Landschaftsarchitekten und Stadtplaner	157
FollyForest, Strathcona School, Winnipeg	49, 74 – 75
Straub, Prof. Dipl.-Ing. Dietmar	75
SUPERFLEX	
Superkilen, Copenhagen	49, 72 – 73
Tauscher, Christoph	63
Theis, Björn	116 – 132, 166
Thiel, Elisabeth	106, 107
Thurmayr, Prof. Dipl.-Ing. Anna	75
thoma architekten	49, 50 – 59
Töpfer, Prof. Dr. Klaus	7, 26 – 37, 166
Topotek 1 Gesellschaft von Landschaftsarchitekten mbH	156
Superkilen, Kopenhagen	49, 72 – 73
Uhrig, Dr.-Ing. Nicole	7, 134 – 151, 167
urbane gestalt johannes böttger landschaftsarchitekten	
Outdoor areas of Buchheimer Weg housing estate, Ostheim, Cologne	143
Vogt, Günther	7, 38 – 47, 102, 167
Vogt Landschaftsarchitekten	38
Wartner & Zeitzler Landschaftsarchitekten bdla und Stadtplaner	158
Gänsdorf Solar Field	76, 82 – 83
Wartner, Helmut	83, 158
Weeramantry, Christopher G.	8
Wegener, Burkhard	65
Weichhart, Peter	151
WGF Landschaft	154
Green Belt: Impuls 2012, Cologne	49, 62 – 63
Yang, Jun	107, 108
Zeitzler, Rupert	83, 158
Zoderer, Beat	
Interior courtyard of the Bundestag, Berlin	118

Ortsregister

Aachen 48, 68, 69
Bad Radkersburg 139
Basel 13, 105
Bergen-Belsen 144, 145
Berlin 18, 32, 38, 39, 48, 51, 60, 61, 69, 73, 76, 79, 88–93, 100, 101, 110–115, 117, 118, 129, 135, 136, 144
Bitterfeld 28, 83, 125
Bonn 32, 79, 149
Bottrop 85
Braunschweig 102
Bremen 76, 86, 87
Castrop-Rauxel 85
Delhi 39
Dessau 28, 125
Dettenhausen 71
Dinslaken 78, 79
Dortmund 48, 66, 67, 78, 79, 85
Duisburg 85, 147
Emscher 88–91
Essen 9, 79, 85, 123
Freiburg/Breisgau 17
Freising 105, 106, 107, 108
Fukushima 33
Gänsdorf 76, 82, 83
Gelsenkirchen 85
Gornja Radgona 139
Hamburg 24, 76, 98, 99, 121, 129, 147
Hannover 29, 37, 113, 115
Heathrow 45
Herne 85
Herten 85
Hyères 139
Jena 16
Karlsruhe 95
Kassel 85, 150
Köln 18, 48, 62, 63, 65, 79, 141, 143
Kopenhagen 48, 72, 73
Landshut 83
Las Vegas 8
Löbau 48, 50–59
London 12, 38, 39, 42, 44, 45, 46
Ludwigsburg 10
Mannheim 76, 94, 95
Memmingen 48, 64, 65
Moers 85
Möhlin 105
Montaione 9
München 35, 75, 105, 106, 131, 139
Murten 39, 41
Nagold 48, 70, 71
Neustadt an der Weinstraße 150
Oberhausen 85, 123
Paris 42
Petershausen 105
Potsdam 37
Rüschlikon 39
Salem 126
Singapur 20
Sissach 13
Staßfurt 151
Stuttgart 10, 76, 96, 131
Tschernobyl 34
Tübingen 14
Überlingen 17, 20, 126
Venedig 42, 44
Venlo 149
Wien 17
Wiesbaden 117
Winnipeg 48, 74, 75
Zürich 8, 38, 39, 41, 42, 102

Index of places

Aachen 49, 68, 69
Bad Radkersburg 139
Basel 13, 105
Bergen-Belsen 144, 145
Berlin 18, 32, 39, 49, 51, 60, 61, 69, 72, 73, 77, 79, 88–93, 100, 101, 109, 110–115, 117, 118, 129, 135, 136, 144, 151
Bitterfeld 28, 83, 125
Bonn 32, 79, 149
Bottrop 85
Braunschweig 102
Bremen 77, 86, 87
Castrop-Rauxel 85
Chernobyl 34
Cologne 18, 49, 62, 63, 65, 79, 141, 143
Copenhagen 49, 72, 73
Dehli 39
Dessau 28, 125
Dettenhausen 71
Dinslaken 78, 79
Dortmund 49, 66, 67, 79, 85
Duisburg 85, 147
Emscher 88–91
Essen 9, 79, 85, 123
Freiburg / Breisgau 17
Freising 105, 106, 107, 108
Fukushima 33
Gänsdorf 77, 82, 83
Gelsenkirchen 85
Gornja Radgona 139
Hamburg 24, 77, 98, 99, 121, 129, 147
Hanover 29, 37, 113, 115
Heathrow 45
Herne 85
Herten 85
Hyères 139
Jena 15
Karlsruhe 95
Kassel 85, 150
Landshut 83
Las Vegas 8
Löbau 49–59
London 12, 39, 42, 44, 45, 46
Ludwigsburg 10
Mannheim 77, 94, 95
Memmingen 49, 64, 65
Moers 85
Möhlin 105
Montaione 9
Munich 33, 35, 75, 105, 106, 107, 108, 131, 139
Murten 39, 41
Nagold 49, 70, 71
Neustadt an der Weinstraße 150
Oberhausen 85
Paris 42
Petershausen 107
Potsdam 37
Rüschlikon 39
Salem 126
Singapore 20
Sissach 13
Staßfurt 151
Stuttgart 10, 77, 96, 131
Tübingen 14
Überlingen 17, 20, 126
Venice 42, 44
Venlo 149
Vienna 17
Wiesbaden 117
Winnipeg 49, 74, 75
Zurich 8, 38, 39, 41, 42, 102

Bildnachweis

Atelier Dreiseitl 22
Baan, Iwan 73 oben, unten
Bierwald, Simon 85
Bozic, Brane 138
Brückner, Heike 29, 124, 125
Case Studio VOGT 43
club L94/Fotoatelier 2 64, 65 oben, unten
De Andrade Adauto Costa, Isabella 108 links, rechts
Dobrzanski, Harry 130 rechts
Dreyße, Claudia 146
el:ch landschaftsarchitekten 34 (Foto: Christian Henke)
Feser, Michael 90, 91 unten
Fromm, Stefan 15, 70, 71 oben, unten links, unten rechts
GAG Immobilien AG Köln 142
Glück, Michael 97 oben, unten
Hager Partner AG 119 (Foto: Felix Bearth)
Helleckes, Stefan 95 unten
Hempel, Jörg 69 oben, unten links, unten rechts
Heppekausen, Sarah 122
hutterreimann Landschaftsarchitektur GmbH 58 oben, 59
IASS Potsdam 26 (Foto: Foto Schulzendorff)
Info&Idee 11
Insta Elektro GmbH 24, 25
Förderverein Goitzsche e.V. 31 (Foto: Klaus-Peter Jaskulski)
Joosten, Hanns 61 oben, unten links, unten rechts, 117, 128 oben, unten
Karle, Fabian 114 links, rechts
König, Evelyn 112, 113
Leek, Mareen 114 links, rechts
Leidorf, Klaus 83 oben
Lichtschwärmer 135, 136, 137
Lichtschwärmer Umschlagfoto, 51, 53, 54, 55, 56 oben, unten 57, 58 unten (Fotos: Christo Libuda)
Lindhe, Jens 72
lohrer.hochrein landschaftsarchitekten bdla 66, 67 unten (Foto: Hans Wulf Kunze)
LOMA architecture.landscape.urbanism 150, 151 (Foto: Wolfgang Schück)
Ludwig, Karl 16
Lützow 7 Cornelia Müller, Jan Wehberg, Landschaftsarchitekten 68
Maier-Harth, Isabel 104, 105
Malzahn, Lasse 110, 111
Marktgemeinde Eugendorf 130 links
Melzer, Dirk 140, 141
Menges, Simon 89, 91 oben
Ortmeyer, Klemens 145 oben, 145 unten
Outside! Landschaftsarchitekten GmbH 98, 99 oben, 99 unten
pg landschaften 12
Planstatt Senner 126, 127
Planergruppe Oberhausen 84
planungsgruppe grün gmbh 87 oben, 87 unten links, 87 unten rechts
PUB Dreiseitl 21
Pytlik, Dennis 104, 105
Rainer Schmidt Landschaftsarchitekten und Stadtplanern 131, 132, 133 (Fotos: Raffaella Sirtolli)
rajek barosch landschaftsarchitektur 17
Rauch, Lucas 110, 111
relais Landschaftsarchitekten 60
RMP Stephan Lenzen Landschaftsarchitekten/ASTOC Architects and Planners in Zusammenarbeit mit Landschaft planen + bauen/Norbert Post · Hartmut Welters, Architekten und Stadtplaner GmbH 79, 80/81 oben, 80 unten, 81 unten
Sankowski, Jutta 67 oben
Schadzek, Franziska 112, 113
Schmidt, Hagen 109 links, rechts
Schulthess, Kathrin 13
Schumann, Ralf 19
sinai Gesellschaft von Landschaftsarchitekten 144
Straub Thurmayr Landschaftsarchitekten und Stadtplaner 74, 75 oben, unten (Fotos: Dietmar Straub)
Su Schnorbusch Architekten 93 oben, unten
Thiel, Elisabeth 106 links, rechts
thomasmayerarchive.de, Thomas Mayer 148, 149
Vogt Landschaftsarchitekten AG 45, 46, 47
Vogt, Christian 39, 41, 42
von Stengel, Stefan 9
Waldmeier, Jürg / VOGT 40
Wartner & Zeitzler Landschaftsarchitekten bdla und Stadtplaner 83 unten
WGF Landschaft Aufmkolk – Hintermeier – Voit – Ziesel Landschaftsarchitekten GmbH 62, 63 oben, unten
Wilhelmsen, Thomas 123
Yang, Jun 108 links, rechts
Zeitnitz, Kai 120

Illustration credits

Atelier Dreiseitl 22
Baan, Iwan 73 top, bottom
Bierwald, Simon 85
Bozic, Brane 138
Brückner, Heike 29, 124, 125
Case Studio VOGT 43
club L94/Fotoatelier 2 64, 65 top, bottom
De Andrade Adauto Costa, Isabella 108 left, right
Dobrzanski, Harry 130 right
Dreyße, Claudia 146
el:ch landschaftsarchitekten 34 (photograph: Christian Henke)
Feser, Michael 90, 91 bottom
Fromm, Stefan 15, 70, 71 top, bottom left, bottom right
GAG Immobilien AG Köln 142
Glück, Michael 97 top, bottom
Hager Partner AG 119 (photograph: Felix Bearth)
Helleckes, Stefan 95 bottom
Hempel, Jörg 69 top, bottom left, bottom right
Heppekausen, Sarah 122
hutterreimann Landschaftsarchitektur GmbH 58 top, 59
IASS Potsdam 26 (photograph: Foto Schulzendorff)
Info&Idee 11
Insta Elektro GmbH 24, 25
Förderverein Goitzsche e.V. 31 (photograph: Klaus-Peter Jaskulski)
Joosten, Hanns 61 top, bottom left, bottom right, 117, 128 top, bottom
Karle, Fabian 114 left, right
König, Evelyn 112, 113
Leek, Mareen 114 left, right
Leidorf, Klaus 83 top
Lichtschwärmer 135, 136, 137
Lichtschwärmer cover, 51, 53, 54, 55, 56 top, bottom 57, 58 bottom (photographs: Christo Libuda)
Lindhe, Jens 72
lohrer.hochrein landschaftsarchitekten bdla 66, 67 bottom (photographs: Hans Wulf Kunze)
LOMA architecture.landscape.urbanism 150, 151 (photograph: Wolfgang Schück)
Ludwig, Karl 16
Lützow 7 Cornelia Müller, Jan Wehberg, Landschaftsarchitekten 68
Maier-Harth, Isabel 104, 105
Malzahn, Lasse 110, 111
Marktgemeinde Eugendorf 130 left
Melzer, Dirk 140, 141
Menges, Simon 89, 91 top
Ortmeyer, Klemens 145 top, 145 bottom
Outside! Landschaftsarchitekten GmbH 98, 99 top, 99 bottom
pg landschaften 12
Planstatt Senner 126, 127
Planergruppe Oberhausen 84
planungsgruppe grün gmbh 87 top, 87 bottom left, 87 bottom right
PUB Dreiseitl 21
Pytlik, Dennis 104, 105
Rainer Schmidt Landschaftsarchitekten und Stadtplaner, Munich 131, 132, 133 (photographs: Raffaella Sirtolli)
rajek barosch landschaftsarchitektur 17
Rauch, Lucas 110, 111
relais Landschaftsarchitekten 60
RMP Stephan Lenzen Landschaftsarchitekten; ASTOC Architects and Planners in cooperation with Landschaft planen + bauen; Norbert Post · Hartmut Welters, Architekten und Stadtplaner GmbH 79, 80/81 top, 80 bottom, 81 bottom
Sankowski, Jutta 67 top
Schadzek, Franziska 112, 113
Schmidt, Hagen 109 left, right
Schulthess, Kathrin 13
Schumann, Ralf 19
sinai Gesellschaft von Landschaftsarchitekten 144
Straub Thurmayr Landschaftsarchitekten und Stadtplaner 74, 75 top, bottom (photographs: Dietmar Straub)
Su Schnorbusch Architekten 93 top, bottom
Thiel, Elisabeth 106 left, right
thomasmayerarchive.de, Thomas Mayer 148, 149
Vogt Landschaftsarchitekten AG 45, 46, 47
Vogt, Christian 39, 41, 42
von Stengel, Stefan 9
Waldmeier, Jürg / VOGT 40
Wartner & Zeitzler Landschaftsarchitekten bdla und Stadtplaner 83 bottom
WGF Landschaft Aufmkolk – Hintermeier – Voit – Ziesel Landschaftsarchitekten GmbH 62, 63 top, bottom
Wilhelmsen, Thomas 123
Yang, Jun 108 left, right
Zeitnitz, Kai 120